U.S. IMPERIALISM
IN LATIN AMERICA

U.S. IMPERIALISM IN LATIN AMERICA

Bryan's Challenges and Contributions, 1900–1920

EDWARD S. KAPLAN

Contributions in Comparative Colonial Studies,
Number 35

GREENWOOD PRESS
Westport, Connecticut • London

Library of Congress Cataloging-in-Publication Data

Kaplan, Edward S.
U.S. imperialism in Latin America : Bryan's challenges and
contributions, 1900–1920 / Edward S. Kaplan.
p.   cm.—(Contributions in comparative colonial studies,
ISSN 0163-3813 ; no. 35)
Includes bibliographical references and index.
ISBN 0-313-30489-0 (alk. paper)
1. Bryan, William Jennings, 1860–1925—Views on Latin America.
2. United States—Foreign relations—Latin America.   3. Latin
America—Foreign relations—United States.   4. United States—
Foreign relations—1865–1921.   5. Imperialism—United States—
History—20th century.   I. Title.   II. Series.
E664.B87K37   1998
327.7308′09′041—dc21   97-37541

British Library Cataloguing in Publication Data is available.

Library of Congress Catalog Card Number: 97-37541
ISBN: 0-313-30489-0
ISSN: 0163-3813

First published in 1998

Greenwood Press, 88 Post Road West, Westport, CT 06881
An imprint of Greenwood Publishing Group, Inc.

Printed in the United States of America

The paper used in this book complies with the
Permanent Paper Standard issued by the National
Information Standards Organization (Z39.48–1984).

10 9 8 7 6 5 4 3 2 1

To my professors at New York University

Contents

Preface

Beginning in 1900, the United States practiced an imperialistic policy toward Latin America that lasted until the "Good Neighbor" policy of Franklin Roosevelt in the 1930s. This book explains the nature of this imperialism—U.S. intervention in the affairs of its southern neighbors—by studying the attitude and policy of William Jennings Bryan toward Latin America.

From the end of the Spanish-American War in 1898 until the time that he became secretary of state in March 1913, Bryan spoke against imperialism and "dollar diplomacy" in Latin America. In 1901, he opposed both the Cuban Platt Amendment and the Supreme Court decision denying Puerto Ricans the same rights as Americans. In place of imperialism and "dollar diplomacy," he urged friendship and understanding. The latter was especially evident in speeches he made during a Latin American tour in 1910. However, when Bryan became secretary of state during the Wilson administration in March 1913, he practiced the very same imperialism and "dollar diplomacy" that he had criticized previously. This was particularly evident in regard to Nicaragua, Haiti, and the Dominican Republic.

For Nicaragua, he formulated a treaty in July 1913, that contained provisions similar to the Platt Amendment; he worked with the same bankers used by the Taft administration. He also defended his treaty against the protests of both El Salvador and Costa Rica.

In Haiti, the threat of German and French financial interests and the prevalence of political instability swayed Bryan into attempting the imposition of a financial agreement calling for control of the customs. His insistence on this only aggravated the political situation, since nationalist sentiment opposed American interference.

In the Dominican Republic, Bryan also feared foreign pecuniary interests and political revolution. Here, he supported the constituted government against all revolutionary groups, while attempting to increase American financial control (the

United States already controlled the customs) by appointing an American financial adviser to control the Dominican budget. James M. Sullivan, the U.S. minister to the Dominican Republic, played a prominent role here. He best exemplified the much used phrase "deserving Democrats," a term denoting a political appointee with no qualifications except his party's label and gratitude. The Sullivan appointment proved most embarrassing to Bryan after an investigating committee linked the minister to American business.

Bryan's policy toward Mexico, the Panama Canal tolls controversy, and the Colombian treaty was similar to his anti-imperialistic attitude before becoming secretary of state. Here, he opposed intervention and spoke of the necessity of improving U.S.-Latin American relations.

Though Bryan reluctantly approved of American intervention at Veracruz in April 1914, he absolutely opposed reinforcing American troops there. He feared that American intervention would unite the Mexican opposition groups in a war against the United States.

Bryan also supported repeal of exemption for American ships engaged in coastwise trade in the Panama Canal tolls controversy. He believed that exemption was morally wrong and aided the fight for repeal in both the House and Senate.

Convinced of America's guilt during the Panamanian revolution in 1903, Bryan attempted to seek redress for Colombia, for its loss of Panama, through a treaty. His role in the formulation of the Colombian treaty in April 1914 demonstrated his earnest desire to improve U.S.-Latin American relations.

After Bryan resigned in June 1915, he continued to support the Wilson administration's policies in Haiti, the Dominican Republic, and Mexico. He also worked successfully for the passage of both the Nicaraguan and Colombian treaties.

1

Introduction

William Jennings Bryan became President Woodrow Wilson's secretary of state in 1913 and remained in that office until June 1915. During that time, he influenced American foreign policy in many areas of the world, especially in Latin America. If we study Bryan's attitude toward Latin America from 1900 to 1913, the years prior to becoming secretary of state, we find him speaking and writing against the imperialism and "dollar diplomacy" practiced by the Taft administration in Latin America. William H. Taft was a firm supporter of American business interests abroad, often using American troops to protect them. Once Bryan became secretary of state in 1913, however, he actually continued and furthered these same policies in three countries: Nicaragua, Haiti, and the Dominican Republic. He only remained consistent with his early anti-imperialistic sentiments in regard to Mexico, the Panama Canal tolls controversy, and the Colombian treaty. Here he worked hard to correct the interventionist policies of past administrations, stressing friendship and understanding with Latin America.

Bryan never realized the inconsistency of his Latin American policy—he never admitted to the ambiguity of his actions. During his tenure as secretary of state, he believed that he was actually eradicating the imperialistic policies of Theodore Roosevelt and William Howard Taft in Latin America.

In explaining this inconsistency, it would be easy to declare that Bryan feigned sincerity when he promised to end the military intervention and "dollar diplomacy" of his predecessors. But Bryan was never insincere; he firmly believed until his death in 1925 that he had helped change the interventionist policies of past administrations.

Before Bryan became secretary of state, he preached constantly against the acquisition of new territory outside the continental boundaries of the United States and military intervention in foreign lands whether it be to protect American business or control the local governments. This anti-imperialistic sentiment was an aspect of Bryan's strong moralistic attitude—an attitude that would later be used to defend his imperialistic policies toward Nicaragua, Haiti, and the Dominican Republic. If we examine Bryan's moralistic behavior, we will find some of the causes of his inconsistency in Latin America.

Bryan was proud of his high moral principles, his idealism, and this was especially true in his attitude toward war. He considered war to be immoral and hoped that all nations would outlaw it as an instrument of national policy. The primary reason Bryan opposed Theodore Roosevelt's Latin American and world policies was because they stressed militarism—the need for a large standing army and navy. Roosevelt was a realist—he thought that war was part of the natural state of man and could only be prevented through both military preparation and the use of force to quell minor disorders before they became major catastrophes. Bryan, on the other hand, was an idealist—he believed that war was unnecessary and could be avoided if all nations would only think of its consequences before they acted. When he became secretary of state, he proposed to end war forever through a series of arbitration treaties (see chapter 2). Bryan asserted that military preparation and intervention acted only to provoke war rather than prevent it and, consequently, that the United States had a moral obligation to refrain from this type of action.

While Bryan's sense of moral obligation disparaged militarism, it also led to his own military intervention in Latin America. He never understood that he held in common with Roosevelt and Taft a belief in the superiority of American political and economic institutions over their Latin American counterparts. It was this feeling that contributed to his interference in the political and economic institutions of Nicaragua, Haiti, and the Dominican Republic. He declared that the United States was morally obligated in these politically unstable countries to instruct the Latin Americans on democratic government.

In March 1913, when the Wilson administration took office, Bryan finally had the opportunity to implement policy. The new secretary of state wanted to eradicate the military intervention of past administrations, but he could not completely do this. Bryan was no longer a public citizen outside the realm of government but now held a position of responsibility; he could no longer afford the luxury of his idealism, but had to act with firmness and dispatch in making crucial decisions.

Bryan's concern with the security of the United States led him to accept the same policies of the Roosevelt and Taft administrations in Nicaragua, Haiti, and the Dominican Republic. He came to believe—through the efforts of James M. Sullivan, his ambassador to the Dominican Republic, and such personnel in the Division of Latin American Affairs as J. H. Stabler and Boaz W. Long—that the political instability in Latin America invited European intervention.

Nicaragua, Haiti, and the Dominican Republic were bankrupt and indebted to European creditors in Great Britain, France, Germany, and Italy. Bryan reasoned that these European nations would justify intervention on the grounds that the claims of their creditors were not met. The secretary of state feared this intervention would not be temporary but would lead to the acquisition of naval bases and coaling stations and perhaps colonization. This whole idea contravened the conception of the Monroe Doctrine to which Bryan became an ardent adherent. He was concerned that the presence of European powers so close to the continental United States would threaten its security. This was especially true in time of war (World War I began in 1914 and probably affected Bryan's thinking) when the fighting for bases would spread to the vicinity of the United States.

Bryan, on the other hand, was not concerned with American security in regard to Mexico, the Panama Canal tolls controversy, and the Colombian treaty. Here, he had the opportunity to enhance American friendship. Unfortunately for Bryan, he used his actions toward these countries to describe and characterize his entire Latin American policy. He permitted his good intentions, especially in regard to the Colombian treaty, to obscure the inconsistency of his policy; this was not done purposely since Bryan never really thought in terms of a dual policy. He did not seem to perceive that the policy he followed in regard to Nicaragua, Haiti, and the Dominican Republic was nothing more than the traditional Latin American policy of past administrations.

Since the formulation of the Monroe Doctrine in 1823, the United States claimed the western hemisphere as its special sphere of influence. This attitude became especially important in the last decade of the nineteenth century with the growing rivalry for colonies among such industrial nations as Great Britain, Germany, France, Italy, Japan, and Russia. The United States feared that this competition for colonies would spread to the western hemisphere and threaten its security.[1] The idea of a major European power controlling naval bases so close to the United States threatened American security, since these bases could be used as invasion points in time of war.

Great Britain was the chief rival of the United States in the early part of the nineteenth century. Though British competition had subsided considerably by the beginning of the twentieth century (Great Britain had withdrawn from much of Central America and had signed the Hay-Pauncefote Treaty with the Roosevelt administration in 1902), the United States remained suspicious of British motives in Latin America. When a territorial dispute began between Venezuela and British Guiana in 1895, the Cleveland administration sympathized with Venezuela and urged the British to arbitrate.[2]

When the Spanish-American War ended in 1898, the United States kept Puerto Rico and imposed the Platt Amendment on Cuba. The McKinley administration, in both cases, wanted to prevent European nations such as Great Britain, France, and Italy from securing naval bases and coaling stations. Article One of the Platt Amendment explicitly prohibited Cuba from entering into any treaty or compact with a foreign nation which would endanger Cuban independence.[3]

President Theodore Roosevelt not only continued but elaborated upon the policies of his predecessors. When Great Britain, Germany, and Italy threatened intervention in Venezuela to collect debts in 1902, Roosevelt at first appeared unconcerned. He said, "We do not guarantee any state against punishment if it misconducts itself, provided that punishment does not take the form of the acquisition of territory by a non-American power."[4] However, after the British and German navies blockaded Venezuelan ports and sunk several Venezuelan gunboats, Roosevelt demanded arbitration—he feared that these powers were using debt collection as a pretext for intervention and really desired territory for a naval base.[5]

The Venezuelan dispute paved the way for the "Roosevelt Corollary" to the Monroe Doctrine. The Hague Tribunal, in February 1904, had supported the intervention of Great Britain, Germany, and Italy in Venezuela—the arbitration committee claimed that these major powers had every right to collect debts owed them.[6] The United States feared that this decision would lead to more European intervention in Latin America. Thus, in 1904, when the Dominican Republic defaulted in payment of its debts to Italian citizens, the Roosevelt administration decided that it must implement a policy to ensure payment of debts to European and American creditors—the United States would assume the responsibility for debt payment in the Western Hemisphere to prevent European intervention there (see chapter 5).

President Taft's Latin American policy differed from Roosevelt's in one important way. He attempted to use the American businessman as a tool to end European financial and political influence. If Taft could eliminate the European creditor and replace him with the American creditor, European nations could not use debt collection as an excuse to interfere in the affairs of Latin America.[7]

Taft attempted to carry out his policy in Nicaragua, but it failed primarily because of the revolution that began in 1909—American businessmen were unwilling to invest in politically unstable countries. When the revolution continued in 1912, Taft sent American marines to restore stability. He then asked the American bankers Brown Brothers and Company and J. and W. Seligman and Company to lend money to the new Nicaraguan government (see chapter 3).

The tragedy of William Jennings Bryan's Latin American policy was not only that he never realized its inconsistency, but also that he insisted that it differed from the traditional policies of the Roosevelt and Taft administrations, even in regard to Nicaragua, Haiti, and the Dominican Republic. Bryan never understood that when he used military force , he was doing the same thing his predecessors did. Nonetheless, as secretary of state, he continued to denounce the militaristic policies of past administrations, declaring that he would never resort to military power. As we shall see, notwithstanding his rhetoric, Bryan was, under certain circumstances, very much an imperialist.

NOTES

1. Samuel Flagg Bemis, *The Latin American Policy of the United States* (New York: Harcourt, Brace and Company, 1943), pp. 386-387.

2. J. Fred Rippy, *The Caribbean Danger Zone* (New York: G. P. Putnam's Sons, 1940), pp. 24-29.

3. Bemis, *The Latin American Policy of the United States*, pp. 138-141.

4. Rippy, *The Caribbean Danger Zone*, p. 32.

5. Bemis, *The Latin American Policy of the United States*, pp. 146-147.

6. Ibid., p. 151.

7. Dana G. Munro, *Intervention and Dollar Diplomacy in the Caribbean, 1900-1921* (Princeton, N.J.: Princeton University Press, 1964), pp. 160-163.

2

Bryan's Early Attitude toward Latin America, 1900–1913

After William McKinley won the presidential election in 1896, he became involved in the Cuban revolt. This uprising had begun in 1868 and continued intermittently. By 1898, however, the cause of Cuban independence was taken up in the American press. The press now wrote stories, often exaggerated, about the suffering of the Cuban people and greatly influenced U.S. public opinion into supporting Cuban independence. This propaganda campaign in the press and the work of leading Cuban insurgents in the United States also had the same effect on members of Congress.[1] The Democratic Cleveland administration, which had been in power during most of the recent uprising, refused to intervene in Cuban affairs. The Republican party, during the campaign of 1896, favored Cuban independence, though McKinley, the party's nominee and the next president, remained reluctant to interfere immediately—he did not want war as the price of Cuban freedom. Nonetheless, by April 1898, McKinley had come to view war with Spain as inevitable. The president had not surrendered to the war hysteria of public opinion as some historians, such as Samuel Flagg Bemis, had declared. What had happened was that the president was already negotiating with Spain for Cuban independence, and he came to believe that the Spanish government was not carrying on these talks in good faith. Therefore, in April 1898, with the support of McKinley, Congress by joint resolution declared war on Spain.[2] Attached to the resolution was the Teller Amendment, which denied any intention of occupying Cuba permanently. It stipulated "that the United States hereby disclaims any disposition or intention to exercise sovereignty, jurisdiction, or control over the said island except for the pacification thereof, and asserts its determination, when that is accomplished, to leave the government and control of the island to its people."[3]

William Jennings Bryan, now an influential private citizen, supported the war resolution; he condemned Spanish tyranny and called the Cuban revolt a fight for humanity. He said, "Yes, the time for intervention has arrived. Humanity demands that we shall act. Cuba lies almost within sight of our shores and the sufferings of her people cannot be ignored unless we, as a nation have become so engrossed in money-making as to be indifferent to distress."[4] Bryan clarified his position not only on the war, but also on imperialism in a speech delivered in Nebraska, in June 1898, when he reiterated that the war was a fight for humanity and at the same time repudiated imperialism; the war was not to extend United States territory, but only to spread democracy and equality among peoples.[5] Here was the first intimation of his suspicion that others might use the war with Spain to build an empire for the United States.

Though Bryan saw no military action, he offered his services to President McKinley as early as April 25, 1898. However, it was Governor Silas Holcomb of Nebraska who authorized Bryan to organize the Third Regiment of the Nebraska Volunteers.[6] He was made a colonel, and when the *New York Times*, one of his critics, learned of his commission, it continually criticized him as having little military experience and charged that his only reason for enlisting was to keep himself in the public view.[7] There was no question that Bryan had an eye on the 1900 campaign, but it was unfair to criticize him for lack of military experience, since many men of influence from wealthy families without military experience received commissions.

As the war progressed, it became evident to Bryan that the United States was embarking on an imperialistic venture. There were rumors to the effect that he was disenchanted with military life and that he would resign as soon as September 1898.[8] He did not resign, as the early *New York Times* reports indicated; he remained in the army until December 11, 1898, one day after the Treaty of Paris was signed.[9]

However, the threat of imperialism caused Bryan's resignation. In December 1898, he held a news conference and condemned imperialism in no uncertain terms. He said:

Now that the treaty of peace has been concluded, I believe that I can be more useful to my country as a civilian than as a soldier. My judgment is that our country is in greater danger just now than Cuba. This nation cannot continue half a republic and half a colony—half free and half vassal. Our opponents quote Jefferson as favoring expansion, but they should distinguish between that which secures contiguous territory for future settlement and expansion which secures us alien races for future subjugation.[10]

How did Bryan define imperialism? Note in the passage just quoted that Bryan, an admirer of Thomas Jefferson, defended Jefferson's purchase of the Louisiana territory from France in 1803. What Bryan meant by imperialism was the acquisition of land outside the continental boundaries of the United States. He was criticizing colonialism—the political rule and economic exploitation of one country over another. Thus, he denounced the United States for its seizure of Cuba, Puerto Rico, and the Philippines, and berated his government for attempting to rule the people of Puerto Rico and the Philippines without regard to the American constitution.[11]

Bryan expanded on his definition of imperialism during the Roosevelt and Taft administrations. It not only meant colonialism, but also militarism. He called Roosevelt and Taft imperialists and denounced their military intervention in Latin America, whether intended to prevent a political revolution or to protect American economic interests.

Bryan had become involved in a full-scale war against imperialism. In a speech delivered in the winter of 1898, in Denver, Colorado, entitled "Naboth's Vineyard," he praised the Teller Amendment of April 1898, which demonstrated that the United States had no desire to possess Cuba, but only free it. He also warned of the dangers of imperialism, emphasizing that subjugation of colonial peoples should be left to the monarchies.[12] For Bryan, democracy and imperialism could not coexist, and the American system of government was endangered by the acceptance of imperialism abroad. He questioned whether a double standard of democracy in the United States and authoritarianism abroad could be applied indefinitely.[13]

Bryan also detested economic imperialism. He claimed that it was a financial burden on the American people, who were forced to pay more taxes in order to give a few speculators an opportunity for exploitation.[14] Bryan, in a speech made in Cuba on May 20, 1902, before Americans assembled at the Inglaterra Hotel to celebrate the birth of the Cuban republic, warned those living in Cuba to behave as good American citizens and to deal fairly with the Cuban people. He emphasized that money-making should not be their only object and that American businessmen should understand that they were only guests in a foreign land, since Cuba belonged to the Cubans. He hoped that American companies doing business in Cuba would give as much if not more than it took.[15] Bryan had a high regard for the Cuban people, and he felt that they were capable self-government. He said, "I believe that the Cubans are able to govern themselves. If any failure comes it is more likely to come from the interference of foreigners and from the attempt of outsiders to monopolize the resources of the island than from the incapacity of the people."[16] Here we see the roots of his hostility toward "dollar diplomacy."

BRYAN, THE ANTI-IMPERIALISTS, AND THE RATIFICATION OF THE TREATY OF PARIS

It is interesting to note that among Bryan's most vociferous critics were prominent anti-imperialists such as Republican Senator George F. Hoar of Massachusetts, ex-Republican President Benjamin Harrison, and Charles Francis Adams, Jr., grandson of one president and great-grandson of another. None of these men voted for Bryan in the 1900 campaign primarily because they questioned his anti-imperialist sentiments. Though some anti-imperialists, such as Carl Schurz, intellectual and reform politician; E. L. Godkin, editor of the *Nation*; and Charles Eliot Norton, intellectual and professor at Harvard University, had voted for Bryan, they also doubted his sincerity, but they could not support

McKinley—an outright imperialist. All of these men, and numerous others, formed the Anti-Imperialist League—a league that opposed the ratification of the Treaty of Paris that ended the Spanish-American War and called for the acquisition of the Philippines, Guam, and Puerto Rico, and the independence of Cuba.

The Anti-Imperialist League was formed in June 1898 in Chicago. Many of its members were political reformers who fought for civil service reform in the 1880s, intellectuals, and clergymen. Some like Norton and Adams opposed imperialism on idealistic grounds, while others, such as Schurz, opposed it on racial grounds. For example, Norton worried that the United States, by pursuing territory, would lose its unique place in the world as a leader in the progress of civilization. Adams could not believe such statements made by William Howard Taft, the civil governor of the Philippines from 1901 to 1904. Taft had declared that the United States would teach the people of the Philippines all about liberty and self-government. Adams saw a paradox between Taft's statement and the actual system established to run the Philippine government. He asked how it was possible to make them a self-governing community and then forbid them absolutely to discuss the principle of self-government. Are we going to make them an independent people by putting them in jail if they mention the word independence? Schurz, on the other hand, feared that the acquisition of new territory would bring a mixing of the races, which he felt would destroy the purity of American society. For example, he worried that the United States would absorb "immense territories inhabited by white people of Spanish descent, by Indians, by negroes, mixed Spanish and Indians, mixed Spanish and negroes, Hawaiians, Hawaiian mixed blood, Spanish Philippinos, Malays, Tagals. These people were savages and half-savages: they were all animated with the instinct, impulses and passions bred by the tropical sun."[17]

In December 1898, while the treaty was being debated in the Senate, President McKinley presented his annual message to the nation. He totally ignored the issue of expansionism and the question of Philippine annexation for one very good reason. His party then lacked the votes to obtain ratification, and he did not want to irritate the undecided senators by pushing the issue.[18]

While McKinley played down the treaty, Senator Hoar vehemently denounced it on the Senate floor. Hoar turned his wrath against Bryan, calling him a hypocrite for supporting the treaty, while touring the country on an anti-imperialistic crusade.[19] The industrialist and anti-imperialist Andrew Carnegie also questioned Bryan's commitment to anti-imperialism. Carnegie, the owner of the Carnegie Iron and Steel Works, which later became, along with other companies, the United States Steel Corporation, had conferred with Bryan during the debate in the Senate. The steel owner had told Bryan that he believed that the treaty was at least two votes short of ratification and that Bryan, by supporting the treaty, had disorganized matters.[20] Senator Wilkinson Call of Florida had wired Bryan to urge him to come to Washington to work against the treaty. He said, "Your friends think you ought to be here aiding Carnegie and others to amend the treaty."[21] Bryan told Call that the treaty was not the issue and that he would not oppose it. What Bryan wanted from McKinley was a resolution declaring U.S. policy in the Philippines. He said, "I believe that the fight should be made in favor of a resolution declaring the nation's policy. To reject the treaty or amend it throws the matter back into the hands of the executive. The resolution declaring policy might be passed before the treaty is ratified or it might be attached to the bill appropriating the twenty millions of dollars."[22]

In February 1899, the treaty was ratified by the Senate by a vote of 57 to 27. The treaty's supporters had acquired the necessary two-thirds vote with one vote to spare. Exactly how much influence Bryan had on the final vote in the Senate is debatable. Carnegie claimed that Bryan turned at least seven votes in favor of the treaty.   Hoar, Bryan's most vociferous critic, probably exaggerated when he declared that Bryan had influenced as many as seventeen votes. He wrote Bryan afterward stating that "next to McKinley, you are the person in the country most responsible for its adoption.[23] The anti-imperialists such as Hoar and Carnegie could never understand Bryan's reasoning for supporting the treaty. The historian Robert Beisner questioned both Bryan's commitment to anti-imperialism and his influence on the vote in the Senate. Beisner claimed that Bryan had little influence on the outcome of the vote. Most of the country favored the treaty, since they equated nationalism with imperialism.[24]

Paxton Hibben, a Bryan biographer, claimed that Bryan had supported the ratification of the treaty in order to find a campaign issue to run on in the 1900 election—he would obtain ratification and then speak against it. This makes no sense, since Bryan's opponents would always claim that he supported the treaty's passage, and Bryan would be in a poor position to make the treaty a campaign issue. In fact, he separated the issue of imperialism from the treaty. As early as December 1898, he urged ratification. He said, "Some think that the fight against expansion should be made against ratification of the treaty, but it will be easier, I think, to end the war by ratifying the treaty and then obtain a declaration of our national policy through Congress."[25] Two months later, at a Democratic banquet in St. Paul, Minnesota, he again defended ratification by telling his fellow Democrats that

the ratification of the treaty instead of committing the United States to a colonial policy really clears the way for recognition of a Philippine republic. Lincoln in his first inaugural message, condensed the unanswerable argument into a brief question when he asked: "Can aliens make treaties easier than aliens can make laws?" The same argument is presented in the question: Could the independence of the Filipinos be secured more easily by diplomacy from a foreign and hostile nation than it can through laws passed by Congress and voicing the sentiments of the American people alone?[26]

Bryan thought that it was best to ratify the treaty, release the soldiers from duty, and end the war expenditure. He emphasized that it was better to trust the United States to eradicate imperialism than Spain.[27]

Bryan also condemned the clause in the Treaty of Paris relating to the island of Puerto Rico. He berated the U.S. government for failing to give the people of Puerto Rico American citizenship and denounced the Supreme Court's decision, in June 1901, that upheld the government's policy. He called that decision unjust, and asked how Congress could deal with Puerto Rico without regard to the limitations of the U.S. Constitution.[28]

In November 1900, the Cuban convention dared to adopt a constitution without provision for future relations with the United States. The American government, anxious to continue its economic and political influence in Cuba, passed the Platt Amendment and then forced the Cuban government to embody it in the new Cuban constitution. The provisions of this amendment were embarrassing to both the Cuban people and the anti-imperialists in the United States. The first and third articles were the most relevant. The first stipulated that Cuba could not enter into any treaty or other compact with a foreign power that would endanger its independence. The third allowed the United States to intervene in Cuban affairs whenever disorder threatened that country's independence.[29]

Bryan backed the anti-imperialistic position and denounced the Platt Amendment. He called it a complete repudiation of the Teller Amendment and accused financial interests of wanting to establish a protectorate over Cuba.[30] In a statement that went beyond Cuba, he declared that "it was not necessary that the United States formally establish a protectorate over any republic on American soil."[31] Bryan completely reversed his position on protectorates in 1913 when, as secretary of state, he attempted, against the opposition of his own party, to form a protectorate over Nicaragua, which, in many ways, went beyond the Platt Amendment that he so vociferously opposed in 1901.

ANTI-IMPERIALISM AND THE PRESIDENTIAL ELECTIONS FROM 1900-1912

Bryan's anti-imperialism was also evident in the Democratic platforms from 1900 to 1912. Until the election of Woodrow Wilson in 1912, Bryan remained the most influential member of the Democratic party. He was not only its nominee in 1900 and 1908, but he also influenced and approved all the party platforms from 1900 to 1912.[32]

Before the Democrats met in Kansas City, Missouri, in July 1900, the question on most delegates' minds was what issue would best unite the party. Free silver had been the main issue in 1896, but it had divided the party between the Cleveland and Bryan Democrats and ensured the election of the Republican candidate William McKinley. Since 1896, the topic of imperialism had become the major issue, providing the Democrats with the opportunity to unite again. It was Bourke Cockran, a Democrat who had supported McKinley in 1896, who put it best when he said in January 1900 that he would support Bryan if the major issue were imperialism.[33]

When the Democratic convention opened in Kansas City in July 1900, Bryan was chosen as the nominee. He wanted to make imperialism the major issue, but he could not put aside the free silver issue of 1896, and demanded that it be put into the Democratic platform. The silver plank was the best thing that could have happened for the Republicans in this election. The Philippine insurrection had driven the Republicans into a defensive position, and they were looking for something that would divide the Democrats. With the silver issue, the Republicans were looking forward to fighting the 1896 election once again. McKinley took up the challenge and in his acceptance letter he stated that the currency question was the major issue in the 1900 campaign.[34]

In the beginning of the campaign, Bryan did stress the imperialism issue. He helped to write a plank into the platform that denounced the keeping of American soldiers in Cuba. It read as follows:

We demand the prompt and honest fulfillment of our pledge to the Cuban people and the world that the United States has no disposition nor intention to exercise sovereignty, jurisdiction or control over the island of Cuba except for its pacification. The war ended nearly two years ago, profound peace reigns over all the island, and still the administration keeps the government of the island from its people, while Republican carpetbag officials plunder its revenues and exploit the colonial theory to the disgrace of the American people.[35]

The Democratic platform also denounced the government's policy toward Puerto Rico (denying the people the rights of American citizens) as pure exploitation of the Puerto Rican people. The plank in the platform embodied the same words used during the American Revolution to describe the situation— "taxation without representation."[36]

The platform also opposed militarism and conquest, but it declared that the Democratic party was not opposed to territorial expansion when it included desirable territory that would become states and whose people would become U.S. citizens.[37] Bryan had said almost the very same thing in December 1898 when he defended Jeffersonian expansionism while denouncing imperialism.[38]

The Democratic platform also supported the construction, ownership, and control of a Nicaraguan canal. After the Spanish-American War, the need for a canal became obvious to both political parties. For example, during the war the U.S.S. *Oregon* had taken many weeks to sail from the Puget Sound around Cape Horn to come to the defense of the East Coast. Now that the United States had acquired Pacific Ocean territory, it became necessary for the American navy to travel quickly from ocean to ocean. By 1900, Nicaragua had become the leading site for the canal that would be eventually built in Panama.[39] A detailed discussion of the Panama Canal and the Colombian treaty is discussed in chapter 9.

McKinley was re-elected in 1900 and imperialism had little to do with his victory. In analyzing the election, Bryan proved his own worst enemy. He opened his campaign by blasting colonialism, militarism, and imperialism, but his audiences were unresponsive, so Bryan turned to attacking the trusts, special privilege, and plutocracy. He pushed the silver issue, forcing many Gold

Democrats and anti-imperialists to choose between the money issue and anti-imperialism.[40]   Anti-imperialists such as Andrew Carnegie and Charles Francis Adams voted for McKinley because they regarded economic chaos, resulting from free silver, as the more immediate danger. The Republican Carl Schurz, on the other hand, was one of the few who concluded that imperialism was worse than free silver and voted for Bryan.[41] McKinley and the Republicans emphasized the gold standard, the protective tariff, and patriotism. The Republicans had warned the working class in the cities that free silver would cause inflation, which would bring an end to the existing prosperity. In the final analysis, the electorate preferred the known weaknesses of McKinley to the wild theories of Bryan.[42]

Bryan's influence in the writing of the platform in 1900 was evident in both the Cuban and Puerto Rican planks. Later, in 1901, he would denounce both the Platt Amendment and the Supreme Court decision relating to Puerto Rico. After the election, Bryan traveled to Europe for a long needed vacation.[43]

When the Democratic convention met in St. Louis in 1904, Alton B. Parker was nominated, much to Bryan's disappointment. Parker, a conservative Democrat was chosen for his safe views and close ties to New York wealth. Bryan initially hesitated about giving Parker his endorsement fearing that the nominee would oppose many of the policies that the Democrats had supported in 1900. As early as April 1904, Bryan had criticized Parker and the New York State Committee for omitting mention of imperialism from its state platform.[44] However, Bryan's concerns proved unfounded—the Democratic platform in 1904 contained a scathing denunciation of imperialism.[45] Bryan praised the platform by formally endorsing it in the *Commoner* a week after the convention ended. He lauded the Democratic opposition to imperialism, criticized the militarism of President Theodore Roosevelt, the Republican presidential candidate, and supported a reduction in the standing army.[46]

Roosevelt, a very popular president, easily won election (he had been vice-president when McKinley was assassinated in September 1901) over Parker who ran a dull campaign. Four years later in July 1908, the Democrats met in Colorado and once again nominated Bryan. The 1908 platform condemned imperialism in the Philippines and demanded that the people of Puerto Rico be given the rights and privileges of a territorial form of government, but more important, it recognized the economic advantages of developing closer ties of friendship between the United States and the countries of Latin America. This was the first time that a major party in the United States adopted a desire for a new relationship with Latin America in its platform.[47]

Once again, Bryan lost in 1908. This time he was defeated by William Howard Taft, a corporation lawyer, governor-general of the Philippines, and Roosevelt's secretary of war. Bryan had the distinction of becoming the first and only major presidential party candidate to be nominated three times and to lose all three times.

In 1912, the Democratic party turned away from Bryan, now its elder statesman, and gave its nomination to Thomas Woodrow Wilson, governor of New

Jersey. When the Democratic convention opened on June 25, Wilson was not the favorite to win the nomination. The leading candidate (in those days a candidate had to have two-thirds of the delegates to secure the nomination) was Champ Clark, speaker of the House of Representatives. Clark had allied himself with New York's Tammany Hall, a formidable political machine. Bryan was upset by the Clark-Tammany Hall alliance. As chairman of the Nebraska delegation, he had promised the people of Nebraska that he would not support a Tammany Hall candidate. Wilson decided to use Bryan's antipathy for Tammany Hall to seek his support for the nomination. Finally, Wilson, on July 2, after forty-six ballots, received the nomination with Bryan's blessing. The platform was a progressive document influenced by Bryan's anti-imperialism. It denounced imperialism in general terms and specifically declared that the Democrats would recognize the independence of the Philippines as soon as a stable government was established there.[48]

THEODORE ROOSEVELT, WILLIAM HOWARD TAFT, AND LATIN AMERICA

Bryan's reaction to the actual policies of Roosevelt and Taft in Latin America from 1901 to 1912 demonstrated his strong stand against imperialism. When Roosevelt made his speech to Congress in December 1901, Bryan ridiculed him for pretending to help the backward peoples to self-government, when in fact his whole policy was based upon force and power.[49] Again, in April 1902, Bryan attacked Roosevelt by detailing the differences between Roosevelt's imperialism and Jefferson's expansionism. He related that "Jefferson favored the annexation of contiguous territory, to be inhabited by American citizens and to be built into American states."[50] In referring to Roosevelt, he said, "Roosevelt favors the conquest of remote islands to be inhabited by subjects and to be held as colonies, taxed without representation and governed without the consent of the governed."[51] The above statement pertained to Republican policies in Puerto Rico, the Philippines, Guam, Samoa, and Hawaii.

The United States government intervened in various areas of Latin America throughout the early twentieth century. Cuba had been a trouble spot ever since the implementation of the Platt Amendment. Political turmoil prevailed there even after American troops departed. Following the Cuban election in 1902, Bryan blamed the Republican party for giving the impression that it had interfered in that election.[52]

In 1902, a crisis in Latin America began to unfold. Great Britain, Italy, and Germany threatened intervention in Venezuela in order to collect debts owed to their citizens. Cipriano Castro had become president of Venezuela in 1899 by the traditional Latin American revolution. Like many of his predecessors, he had failed to improve the economy and had incurred a large debt that he refused to pay. The Roosevelt administration had refused to help the corrupt Cipriano Castro government. In fact, Roosevelt had contemptuously referred to the Venezuelan president as an "unspeakably villainous little monkey."[53] In December 1902, Britain, Italy, and Germany prepared a naval expedition. They seized four Venezuelan gunboats, sinking three of them and then proceeded to blockade five principal Venezuelan ports.[54] Roosevelt, at first, did not seem to object to the European intervention, since he was led to believe by Germany and Great Britain that it would not involve the annexation of any territory. Furthermore, nothing in the Monroe Doctrine prevented foreign nations from collecting debts. In July 1901, Vice-president Roosevelt had stated that "if any Southern American country misbehaves toward any European country, let the European country spank it."[55] Roosevelt had known that these countries had offered Castro early arbitration to settle the debt dispute, but the Venezuelan president had refused to consider it. U.S. public opinion favored the foreign nations since most of the press also believed that Castro was obligated to pay his country's debts. However, when a German warship bombarded Fort Carlos and the surrounding Venezuelan village, both Roosevelt and public opinion in the United States began to change. The American president became suspicious of Germany's intentions, believing that it was prepared to seize territory in Venezuela as compensation for debts owed.[56] At this point, Roosevelt suggested arbitration, and the matter was settled by the Hague Permanent Court of Arbitration.[57] Bryan had supported the arbitration proceedings, but condemned Roosevelt for delaying and, thereby, endangering Venezuela. He argued that immediate arbitration should have been undertaken when Great Britain, Italy, and Germany approached Roosevelt with their intentions.[58]

In 1903, an incident occurred that threatened U.S.-Colombian relations. The United States had bargained with the New Panama Canal Company to build an Isthmian canal. This company already had an agreement with the Colombian government, which was sovereign over Panama. Colombia, wanting more money, refused to allow the United States permission to build the canal. A revolution then occurred in Panama, which declared its independence from Colombia. When the Colombian government sent soldiers to quell the revolution, the U.S. Navy successfully blockaded their entry into Panama, and the U.S. government recognized the new Panamanian regime.[59] Roosevelt was open to the charge that he had fomented the revolution, and the image of the United States suffered considerably in other Latin American countries as well as among critics at home. This incident will be dealt with more thoroughly in chapter 9. Nevertheless, we should note that Bryan had become one of the most vociferous critics of the Roosevelt administration's Panama policy. He criticized the administration for recognizing so quickly the independence of Panama—only three days after the revolt.[60] Bryan called Roosevelt's action a clear violation of international law and a change of policy from McKinley, who in 1898 had refused to recognize the independence of Cuba.[61] Bryan also denounced Roosevelt for interpreting the 1846 treaty with Colombia in a way favoring the United States. He admitted that the United States could intervene, according to the treaty, in case of chaos, but Colombia, by the same treaty, was guaranteed sovereignty over the area.[62]

When John Barrett, a diplomatic appointee to Panama, wrote an article in October 1904 praising Roosevelt's "big stick" diplomacy as ennobling the United States among world powers, Bryan criticized the article and charged that Roosevelt was changing the ideals of the nation by substituting "big stick" for liberty.[63] Bryan perceived the United States as a beacon of liberty and a model of republican virtue. Like Roosevelt, he eagerly wanted the United States to be a world leader, but that leadership should be by example and not military force. He declared that "if this nation enters upon a career of imperialism it ceases to be a moral factor in the world's progress."[64] Bryan continued to deplore Roosevelt's warlike attitude whenever the opportunity presented itself.

In 1905, the Roosevelt administration, worried about the deteriorating financial situation in Santo Domingo and elsewhere, proceeded to make an agreement with Santo Domingo by which an American would control the receivership. This was not a quick decision by the president. As early as 1903, a dictatorship had squandered the treasury, and the country was unable to meet its financial obligations to citizens of France, Italy, and Germany. By the end of that year, it was rumored that a German naval squadron was headed for the Dominican Republic to force the issue. The French and Italian governments, on behalf of their citizens, were also threatening to use force. Meanwhile, numerous journals in Great Britain were taking the position that if the United States wanted to protect Latin American countries from foreign intervention, then the United States had to assume some responsibility for debt collection.[65]

Roosevelt, however, refused to take any action until after the 1904 election. After his election victory in November 1904, the president officially proclaimed what became known as the Roosevelt Corollary to the Monroe Doctrine to the Congress in December 1904. He stated that the United States would not intervene in the affairs of countries that conducted themselves "with decency in industrial and political matters" and met their financial obligations. But he declared that "brutal wrongdoing, or an impotence which results in a general loosening of the ties of civilized society, may finally require intervention by some civilized nation, and in the Western Hemisphere the United States cannot ignore this duty."[66]

With the Roosevelt Corollary in place, the State Department, in January 1905, recommended to Roosevelt that an American be appointed as the collector of Dominican customs and director of national finance. The agreement called for 45 percent of the total receipts to be given to the Dominican government for operating expenses, and the rest to be placed in a trust fund to pay the international debts and obligations.[67]

Although the plan appeared practical, Bryan blamed the United States and foreign countries for the receivership. He noted that European governments had been in the habit of backing up the "usurious claims" of their citizens and now charged that the United States was doing the same.[68] Bryan went further in stating that loans should be entirely free of fraud, and pointed out that if a nation wanted to back its citizen's claims, it should force them to lend at fair interest rates.[69]

In a speech delivered at Madison Square Garden on August 30, 1906, Bryan had alluded to the Dominican situation by strongly opposing the use of the navy for the collection of private debts. He added that any person who conducted business abroad must be subject to the laws of the country in which his transactions occur.[70] Here we witness Bryan's hostility to "gunboat diplomacy," and his attack on the use of the navy. In 1910, he enlarged on his criticism of the navy. He said:

I believe that our nation can take a long step in advance now by announcing that the navy will not be used for the collection of debts; that as we do not imprison people for debt in this country, we will not man battleships and kill people because they owe people in this country; that we will apply to international affairs, the very doctrine we apply to our national affairs, and if anyone in the United States wishes to invest money in another country, he must do so according to the laws of that country. Then every nation would be open to American investments. For that is the kind of investments they look for. They have had enough of the investments which are preceded by the purchase of a little land to be followed by a battleship that takes the rest of the country.[71]

In 1906, the Roosevelt administration had to confront the growing crisis in Cuba. The background to this crisis stemmed from 1904 when the Moderate party was founded, and President Estrada Palma decided to run on its ticket for a second term. The Liberal party chose Jose Miguel Gomez to oppose him.[72] When it appeared that the Moderates would win the election, the Liberals withdrew from the contest, proclaimed it fraudulent, and threatened revolution. In December 1905, Palma was re-elected and sporadic fighting began, initiated by the Liberals who hoped for American intervention and new elections.[73] In September 1906, Roosevelt, after unsuccessful mediation, appointed William Howard Taft provisional governor of Cuba. In October 1906, Charles E. Magoon succeeded Taft and American occupation lasted until 1909.[74]

During the Cuban crisis, Bryan urged Roosevelt to withdraw American troops from Havana. He favored mediation, and when Roosevelt attempted it, Bryan supported him.[75] When intervention did occur in the form of a provisional government in September 1906, Bryan reminded the Republican administration that the United States must not tarnish its name by using this opportunity to acquire territory.[76]

When William Howard Taft became president in 1909, he also had to contend with the sharp criticism of Bryan. In his newspaper, the *Commoner*, Bryan denounced Taft for following Roosevelt's policy of building a large navy. Bryan believed it would mean more intervention and belligerency. He opposed interventionism as a policy, stating that he wanted his country to be "the supreme moral factor in the world's progress, a republic whose flag is loved while other flags are only feared.[77]

When civil war in Nicaragua broke out in 1910, Bryan opposed intervention, firmly believing that the Nicaraguan government could resolve its own problems. The United States did intervene in 1912, but this will be discussed in chapter 3.[78]

In 1910, Bryan visited the Latin American region. He went to Panama, Cuba, Bolivia, Argentina, Chile, Uruguay, and Brazil. He learned firsthand about the problems facing the people and government and made speeches about the necessity of increasing friendly relations between the United States and its southern neighbors.[79] Visiting the Panama Canal Zone in March 1910 Bryan incessantly praised the building of the canal as a great engineering feat and declared that it would bring the two regions closer together economically.[80] Perhaps it was his growing attachment to the importance of the canal that prompted him to act as Roosevelt and Taft had in Nicaragua, Haiti, and the Dominican Republic in 1913. As early as 1910, Bryan wrote that the canal should be freely used by all nations without charge other than that necessary to cover the operational expenses. One reason for his liberality was the fear that Europeans would also build a canal somewhere in Latin America, and like Roosevelt and Taft, he opposed the extension of European influence in the Western Hemisphere.[81]

Bryan spoke in Lima, Peru, in February 1910 about the importance of the Isthmian Canal. He spoke of neighborly love and American interest that derived from proximity. He favored a program of student exchange as the best way of maintaining peace and understanding between North and South America.[82]

In Brazil, Bryan stressed the role the United States had to play if it wanted to help the Latin American people and gain their friendship and trust. He emphasized the need to send machines and tools to the Latin American people to help them increase their productivity. He also pointed out that the illiteracy rate in many Latin American countries was too high, and he stressed the need to help their governments improve their educational facilities. Bryan believed that it was important that our southern neighbors feel an attachment toward the United States. He said, "If our influence is to be paramount in the southern half of the western hemisphere, we must make it so by disinterested and helpful service in the development of the younger republics, and the advancement of their welfare."[83]

Perhaps Bryan's interest in American conduct toward Latin American can best be concluded by his speech to the Puerto Rico Association in San Juan, Puerto Rico, on April 9, 1910. Bryan told of the advancements of Americans in all fields; he noted that the government of the United States, with its technology, had the opportunity to speed or retard the progress of the Puerto Rican people. Since an opportunity existed, Bryan had hoped that not only the government of the United States, but also American businessmen in Puerto Rico would treat the people there fairly.[84]

In conclusion, Bryan's interest in Latin America really began with the ratification of the Treaty of Paris, which brought the Spanish-American War to a conclusion. By 1900, he became disenchanted with what he viewed as the beginning American imperialism. He attacked the Platt Amendment in Cuba and the Supreme Court decision involving Puerto Rico's status. He not only was responsible for the anti-imperialistic planks of the Democratic party platforms from 1900 to 1912, but he also condemned the Latin American policies of the Roosevelt and Taft administrations. Bryan's interest in cultivating good relations with Latin America continued to be one of his most important goals. During his extensive visit there in 1910, he demanded the termination of "dollar diplomacy" and imperialism and the substitution of friendship and increased economic and cultural exchange.

NOTES

1. Samuel Flagg Bemis, *The Latin American Policy of the United States* (New York: Harcourt, Brace and Company, 1943), p. 133.

2. H. Wayne Morgan, *America's Road to Empire: The War with Spain and Overseas Expansion* (New York: Wiley, 1965), pp. 60-63; Paul S. Holbo, "Presidential Leadership in Foreign Affairs: William McKinley and the Turpie-Foraker Amendment," *American Historical Review* 72 (July 1967): 1321-1335; Bemis, *The Latin American Policy of the United States*, pp. 131-137.

3. Bemis, *The Latin American Policy of the United States*, p. 138.

4. *New York Times*, April 1, 1898.

5. Ibid., June 15, 1898.

6. Ibid., May 18, 1898.

7. Ibid., May 27, 1898.

8. Ibid., September 21, 1898.

9. Ibid., December 12, 1898.

10. Ibid., December 14, 1898.

11. Ibid.

12. William Jennings Bryan, *Speeches of William Jennings Bryan*, vol. 2 (New York: Funk and Wagnalls, 1909), pp. 7-8.

13. Ibid., p. 12.

14. *New York Times*, April 7, 1899.

15. *Commoner*, June 6, 1902.

16. Ibid.

17. Irwin Unger, *These United States: The Questions of Our Past*, 4th ed. (Englewood Cliffs, N.J.: Prentice-Hall, 1989), p. 575.

18. Paul W. Glad, ed., *William Jennings Bryan: A Profile* (New York: Hill and Wang, 1968), p. 59.

19. Ibid., pp. 62, 67.

20. Ibid., p. 63.

21. Ibid., p. 64.

22. Ibid.

23. Ibid., p. 67; Louis W. Koenig, *Bryan: A Political Biography of William Jennings Bryan* (New York: G. P. Putnam's Sons, 1971), p. 293.

24. Robert L. Beisner, *Twelve Against Empire: The Anti-Imperialists, 1898-1900* (New York: McGraw-Hill, 1968), pp. 130-131.

25. Paxton Hibben, *The Peerless Leader William Jennings Bryan* (New York: Russell and Russell, 1967), p. 222; *New York Times*, December 14, 1898.

26. *New York Times*, February 15, 1899.

27. *Commoner*, May 17, 1901.

28. Ibid.; Ibid., June 7, 1901.

29. Bemis, *The Latin American Policy of the United States*, p. 141.

30. *Commoner*, March 15, 1901.

31. Ibid., February 6, 1901.

32. *New York Times*, July 6, 1900.

33. Ibid., January 27, 1900.

34. Glad, *William Jennings Bryan*, p. 78.

35. *New York Times*, July 6, 1900.

36. Ibid.

37. Ibid.

38. Ibid., December 14, 1898.

39. Ibid., July 6, 1900.

40. Glad, *William Jennings Bryan*, pp. 78, 80.

41. Ibid., p. 80.

42. *New York Times*, July 6, 1900.

43. *Commoner*, March 15, 1901, and May 17, 1901.

44. *New York Times*, April 24, 1904.

45. Ibid., July 8, 1904.

46. *Commoner*, July 15, 1904.

47. *New York Times*, July 10, 1908.

48. Ibid., July 3, 1912; Arthur S. Link, *Wilson: The Road to the White House* (Princeton, N.J.: Princeton University Press, 1947), p. 463.

49. *Commoner*, December 13, 1901.

50. Ibid., April 11, 1902.

51. Ibid.

52. Ibid., January 31, 1902.

53. George E. Mowry, *The Era of Theodore Roosevelt and the Birth of Modern America, 1900-1912* (New York: Harper and Row, 1958), p. 157.

54. Bemis, *The Latin American Policy of the United States*, p. 146.

55. Henry Pringle, *Theodore Roosevelt* (New York: Harcourt, Brace, Jovanovich, 1956), p.198.

56. Mowry, *The Era of Theodore Roosevelt*, p. 157.

57. Bemis, *The Latin American Policy of the United States*, p. 147.

58. *Commoner,* January 2, 1903.

59. Dana G. Munro, *Intervention and Dollar Diplomacy in the Caribbean, 1900-1921* (Princeton, N.J.: Princeton University Press, 1964), p. 53.

60. *Commoner*, November 13, 1903.

61. Ibid.

62. Ibid., November 20, 1903.

63. *New York Times*, October 27, 1904.

64. Leroy Ashby, *William Jennings Bryan: Champion of Democracy* (Boston: Twayne Publishers, 1987), pp. 85-86.

65. Mowry, *The Era of Theodore Roosevelt*, pp. 158-159.

66. Ibid., p. 159.

67. Ibid., pp. 159-160.

68. *Commoner*, March 24, 1905.

69. Ibid.

70. Bryan, *Speeches of William Jennings Bryan*, vol. 2, p. 67.

71. Merle F. Curti, "Bryan and World Peace," *Smith College Studies in History* 16 (April-July 1931): 140.

72. Munro, *Intervention and Dollar Diplomacy in the Caribbean*, p. 126.

73. Ibid., p. 127.

74. Ibid., p. 133.

75. *Commoner*, September 21, 1906.

76. Ibid., October 5, 1906.

77. Ibid., April 16, 1909; Ashby, *William Jennings Bryan*, p. 151.

78. *Commoner*, January 7, 1910.

79. Ibid., June 17, 1910.

80. Ibid., March 11, 1910.

81. Ibid.

82. Ibid., February 25, 1910.

83. *New York World Magazine*, June 19, 1910.

84. Address of William Jennings Bryan to the Porto Rico Association at San Juan, April 9, 1910, Bryan Papers, Library of Congress.

3

The Beginnings of a Latin American Policy

BRYAN'S APPOINTMENT AS SECRETARY OF STATE

After the election of Woodrow Wilson to the presidency in November 1912, he set to work, during the pre-inauguration period, choosing his cabinet and advisers, and beginning the formulation of a foreign and domestic policy. The choice of the cabinet was the most important, and among its positions, the secretary of state held the highest status. The individual who accepts this position must work in harmony with the president, advise him, and have a knowledge of the workings of foreign policy. President-elect Wilson chose William Jennings Bryan as his secretary of state.

Arthur S. Link, a Wilson biographer and historian, has written that Bryan received his position because of the part he played in securing the nomination for Wilson at the Baltimore Convention in the summer of 1912.[1] In fact, Wilson had recognized Bryan's importance a year earlier when he had declared that "no Democrat can win whom Mr. Bryan does not approve."[2] Since Bryan did not support the leading contender, Champ Clark of Missouri, and later came out for Wilson during the convention, and campaigned actively for him during the election—Bryan had spent seven weeks on the campaign trail, making numerous speeches on his behalf—Wilson felt indebted to him.[3]

Most Democrats recognized that Bryan had to be given an important post in the new administration. He was still the most important Democrat in the party aside from Wilson. He had been its nominee in 1896, 1900, and 1908; had much to say about the formulation of the party platforms; and had a great number of influential friends in the Democratic party. Right after the nomination and just prior to the election, Wilson asked Albert S. Burleson of Texas, his future postmaster general, "If I am elected, what in the world am I going to do with W. J. Bryan." Burleson had replied, "Make him Secretary of State."[4] Wilson did not make any decision on Bryan at that time but waited until after the election.

Immediately after the election in November, Edward M. House, Wilson's close personal adviser and friend, met with the president-elect four times to discuss appointments to the cabinet. When Bryan's name was raised, it was first decided that he should be given a diplomatic post, but later, both House and Wilson agreed that it would be best to keep Bryan in Washington, close to the administration and friendly toward it, since he held great influence in the party.[5]

On December 21, 1912, Bryan met Wilson in Trenton, New Jersey. For three hours they talked about cabinet appointments when Wilson finally asked him to be his secretary of state. Bryan told the president-elect that he would have preferred being secretary of the treasury, but he would accept this appointment on two conditions; (1) he would not have to serve alcoholic beverages at State Department functions (Bryan was a teetotaler); and (2) Wilson would allow Bryan to negotiate a series of peace treaties that would outlaw war forever. Wilson told Bryan to follow his conscience when it came to serving alcoholic beverages and that he had no objections to these peace treaties.[6]

Many historians, including Link, claim that Wilson's choice of Bryan reflected political realities more than enthusiasm or confidence in Bryan's abilities. They state that the president-elect had little respect for Bryan's judgment and dreaded the prospect of potential disagreements.[7] It was Bryan's personal following among the party leaders, his devotion to the Democratic party, and the comparative lack of importance given to foreign affairs in 1912-1913, as much as it was his aid in securing the nomination for Wilson that made Bryan Wilson's first secretary of state.[8]

Though Bryan accepted the appointment in December 1912, it was not made public until the end of January 1913. In fact, Bryan's own paper, the *Commoner*, as late as January 10, 1913, repudiated outright the assertion that its editor and chief had been offered any position in Wilson's cabinet.[9] When the appointment was made public later that month, the *New York Times* noted that Bryan had been the man Wilson wanted for secretary of state even before election day, that the Democratic leaders supported Bryan's appointment, and that he had made no request for the job.[10]

BRYAN, PEACE, AND THE ARBITRATION TREATIES

As early as 1900, Bryan in a speech accepting the Democratic nomination, indicated the type of policy he would favor. He held that the United States should set an example by its own conduct and become "the supreme moral factor in the world's progress and the accepted arbiter of the world's disputes."[11] Morality became an instrument in the working of foreign policy. Bryan possessed the fixation that things were either right or wrong; he seldom saw two sides of an issue. This inflexibility and adherence to morality, perhaps, came from his religious zeal. He was Presbyterian, attended church frequently, and considered himself a pious Christian. He believed that all men were brothers and should act toward each other with kindness and love.[12] Because of this attitude, the one thing he feared above all else was war. To Bryan, it was the most un Christian act that humanity could inflict upon his fellow man. In 1902, when he visited Europe and Asia, he met his great hero, Leo Tolstoy, the apostle of peace; it was Tolstoy who influenced Bryan more than any other individual.[13] When he became secretary of state, Bryan applied his Christian and moral principles to foreign policy, noting little difference between the behavior of individuals and nations.[14] He believed that the first objective of the president and secretary of state must be peace, and one of the first steps he took was to formulate treaties of arbitration. He wanted to conclude treaties with all nations requiring the submission of belligerent disputes to investigation by an international commission. The disputing parties would agree not to declare war for one year, giving the arbitration commission time to make suggestions for a settlement. Bryan gave this plan his full attention, and by the end of his first year in office, it had been adopted by five Central American states and the Netherlands.[15]

BRYAN'S RELATIONSHIP WITH WILSON

When Bryan became secretary of state there was some question whether he would be able to work well with Wilson. For years, the new secretary of state had been the leader of the Democratic party and now that position had shifted to Wilson. Wilsonian historians Ray Stannard Baker and Link both claim that Bryan, upon becoming secretary of state, accepted Wilson's leadership and worked harmoniously with him. According to Link, Bryan was so loyal to Wilson that he suppressed all his political ambitions. Wilson, on the other hand, hoping to concentrate on his domestic "New Freedom" programs, was willing to listen to Bryan's advice on foreign policy. The president allowed Bryan to negotiate his arbitration treaties, and he gave him a free hand in Nicaragua, Haiti, and the Dominican Republic.[16] Baker went even further than Link by not only stressing the mutual loyalty between the two men, but also emphasizing their closeness and admiration for each other.[17] The overwhelming amount of materials in the National Archives, including the Bryan-Wilson Correspondence, attests to the fact that both of these men corresponded frequently, making suggestions on important foreign policy decisions and respecting each others opinions. This is not to say that Wilson accepted all of Bryan's suggestions or that Bryan agreed with all of Wilson's decisions, but only that before important decisions were made, Bryan and Wilson conferred extensively.

After a few days in office, Wilson called a cabinet meeting where Latin American relations were discussed. Wilson read a statement on future policy in Latin America and gave a copy to Bryan to send to American diplomats in South and Central America. David F. Houston, the secretary of agriculture, noted in his diary that Bryan accepted the Wilsonian statement without reservation, adding that it appeared that the president would be his own secretary of state.[18] This assumption was premature and proved incorrect. There was little question that Wilson determined American foreign policy in the last analysis, but he gave his secretary of state a free hand in Nicaragua, Haiti, and the Dominican Republic; the formulation of the Colombian treaty was also Bryan's work. Wilson determined Mexican policy and appeared in the vanguard in the fight for repeal of exemption in the Panama Canal tolls controversy. Nevertheless, as we shall see later, Bryan contributed to both the Mexican and Panama Canal tolls policies.[19]

Bryan supported the Wilsonian statement issued at the cabinet meeting on March 11, 1913, not to appease his chief, but because it embodied many of the same principles he had supported previously. The statement began with the following objectives: the desire to cultivate friendship and gain the confidence of "our sister republics of Central and South America." It warned about the necessity of maintaining orderly and democratic government and concluded that

the United States has nothing to seek in Central and South America except the lasting interests of the peoples of the two continents, the security of governments intended for the people and for no special group or interest, and the development of personal and trade relationships between the two continents which shall redound to the profit and advantage of both and interfere with the rights and liberties of neither.[20]

Wilson's statement embodied many of the things that Bryan had said in some of his earlier speeches against imperialism and on his Latin American speaking tour in 1910. In fact, in his speeches in Cuba, in May 1902, and in Puerto Rico, in April 1910, Bryan had advocated the need to deal fairly with our Latin American neighbors in order to cultivate friendship and understanding.[21] Bryan's support of Wilson's statement that the United States would not seek in Central and South America additional territory or advantage came as a result of his own opposition to the Platt Amendment.[22] Bryan also favored Wilson's position regarding the opening of trade relations between North and South America. When visiting the Panama Canal Zone in 1910, Bryan noted that the opening of the canal would be economically advantageous to both the United States and Latin America.[23] Thus, the comment that Houston had made in his diary that Bryan agreed with Wilson on his Latin American statement was true but not because, as Houston implied, Wilson dominated and Bryan acquiesced, but because Bryan believed that what the president said embodied his own thought.

BRYAN'S NEW LATIN AMERICAN POLICY

Only two days after the Wilson statement was sent to the American embassies in Latin America, Bryan attended a dinner given by John Barrett, the director-general of the Pan-American Union. In attendance were numerous diplomats from South and Central America who were interested in what the new secretary of state had to say regarding their region. Many of them were upset with the Roosevelt Corollary to the Monroe Doctrine, which made the United States the self-appointed policeman of the Western Hemisphere. Though Bryan did not directly address the corollary, he did try to mitigate their hostility toward the United States by emphasizing the need for increased trade and cultural exchange between the two regions. He attacked the "evil" U.S. business interests who exploited the Latin American peoples, and promised that as secretary of state, he would see that the United States government would act honorably toward all foreign nations.[24]

Bryan had never been a friend of big business. From 1901 to 1904, he had attacked trusts and monopolies. John D. Rockefeller, the oil baron, became one of Bryan's frequent targets. In a speech in 1904, he lambasted Rockefeller by declaring that "no criminal now incarcerated for larceny has shown more indifference to human rights and property rights."[25] Just prior to the 1904 election campaign, Bryan welcomed business opposition to his candidacy. He declared, "We want the trust magnates against us, not for us." [26] Even though he did not get the nomination that year, he continued, throughout his life, to fight against what became know as the "Wall Street influence."

In May 1913, Bryan spoke to the ministers of the twenty Central and South American republics at a dinner at the Waldorf Astoria in New York City. He stated that American capital and enterprise could help in the development of latent resources in Latin America, but only on the basis of a "dollar of service, for every dollar of earning."[27] Perhaps Bryan's sincerity could be measured by his statement denouncing "dollar diplomacy." He said, "The Lord has made us neighbors: let justice make us friends.[28]

It appeared that "dollar diplomacy" would finally be eradicated by the Wilson administration. The new secretary of state had opposed it as a private citizen, and he certainly gave no indication in the spring of 1913 that he had changed his mind. In fact, Bryan made explicit his views on the subject in the *Commoner* in May 1913. He defined "dollar diplomacy" by declaring that "it is a phrase coined to describe a policy of government under which the State Department has been used to coerce smaller nations into recognizing claims of American citizens which did not rest upon a legitimate basis—claims that were exaggerated until they represented an unfair demand.[29] He urged that the United States be scrupulous in dealing with Latin America and also reiterated what he had said in a speech in 1910—that gunboats should not be used to protect American investment.[30]

As secretary of state, Bryan wasted no time in attacking the methods that the Roosevelt and Taft administrations used to arbitrate disputes between American companies and the governments of foreign nations. Previously, the arbitrators represented the corporations involved in the dispute, but Bryan considered this to be unfair to the foreign governments, since arbitrators should be impartial. In fact, he took immediate action in recalling Henry Jones, who was delegated by the Taft administration to act as one of the arbitrators in a claims dispute between the government of Ecuador and the Guayaquil and Quito Railroad Company, an American corporation. According to Bryan, Jones failed to meet the requirements of an impartial arbitrator, since for more than a year, he had assisted the railroad officials in preparing the case against Ecuador.[31]

Bryan noted that these policies of past administrations left an almost indelible stain on future U.S.-Latin American relations. He stressed that it would take time and patience to eliminate the distrust of our southern neighbors. He compared "dollar diplomacy" with a splinter lodged in a human hand, observing that "a splinter in the hand will make a sore and the sore will continue as long as the splinter remains. But when the splinter is withdrawn, nature heals and heals quickly."[32]

The seemingly righteous rejection of "dollar diplomacy" by the Wilson administration did not go unchallenged. In May 1913, the *New York Herald Tribune* pounced upon Bryan for his so-called anti-economic policies in Latin America. This Republican, business-oriented newspaper praised former President Taft for encouraging the development of natural resources in Central and South America, while Bryan was depicted as endangering the continuation of this far-sighted policy.[33] The paper also criticized the new secretary of state for endangering the lives and property of American citizens in Latin America by his insistence that all subjects of foreign nations be compelled to obey the laws of the country in which they resided and by implying that American gunboats would not intervene in times of crisis. Bryan denied that he was implementing a new diplomacy, insisting that he was only returning to the "common sense and mor-ality of former years."[34] He stated that he was not hostile to American financial interests operating in foreign countries as long as they operated fairly; however, he pointed out that "dollar diplomacy" implied that the U.S. government would protect with force all American investment. In actuality, this menaced American interests and closed the door of opportunity to American capital, since smaller nations were unwilling to allow any investment when it meant interference in their sovereignty.[35]

The verbal culmination of Bryan and Wilson's hostility toward "dollar diplomacy" came on October 27, 1913, when the president delivered a speech to the Southern Commercial Congress in Mobile, Alabama.[36] It clarified and enlarged on Wilson's statement of March 11, 1913, regarding Latin America. If we look at various parts of the speech, we can detect Bryan's influence on the president.

Wilson began by assuring the delegates assembled that the future policy of the United States toward Latin America would differ from the past. He hoped to draw closer to Latin America by a "common understanding." He said, "Interest does not tie nations together. It sometimes separates them; but sympathy and understanding does unite them, and I believe that by the new route that is just about to be opened, while we physically cut two continents asunder, we spiritually unite them. It is the spiritual union which we seek."[37] Bryan, for the past twelve years, had been urging friendship and understanding with Latin America. As early as 1901, he had repudiated the Platt Amendment, fearing that it would destroy any good the United States had accomplished in freeing Cuba from Spain.[38] When Bryan had visited Brazil in 1910, he also emphasized that the United States must gain the friendship and trust of her southern neighbors; he even went further than Wilson by suggesting that this could be accomplished by an aid program.[39]

Wilson had made several references to the benefits of the Panama Canal for both North and South America. He said, "The Latin American states which to their disadvantage have been off the main lines, will now be on the main lines."[40] He had meant that the opening of the Panama Canal would increase the amount of trade between the United States and Latin America. Bryan had this in mind as early as 1910, when he had visited the Canal Zone; he told of the trade advantages that would emanate for all.[41] In fact, Wilson said almost the same thing that Bryan had stated in 1910 in describing how close the Panama Canal would bring New York to the western coast of South America.[42]

Perhaps the most important part of Wilson's Mobile speech dealt with foreign investment and loans to Latin America. Wilson promised to free Latin America from unfair investment, which would lead eventually to subordination by American and foreign capitalists due to the heavy interest rates charged. The president related that "interest has been exacted of them that was not exacted of anybody else, because the risk was said to be greater; and then securities were taken that destroyed the risk."[43] Bryan had been aware of this problem as early as 1905 when referring to the Dominican Receivership; he criticized American and foreign financial interests for charging loans at excessive interest rates, and when the money could not be repaid, American and foreign gunboats were used to collect.[44] Thus, Bryan had previously stated and supported many of the same points that Wilson referred to in his Mobile speech. They both agreed on the necessity of increasing friendship and trust between the United States and Latin America; they both believed that the Panama Canal would benefit, economically, North and South America; finally, they wanted an end to the high interest rates charged to Latin American nations for loans. Perhaps this last point, more than any other, showed Bryan's influence on Wilson's Mobile speech. The secretary of state did not only speak against "dollar diplomacy," but he also formulated a financial plan that he offered Wilson as a remedy.[45] Bryan wanted the American government to lend its credit, issuing its own bonds at three percent, and then take the bonds of other countries at four percent. The difference would be put into a sinking fund and be used for the retirement of the bonds. As much as Wilson disliked high interest rates, however, he never accepted Bryan's plan. He believed that it "would strike the whole country as a novel and radical proposal."[46]

Writing in November 1913, Bryan praised Wilson's Mobile speech. He said, "It is rich in epigrams and full of meaty phrases. It lifts the nation's thought from the level of material interests to the plane of free government and into the realm where moral considerations have weight. It is the Monroe Doctrine interpreted in the language of today, and applied to the conditions that confront our sister republics."[47]

One day after the Mobile speech, Bryan offered the president his own suggestions on how to improve relations with the governments and peoples of Latin America. He declared that "we must protect the people of these republics in their right to attend to their own business, free from external coercion, no matter what form that external coercion may take."[48] In making a direct reference to the responsibility of the United States, he said:

We must be relieved of suspicion as to our motives. We must be bound in advance not to turn to our advantage any power we employ. If we have the occasion to go into any country, it must be as we went into Cuba, at the invitation of the government, or with the assurances that will leave no doubt as to the temporary character of our intervention. Our only object must be to secure to the people an opportunity to vote, that they may themselves select their rulers and establish their government.[49]

BRYAN'S DIPLOMATIC APPOINTMENTS

Bryan and Wilson not only worked together in the formulation of foreign policy, but they also consulted one another in the selection of diplomatic appointments.[50] Wilson had the final say on all appointments, but the secretary of state was influential, since he had been leader of the Democratic party since 1896 and knew to whom debts were owed. Bryan has been criticized for many reasons, but the most vociferous condemnation appeared to center around his choices for diplomatic posts. During the McKinley administration, Secretary of State John Hay had begun building a professional diplomatic corps, especially in Latin America. Many of the appointees before Bryan became secretary of state came from the East Coast and attended Ivy League colleges such as Harvard, Yale, and Princeton. Both Bryan and Wilson were suspicious of the professional foreign service personnel. Bryan especially had a distaste for the aristocratic leanings and upper class pretensions of this group. Ray Stannard Baker, in evaluating Wilson and Bryan on the matter of appointments, noted that the secretary of state was much more personal in his policies. Bryan had a distrust of the Civil Service laws that encouraged an undemocratic, permanent, office-holding clique. He believed that rank and file citizens in a democracy should serve in government positions. He felt that they would excel in their positions because they possessed an innate wisdom to handle the job better than any stuffy foreign service diplomat. He had so much faith in the common man's ability to hold any office, that he refused to believe that training and experience could make the difference in the ability to perform. Bryan had no problem with the nineteenth century "spoils system" by which supporters of the party in power reaped the rewards of victory. Wilson, on the other hand was an academic and former president of Princeton University. He certainly had more in common with the Ivy League intellectuals than Bryan.[51]

Alan Ashby, a Bryan historian, viewed the secretary of state simply as a "spoilsman." He declared that Bryan in selecting people to diplomatic posts only cared about their devotion to the Democratic party.[52] Link, on the other hand, refused to accept the notion that Bryan was just a "spoilsman" in the traditional sense. The Wilson historian points out that the Democrats had been out of power for almost sixteen years, and it was expected that there would be many changes.

However, Link contended that Bryan actually felt that a complete sweep of the Republican diplomatic officeholders was necessary, since many were incompetent and were fast becoming a snobbish professional elite. The secretary of state stated:

We find that those who have been occupying the legations and embassies have been habituated to a point of view which is very different, indeed, from the point of view of the present administration. They have had the material interests of individuals in the United States very much more in mind than the moral and public considerations which it seems to us ought to control. They have been so bred in a different school that we have found, in several instances, that it was difficult for them to comprehend our point of view and purpose.[53]

It is interesting to note that Bryan never saw himself as a "spoilsman"— selecting people only because they were good Democrats. As early as January 1913, Bryan wrote in the *Commoner* that positions in the Wilson administration should not be given as debt payment to loyal Democratic party members. He contended that they should be distributed to responsible people, but his definition of that term left something to be desired. For example, responsible people did not necessarily have to be qualified for the office that they were given. They only had to be Democrats he approved of and who would contribute to ennobling the Democratic party. In making appointments, Bryan attempted to satisfy loyal Democrats—Democrats who had supported the secretary of state as far back as 1896 and who had continued to back the party and its platforms. The method of appointment was to take into consideration the states—each state should be represented in the administration by a "deserving Democrat."[54] The secretary of state seldom spoke of efficiency or long service or experience when making appointments but rather of places for good, loyal Democrats. He wrote Wilson in August 1913 that "we have plenty of friends who have not yet been taken care of. I am especially anxious to get something for Arkansas. We have not done anything for that state so far and it is one of our most reliable states."[55]

Bryan, aware of the criticism regarding some of his appointments, wasted little time in defending his position. In November 1913, he asserted that his appointees were not only heartily received abroad, but they were of the highest quality—journalists, literary men, politicians, and businessmen. He readily admitted to their inexperience but defended his position by pointing out that the Democrats had not much chance in the Republican administrations during the last sixteen years to acquire that experience.[56] He even declared that experience meant very little. He said, "It is a mistake to suppose that experience in the diplomatic service necessarily fits one for a diplomatic appointment. Experience may acquaint one with the formalities of such a life, but these are of little importance compared with the more substantial qualities required."[57] Those qualities that Bryan had in mind were a thorough knowledge of the United States, sympathy for American institutions, and acceptance of the administration's policies.[58]

In July 1913, the *New York Times* in an editorial entitled "Diplomatic Appointments" attacked Bryan for ignoring qualified men (he had dismissed all ministers who had earned their posts by merit and installed hacks and party friends) who had taken the examinations given by the State Department. Bryan had replaced George T. Weitzel and Lewis Einstein, ministers to Nicaragua and Costa Rica, respectively, who served in the Taft administration. The *New York Times* also criticized the ouster of James T. Dubois, the minister to Bolivia, and Arthur M. Beaupre, the minister to Cuba. The newspaper editorial pointed out that all these men had risen from the very bottom of the diplomatic service, had experience, and were more than qualified for their positions. They were replaced by people who had no diplomatic training but were good "deserving Democrats."[59]

As secretary of state, Bryan had disregarded diplomatic formalities and looked like a hapless amateur. For example, he carried a lunch box to work, wore wrinkled suites, seldom shaved, and paid little attention to administrative duties or organizational details.[60] He chose as his own confidential secretary Manton M. Wyvell, a middle-aged lawyer from New York City. Wyvell had no experience in foreign policy, and his only claim to that position was that he was an old friend of the secretary of state. They had met at a political rally at Cornell University during the campaign of 1900, where Wyvell had become an ardent supporter of Bryan and remained so throughout the years.[61]

Bryan continued to select "deserving Democrats" to work in the State Department or be part of the diplomatic corps. As his assistant secretary of state, he chose John E. Osborn to replace Huntington Wilson, an experienced career officer. Osborne, a former druggist and sheep rancher, had no experience in foreign policy matters. He was Bryan's friend who had been a former governor of Wyoming and was a Democratic national committeeman.[62]

In May 1913 Bryan wrote Wilson that he would like to replace the minister to Ecuador Montgomery Schuyler. The secretary of state admitted to the president that Schuyler was doing a good job. However, what troubled Bryan was that Schuyler had been appointed by the Taft administration, and he needed a job for Charles S. Hartman of Montana. Hartman was a good Democrat, but more importantly, he was a good friend of Montana senator Thomas J. Walsh who was seeking an appointment from his state.[63] When Wilson wrote to Bryan claiming that he had never heard of Hartman, Bryan, disappointed, sent a note to the president stating that "he is one of the most reliable of our Democrats and I think he would fit into the Ecuador situation to perfection."[64] Wilson followed Bryan's advice in this matter, and Hartman was sent to Ecuador to replace Schuyler.[65] Not long after the appointments, a *New York Times* editorial sharply condemned the secretary of state for this political move. Hartman had been a Silver Republican and a follower of Bryan as a member of the House of Representatives from 1893 to 1899. The newspaper editorial sadly remarked that once again an appointment was made without regard to merit. Schuyler had no political connections to protect him, though he was well educated and possessed great ability in the diplomatic field.[66]

Bryan's selection of people who only cared about their devotion to the party went to the absurd when the secretary of state chose Walker W. Vick to head the

Dominican Receivership. Vick had played a prominent role in the election campaign of 1912, and Bryan wished to reward him. He had no experience in the customs service and no knowledge of the Spanish language.[67] After his appointment, the secretary of state wrote to Vick and asked him, "Can you let me know what positions you have at your disposal with which to reward 'deserving Democrats'? You have enough experience in politics to know how valuable workers are when the campaign is on and how difficult it is to find suitable rewards for all of the deserving."[68]

Perhaps, the most controversial appointment of Bryan's career was that of James M. Sullivan as minister to the Dominican Republic. The appointment of Sullivan and the scandal that occurred will be dealt with in chapter 6.

Though Bryan did tamper with the diplomatic service, he refused to alter the merit system in the consular service. Civil service principles were adhered to in the lower divisions of government.

In conclusion, William Jennings Bryan, as secretary of state, played a conspicuous role in aiding Wilson to formulate his Latin American policy. In both the president's statement on Latin America in March 1913 and in his Mobile speech of October 13, 1913, Bryan's influence was discernible. He also guided Wilson in the making of diplomatic appointments, albeit not always wisely.

NOTES

1. Arthur S. Link, *Wilson: The New Freedom* (Princeton, N.J.: Princeton University Press, 1956), p. 7.

2. Leroy Ashby, *William Jennings Bryan: Champion of Democracy* (Boston: Twayne Publishers, 1987), 141.

3. Ibid.

4. Link, *Wilson: The New Freedom*, p. 7.

5. Paxton Hibben, *The Peerless Leader William Jennings Bryan* (New York: Russell and Russell, 1967), p. 320.

6. Link, *Wilson: The New Freedom*, pp. 7-8.

7. Ibid., p. 8.

8. Ibid.

9. *Commoner*, January 10, 1913.

10. *New York Times*, January 31, 1913.

11. Samuel Flagg Bemis, *American Secretaries of State and Their Diplomacy*, vol. 10 (New York: Pageant Book Company, 1929), p. 8.

12. Merle F. Curti, "Bryan and World Peace," *Smith College Studies in History* 16 (April-July 1931): 114.

13. Ibid.

14. Ibid.

15. Bemis, *American Secretaries of State and Their Diplomacy*, vol. 10, pp. 9-10.

16. Link, *Wilson: The New Freedom*, pp. 96-97.

17. Ray Stannard Baker, *Woodrow Wilson: Life and Letters*, vol. 4 (Garden City, N.Y.: Doubleday, Page and Company, 1927), p. 88.

18. David F. Houston, *Eight Years with Wilson's Cabinet*, vol. 1 (Garden City, N.Y.: Doubleday, Page and Company, 1926), pp. 43-44.

19. Link, *Wilson: The New Freedom*, p. 97; Selig Adler, "Bryan and Wilsonian Caribbean Penetration," *Hispanic American Historical Review* 20 (May 1940): 202; Paolo E. Coletta, " William Jennings Bryan and the United States-Colombia Impasse, 1903-1921," *Hispanic American Historical Review* 47 (November 1967): 486-501.

20. Statement regarding Latin America, March 12, 1913, Bryan Papers, Library of Congress.

21. *Commoner*, June 6, 1902; Address of William Jennings Bryan to the Porto Rico Association at San Juan, April 9, 1910, Bryan Papers, Library of Congress.

22. *Commoner*, March 15, 1901.

23. Ibid., March 11, 1910.

24. Ibid., April 4, 1913.

25. Ashby, *William Jennings Bryan*, p. 111.

26. Ibid.

27. *New York Times*, May 16, 1913.

28. Ibid.

29. *Commoner*, May 2, 1913.

30. Ibid.

31. Ibid.

32. Ibid.

33. *New York Herald Tribune*, May 2, 1913.

34. Ibid.

35. Ibid.

36. The President, at the Southern Commercial Congress, Mobile, Alabama, October 27, 1913, Wilson Papers, Library of Congress.

37. Ibid.

38. *Commoner*, March 15, 1901.

39. *New York World Magazine*, June 19, 1910.

40. The President, at the Southern Commercial Congress, Mobile, Alabama, October 27, 1913, Wilson Papers, Library of Congress.

41. *Commoner*, March 11, 1910.

42. Ibid.; The President, at the Southern Commercial Congress, Mobile, Alabama, October 27, 1913, Wilson Papers, Library of Congress.

43. Ibid.

44. *Commoner*, March 24, 1905; William Jennings Bryan, *Speeches of William Jennings Bryan*, vol. 2 (New York: Funk and Wagnalls, 1909), p. 67; Curti, "Bryan and World Peace," p. 140.

45. Bryan to Wilson, October 28, 1913, Bryan Papers, Library of Congress.

46. Ibid.; Dana G. Munro, *Intervention and Dollar Diplomacy in the Caribbean, 1900-1921* (Princeton, N.J.: Princeton University Press, 1964), p. 392.

47. *Commoner*, November, 1913.

48. Bryan to Wilson, October 28, 1913, Bryan Papers, Library of Congress.

49. Ibid.

50. Wilson to Bryan, February 14, 1913, Bryan Papers, Library of Congress.

51. Baker, *Woodrow Wilson: Life and Letters*, vol. 4, p. 42; Ashby, *William Jennings Bryan: Champion of Democracy*, p. 144.

52. Ashby, *William Jennings Bryan: Champion of Democracy*, pp. 144-145.

53. Link, *Wilson: The New Freedom*, p. 105.

54. Bryan to Wilson, May 24, 1913, Bryan-Wilson Correspondence, National Archives.

55. Ashby, *William Jennings Bryan: Champion of Democracy*, p. 145; Link, *Wilson: The New Freedom*, p. 103.

56. *Commoner*, November 13, 1913.

57. Ibid.

58. Ibid.

59. *New York Times*, July 11, 1913.

60. Ashby, *William Jennings Bryan: Champion of Democracy*, p. 146.

61. Louis W. Koenig, *Bryan: A Political Biography of William Jennings Bryan* (New York: G. P. Putnam's Sons, 1971), p. 504.

62. Ibid., pp. 504-505.

63. Bryan to Wilson, May 26 and June 30, 1913, Bryan-Wilson Correspondence, National Archives.

64. Ibid., July 1, 1913.

65. Wilson to Bryan, July 3, 1913, Bryan-Wilson Correspondence, National Archives.

66. *New York Times*, July 20, 1913.

67. Wilson to Bryan, May 22, 1913, Bryan-Wilson Correspondence, National Archives; *New York Times*, August 29, 1913.

68. Link, *Wilson: The New Freedom*, p. 105.

4

Nicaragua

No other area of Latin America exemplified more the return to "dollar diplomacy" than did Nicaragua during the Wilson-Bryan period. Here, Bryan continued and furthered the political and economic policies of the Taft administration. Since Nicaragua's economic and political problems existed years prior to Bryan becoming secretary of state, we will discuss briefly its history.

NICARAGUA BEFORE BRYAN

Nicaragua, located in Central America, is bordered by Honduras to the north, the Caribbean Sea to the east, Costa Rica to the south, and the Pacific Ocean to the southwest. It is the least densely populated Central American nation with most of the people living mainly on a narrow volcanic belt between the Pacific and lakes Managua and Nicaragua. The economy of Nicaragua consists of mining, manufacturing, and, most importantly, agriculture. Nicaragua exports coffee, sugarcane, and bananas. The first colonial cities in Nicaragua were founded by the Spanish in 1524. Ruled as part of Guatemala, Nicaragua became a separate republic in 1838. Throughout most of the nineteenth century, the country suffered a great deal of violence, because of extreme liberal-conservative antagonism. Foreign interference was frequent, especially by the United States, which from the early nineteenth century expressed interest in an inter-ocean waterway in Nicaragua.[1]

In 1855, William Walker, a soldier of fortune from Tennessee, invaded Nicaragua with a small force of fifty-seven men. With the help of the Nicaraguan Liberal Party, he seized control of the government. Walker had hoped to make considerable fortune by dominating the isthmian trade; he also tried to get the United States to annex Nicaragua as a possible slave state. The American adventurer committed a serious blunder when he tried to interfere with Cornelius

Vanderbilt's transit company which had financial interests in Nicaragua. Vanderbilt collected ships and adventurers and, with support of the Nicaraguan Conservative Party, ousted Walker in 1857.[2] After his overthrow, the Liberal Party was no longer a factor in government until 1893. In that year, Conservative Party rule ended and José Santos Zelaya, a liberal from Managua, became Nicaragua's next president.[3]

Zelaya ruled as a depraved and brutal dictator, a contemptible little tyrant who lost little time in persecuting the Conservative Party. He was a vain individual who believed himself a great benefactor—he envisioned himself to be the initiator of Liberal reforms and had hoped to impose these reforms throughout Central America. However, he was best known for his persecution of foreigners. Twice the British government sent warships to Nicaragua as a warning to Zelaya to stop harrassing British citizens.[4]

When the United States chose Panama as its canal site, Zelaya, irritated by that decision, threatened to sell Nicaragua's transit rights to Japan. The only good thing that could be said about Zelaya's rule was that the country had internal peace for sixteen years and the coffee industry grew considerably.[5]

When Taft became president in 1909, he chose as his secretary of state Philander Knox, a corporation lawyer born in Pennsylvania. Knox, a friend of big business, had helped form the giant United States Steel Corporation. He served as attorney general of the United States and was a U.S. senator before entering the State Department. Both Taft and Knox favored peace and stability in Nicaragua for economic progress. They both urged American business and bankers to invest in Nicaragua, and both had every intention of backing that investment with American military force.[6]

By 1909, the Taft administration had become disenchanted with Zelaya's anti-Americanism. He had two American citizens killed, was threatening to negotiate with foreign nations to allow them to build a canal in Nicaragua, and was interfering in the affairs of other Central American countries.[7] In October 1909, a revolution began against Zelaya and his Liberal Party followers. The Taft administration gave encouragement to the anti-Zelaya forces which succeeded in ousting the president. José Madriz became the provisional president until August 1910, when he too was forced to resign—the U.S. government failed to recognize him because he embodied too many of Zelaya's beliefs.[8] In January 1911, a constitutional convention was called, and it elected Juan Estrada as president and Adolfo Díaz as vice-president. It was hoped that the fighting would cease and peace would prevail, but the animosity between the political parties—Estrada was a leader in the Liberal Party, while Díaz was the same in the Conservative Party—led to continued fighting.[9] Finally, in May 1911, the Nicaraguan army turned against Estrada when he began arming his liberal followers and tried to remove his rival, Luis Mena, the minister of war. With the support of the Nicaraguan army and the Taft administration, Díaz now became president, and Estrada fled the country.[10]

The political instability in Nicaragua caused serious economic problems for the new government. Great Britain, France, Italy, and Germany demanded payment of debts owed their citizens and threatened Nicaragua with military intervention to collect. The United States, wanting to avoid foreign interference and keep the new Díaz government in power, had found a solution to Nicaragua's economic problems with the passage of the Knox-Castrillo Treaty signed on June 6, 1911.[11] The terms of this treaty provided for a $15 million loan from the American bankers Brown Brothers and J. and W. Seligman of which the proceeds were to be used in paying claims against the Nicaraguan government, in consolidating the debt, in stabilizing the currency, and in building a railroad to the eastern coast. Until the debt was paid, the customs of Nicaragua were to be placed in charge of a collector-general, appointed by the Nicaraguan president but nominated by the bankers and approved by the State Department.[12] This treaty, sent to the U.S. Senate for ratification three times, was emphatically rejected each time by the anti-imperialists, the majority of whom were Democrats.[13]

Since the treaty could not be ratified and desperate financial conditions continued in Nicaragua, a loan contract was signed between the Díaz government and Brown Brothers and J. and W. Seligman of New York. The Nicaraguan government wanted the loan for $15 million, the same amount stipulated in the treaty, but the bankers had little faith in the Díaz government and were prepared to lend only $1.5 million in exchange for treasury bills to be secured by the customs revenue.[14] In addition, the bankers demanded and received majority control of stock in the Nicaraguan National Bank and an option on 51 percent of stock in the state-owned Pacific Railways. The purchase of the railroad and bank stock by the American bankers and the control of the customs by the U.S. government indebted Nicaragua to American interests.[15]

Many of Nicaragua's leaders opposed these financial agreements, but none so much as Luis Mena. In May 1911, Mena still held his position in the Díaz cabinet as minister of War. He urged Díaz to oppose the agreements, claiming that they would threaten the country's future sovereignty.[16] When Díaz accepted the financial arrangements with the bankers, Mena turned against him, forcing the president to dismiss him from the cabinet in July 1912; shortly afterwards, Mena and his followers began another revolution.[17] Díaz, unable to cope with the new uprising, which gathered strength when many of Zelaya's liberals joined Mena, asked the Taft administration for aid in repulsing the revolt and in protecting American citizens.[18] In August, 100 American marines landed in Managua, Nicaragua's capital, to protect American citizens and to support the Díaz government, and by September, that number had increased to 2,700. On September 25, 1912, the revolt ended as Mena and his followers surrendered to the superior American forces.[19]

There is little question that without the American marines the Díaz government would have been overthrown, and the Taft administration could not have allowed that to happen. If Mena and his allies, Zelay's Liberal Party followers, had succeeded, they would have abolished all the financial agreements, including the customs agreement that the Taft administration had worked so hard

to obtain. Nicaragua, again, would have experienced political instability and
financial chaos—a situation that could have invited foreign intervention.[20]

In November 1912, Wilson won the presidential election, but he would not
take office until March 1913. Meanwhile in February 1913, Knox was forced to
sign a second Knox-Castrillo Treaty with the Nicaraguan government, since
conditions in Nicaragua had deteriorated after the failed revolution by Mena. The
national treasury was empty, and the bankers refused to lend more money to the
Nicaraguan government. Knox felt that this treaty was crucial to Nicaragua's
political and economic survival. It called upon the United States to pay Nicaragua
$3 million for the exclusive option on the Nicaraguan canal route. Since the
United States had no intention of building another canal in the area, this was to
keep Nicaragua from granting the option to another foreign nation. The treaty
also gave the United States the right to build a naval base on the Pacific side of the
Gulf of Fonseca and provided the United States with a ninety-nine-year lease on
the Great and Little Corn Islands in the Caribbean.[21] This was the political and
financial situation that confronted the Wilson-Bryan administration when it took
office in March 1913.

BRYAN'S NICARAGUAN POLICY

Both President Wilson and Secretary of State Bryan opposed American
intervention in Nicaragua. Wilson had criticized the Republican administration
during the campaign of 1912, while Bryan, as early as 1910, during the early
stages of the revolt, had warned of the consequences of intervention, asserting that
it would further tarnish the image of the United States in Latin America.[22]

The day after taking the oath of office, Wilson received a telegram from
Mena, who was recuperating from illness in an American army hospital in the
Panama Canal Zone (he had been detained after his capture by American marines
the previous September). Mena hoped the new administration would be more
amenable to his position, especially after both Wilson and Bryan had criticized
Taft's intervention in Nicaraguan affairs. Mena's telegram told how he had been
unlawfully ousted from his post as minister of war; he also claimed that American
occupation forces were suppressing the will of his people by actively supporting
the Díaz dictatorship.[23] Mena informed Wilson that the only way to avoid more
bloodshed was to withdraw the American marines and to allow his followers,
supported by the people, to assume power in Nicaragua.[24]

Mena's pleas were ignored by the new administration primarily because of the
influence of the State Department's Division of Latin American Affairs. Bryan
had received information from William Doyle, chief of the Division of Latin
American Affairs (Doyle had worked for the Taft administration and would
shortly be replaced by Boaz W. Long) claiming that Díaz was the only leader who
could bring stability to Nicaragua. Doyle had warned the new secretary of state
that political revolutionaries, hostile to the United States, were stationed on

Mexican soil and working to undermine the Díaz government.[25] The division's support of Díaz stemmed primarily from its desire to protect the American bankers in Nicaragua, Brown Brothers and J. and W. Seligman, and to maintain political stability. Neither Bryan nor Wilson were ardent advocates of American business and could have changed the course of events in Nicaragua by withdrawing the marines and allowing the Nicaraguan people to choose their own president. Here was an opportunity for Bryan to show other Latin American countries that the United States had no intention of intervening in their affairs. Instead, Doyle successfully convinced Bryan of the need to maintain political stability while he downplayed the importance of protecting the bankers.[26] Thus, the marines remained in Nicaragua to maintain the Díaz government, political stability, and peace and to prevent chaos that, most certainly, according to Doyle, would lead to foreign intervention.[27]

The financial situation in Nicaragua remained critical as Bryan became secretary of state. He carefully studied both of the Knox treaties that had been rejected by the Senate and wrote Wilson that a new treaty should be drawn up based upon some of the provisions of the previous ones and sent to the Senate for ratification.[28] He hoped that its passage would enable Nicaragua to obtain the necessary funds to pay debts owed to Great Britain, France, Italy, and Germany. Bryan was very concerned that the European nations would use debt collection as an excuse to send troops to Nicaragua.[29] He became so obsessed with the treaty that he urged Wilson to meet with the Nicaraguan minister of finance, Pedro Rafael Cuadra, who arrived in Washington in August 1913 to acquaint the president with the magnitude of the financial crisis.[30]

As much as Bryan wanted to help Nicaragua through its financial crisis and protect it from being hounded by foreign creditors, he vehemently opposed those conditions in the Knox-Castrillo Treaty that gave the bankers over half of the stock in the National Bank and the Pacific Railway.[31] The secretary of state proposed a plan to Wilson that would extricate Nicaragua from the usurious bankers. Bryan informed the president that the Nicaraguan government owed the bankers $711,000, but gave the bankers security that was outrageous—the customs returns from its railroad option on 51 percent of the railroad stock. Bryan calculated that the bankers' profits amounted to $1.5 million, and he had a plan to help Nicaragua without the bankers' involvement. The secretary of state told the president that the U.S. government must become "a good Samaritan and help those who have fallen among thieves." Bryan wrote to Wilson that he felt "that we have an opportunity to help thses nations in a disinterested way that will cement them to us and give us a standing among Latin American countries which no outside influence can shake. He proposed that Nicaragua issue bonds to be taken by the U.S. government at low interest. This would prove to be a great saving over private alternatives, but the president rejected the idea and Bryan was forced to look for alternative funding.[32]

In late May 1913, Bryan, concerned about the critical economic conditions in Nicaragua, began pushing for the ratification of the second Knox treaty of

February 1913. He could not understand why these provisions calling for a canal option and naval base for the United States, for payment of $3 million to Nicaragua, could not be ratified. Bryan informed Wilson that the senators should be told that the United States, by holding the canal option, would eliminate any foreign nation from building a canal in the area. To Bryan, this and the $3 million for Nicaragua, were the most important parts of the treaty.[33]

When the Senate refused to consider the treaty, the secretary of state blamed the bankers, Brown Brothers and J. and W. Seligman. These bankers worked with the Taft administration and made several loans to Nicaragua, charging excessive interest rates and demanding that their claims of stock ownership in both the railroad and bank be recognized. The anti-imperialists in the Senate, such as William Borah of Idaho and William Smith of Michigan, fearing the close ties between the State Department and the bankers, refused to ratify any treaty.[34] When hope of having the February 1913 treaty ratified diminished, Wilson allowed Bryan to take any necessary steps to alleviate the financial conditions in Nicaragua.[35]

On July 20, 1913, Bryan outlined a revised treaty similar to the one Knox had formulated the previous February, except that instead of relying so heavily on the bankers, it attempted to increase American government control over Nicaragua through a clause similar to the Platt Amendment in Cuba. This clause would ensure stability in Nicaragua by the threat of American intervention and would make any loan to Nicaragua, whether government or private, more secure. Bryan hoped that this would provide lower interest rates—the benefit of establishing a virtual protectorate over Nicaragua. Instead of the bankers running the show, the State Department would dictate the terms of the loan with the bankers providing the funds.[36]

The Bryan treaty proposal provided that the United States would pay Nicaragua $3 million in return for the exclusive canal rights across Nicaragua and a new naval base in the Gulf of Fonseca.[37] This part read almost exactly as the Knox treaty of February 1913 but added to this were terms used in the Platt Amendment. It read:

(1) That war should not be declared without the consent of the United States. (2) That no treaties would be made with foreign governments that would try to destroy her independence or that would give those governments a foothold in the republic. (3) That no public debt would be contracted beyond the ordinary resources of the government, as indicated by the ordinary revenues. (4) That the United States should have the right to intervene at any time to preserve Nicaraguan independence.[38]

The day after the treaty was released to the press and public, an editorial in the *New York Times* criticized the terms of the Platt Amendment in the Bryan treaty, comparing it to the original Platt Amendment in Cuba.[39] It praised the original Platt Amendment as inevitable and necessary, since Cuba was liberated in the Spanish-American War. No established government existed in Cuba because of the chaotic conditions emanating from the war. However, Nicaragua was an independent country with an established government, which made the amendment unnecessary.[40] The editorial had supported the Knox-Castrillo Treaty, calling for the supervision of the customs collections, and also the Knox treaty of February 1913, providing for the canal option and naval base, but the Bryan treaty, with the Platt Amendment provisions, was a return to the "dollar diplomacy" of the Taft administration.[41]

Some members of the Senate Committee on Foreign Relations, such as William Borah, viewed the Bryan treaty as a new policy designed to seize control of countries surrounding the Panama Canal and to stabilize and dominate the republics of Central and South America.[42] Senator Borah denounced the treaty as outright imperialism, and he accused Bryan of repudiating his anti-imperialistic views.[43] But Borah was the only Republican senator on the committee to condemn it. Both senators Elihu Root, former secretary of state in the Roosevelt administration, and Henry Cabot Lodge, a good friend of Roosevelt and an ardent supporter of his "big stick" diplomacy, praised the Bryan treaty.[44]

This treaty caused a furor in the Senate and was responsible for hostile feelings in other Central American states. Once again, the United States was viewed as the colossus of the north interfering in the affairs of its neighbors, and this caused many Republicans who had supported the terms of the Platt Amendment to oppose it.[45]

After Bryan appeared before the Senate Committee on Foreign Relations twice during July 1913, he finally realized that he could not obtain approval of his treaty. Senator Augustus O. Bacon, chairman of the Foreign Relations Committee, told the secretary of state that there would be less difficulty in securing the treaty if it contained only the purchase of the canal option and the acquisition of the naval base on Fonseca Bay, but the Senate would never accept the provisions of the Platt Amendment.[46]

When the Foreign Relations Committee met on August 2, 1913, it rejected the treaty with the provisions of the Platt Amendment by a vote of 8 to 4, asserting that it was too imperialistic and also unacceptable to the other countries in Central America.[47] Bryan, however, had no intention of quitting; he resubmitted the treaty in identical form during the next Senate session. He firmly believed that if he could make an intense effort in lobbying specific senators, he would eventually prevail.[48]

Nevertheless, the defeat of the treaty placed Bryan in a precarious situation. He had hoped to use the $3 million to help the Nicaraguan government meet its debts. Charles C. Eberhardt, the consul general in Bluefields, Nicaragua, wrote the State Department concerning the financial situation throughout the country. His opinion was that

Nicaragua is facing a very critical period today. She is bankrupt, and general conditions are such that, if she is unable to secure more money immediately or very soon after June 30th next, great political disorder will result; in fact, it would seem that had we not had our marines stationed in the Republic, such disorder would long since have transpired. Even under best conditions, I do not see how political intrigue, if not open revolt, is long to be avoided, and Bluefields, a district from which a great deal of the revenue of the Republic is derived is bound to be very active and play an important part.[49]

The Nicaraguan government as of July 1913 owed $6.2 million to the Ethelburga Syndicate of England; $750,000 to Brown Brothers and J. and W. Seligman, the bankers of the Taft administration; and $1.5 million to miscellaneous creditors of the government for salaries unpaid, supplies furnished, and advances made; and $3 million in claims made against the Nicaraguan government for destruction of property and loss of life as a result of the recent revolutions.[50] Thus, when the Nicaraguan finance minister arrived in Washington in August 1913 pleading for aid, Bryan was already aware of Nicaragua's dangerous financial situation and that it could not be remedied by his treaty—a casualty of the Senate earlier that month. Now the secretary of state had no choice but to turn to the same bankers used by the Taft administration to secure a loan on the best possible terms.

After two months of tense negotiations, a loan was secured between the bankers and the Nicaraguan government in October 1913. In addition to the 51 percent of the stock that the bankers had already purchased in the Pacific Railways and the National Bank in the 1911 loan, they now received the remaining 49 percent of the stock in the railway as security for the new loan.[51] The bankers also "discounted at par $1.06 million one-year treasury bills of the Republic of Nicaragua dated October 1, 1913, and maturing October 1, 1914, drawing six percent."[52] These treasury bills were secured by a lien on the customs, and the customs administration was led by an American collector-general, recommended by the bankers.[53]

Bryan disliked the terms of this loan, especially the acquisition of the remainder of the railway stock by the bankers. However, the secretary of state was so concerned about Nicaragua's financial and political stability that he had little choice but to deal with the bankers on their terms.[54]

Only three months after the loan was approved, Bryan received a request by the Nicaraguan minister of finance, asking for an increase in the loan of between $250,000 and $500,000.[55] He did not want the loan augmented, as he was already disturbed by the financial exactions made upon Nicaragua by the bankers, but the secretary of state found himself under increasing pressure from both the Nicaraguan government and Boaz W. Long, the new chief of the Division of Latin American Affairs. Long, like his predecessor, William Doyle, supported business ventures abroad. Long had close ties to Wall Street and had been in the commission business in Mexico from 1899 to 1913. He also had close personal ties with an attorney for the United Fruit Company—an American business concern with vast interests in Latin America. Long owed his appointment to head the Division of Latin American Affairs to his close association with Wilson's vice president, Thomas Marshall.[56] The new division chief remained concerned about the economic conditions and the political situation in Nicaragua. Knowing that Bryan distrusted the motives of bankers and business in general, Long sent his boss a letter written by Judge Otto Schoenrich, the president of the Mixed Claims Commission, which told of the dire situation facing the Nicaraguan government. Schoenrich visited the country in January 1914, and found complete economic chaos. Commerce was stagnant, business was depressed from lack of investment, and both foreign and domestic creditors clamored for repayment of debts owed them. Long vouched for the accuracy of Schoenrich's letter and urged Bryan to increase the Nicaraguan loan as soon as possible.[57]

Bryan, feeling the pressure of the Nicaraguan crisis, once again turned to his treaty with the Platt Amendment provisions. He wrote Wilson in late January 1914 and asked him to make a public statement supporting the treaty. The secretary of state told the president that given the hostility of the treaty in the Senate, Wilson's statement should be contingent upon a written declaration by the Nicaraguan president praising the benefits of the Platt Amendment provisions.[58] Bryan informed the president that he had already prepared the way for the necessary statement. He had met with the Nicaraguan minister in Washington, Emiliano Chamorro, who had assured him that President Díaz wanted to send such a message. However, the Nicaraguan president wanted Bryan to word the message for him, and the secretary of state had agreed to do so.[59] It is interesting to note that Bryan saw nothing wrong with this request, and in fact, he informed Wilson that he had already "guessed at Díaz's views as best he could."[60] Bryan hoped that the Díaz statement would convince enough senators that the United States had no imperialistic designs on Nicaragua, and it was the Nicaraguan government that wanted the Platt Amendment provisions. Hopefully, this would end the hostility of the other Central American states toward the treaty and would lead to its ratification by the U.S. Senate.[61]

On February 12, 1914, the Díaz message arrived in Washington and was made available to the Senate Foreign Relations Committee. It read as follows:

The effect of the Platt Amendment on Cuba has been so satisfactory that, since your Government is considering a canal convention with Nicaragua, I respectively request that said convention be made to embody the substance of the Platt Amendment so that my countrymen may see Nicaragua's credit improved, her natural resources developed, the peace assured throughout the land. I believe that revolutions will cease if your Government can see its way clear to grant the addition of the Amendment as requested.[62]

The Bryan-Díaz message praised the Platt Amendment in Cuba, the same amendment that Bryan had opposed in 1901 and now asked for its implementation in Nicaragua. Bryan had done a complete about face concerning the amendment. As a private citizen he had not been privy to the inside information concerning foreign policy. Now, as secretary of state, he saw first hand that the Nicaraguan government needed to end the economic chaos in order to have political stability. However, Bryan was reluctant to use the bankers, and the Nicaraguan treaty, with its controversial Platt Amendment provisions, seemed the only way to go.

The Díaz statement did not help Bryan's cause and, in fact, might have hindered it. In June 1914, the Senate Foreign Relations Committee began hearings on Bryan's relationship as mediator between the Nicaraguan government and Brown Brothers and J. and W. Seligman. Senator Smith, criticized the secretary of state for promoting the October 13th loan that gave the additional stock in the Pacific Railways to the American bankers as security (Bryan, by this time, had conceded to the pleas of Long, Schoenrich, and the Nicaraguan government and had the bankers augment the October loan by $205,000).[63] Both Bryan and Charles A. Douglas, the legal representative of Nicaragua, appeared before the Senate committee to defend the State Department's action. They claimed that Nicaragua needed the money desperately to pay its debts, and if the loan had not been made, armed revolt would have resulted.[64] Douglas testified that Nicaragua's debt exceeded $13 million and urged the Senators to approve the treaty so that a vote on ratification could take place as soon as possible.[65] Some senators, including Senator Smith, who led the investigation, remained unconvinced that ratification of the treaty and the payment of the $3 million would alleviate the financial situation in Nicaragua. In fact, they believed that the payment would have a detrimental effect on the inept Nicaraguan government, burdened already with a magnified debt.[66]

When Chamorro appeared before the Foreign Relations Committee in late June 1914, he took the offensive by warning the committee members that if they failed to ratify the treaty, his government would accept an offer made by the German government, exceeding the $3 million. Germany desired more influence in the Caribbean and had an opportunity to build a naval base in the Gulf of Fonseca and buy an canal option from Nicaragua.[67]

Chamorro was questioned on the presence of American marines in Nicaragua by senators Smith and Borah, who believed that the Díaz government used the marines to maintain power. Borah was particularly vocal about how he heard that the marines used force to threaten Díaz's opposition, a point that Chamorro vigorously denied. The Nicaraguan minister declared that he did not know who requested the marines, but saw no danger to his people by their continued presence.[68]

About one month after Chamorro's appearance before the Senate Foreign Relations Committee, he told Bryan that, in his opinion, the chief obstacle to the treaty was the presence of the American marines and the belief of many of the senators that Díaz would remain in power past his term, which expired in December 1916.[69] He sent to Bryan a message from Díaz, forwarded to the Senate Foreign Relations Committee, reassuring its members that the Nicaraguan president had no desire to continue in office after his term expired.[70]

Bryan, realizing that he could not obtain favorable action by the committee on his treaty, formulated a revised one, calling for the payment to Nicaragua of $3 million for the perpetual rights to an inter-oceanic canal and a naval base in the Gulf of Fonseca. The newly revised treaty, signed on August 5, 1914, unlike the original, precluded the terms of the Platt Amendment.[71]

Bryan believed that by deleting the provisions of the Platt Amendment from the treaty, the Senate would quickly ratify it. Unfortunately, Bryan miscalculated the prevailing mood in the Senate—many senators remained suspicious of the secretary of state's relationship with Brown Brothers and J. and W. Seligman. Also senators Borah and Smith, among others, continued to believe that the Nicaraguan people did not want Díaz in power and that Bryan and the American marines were keeping him there.[72] Thus, when Bryan continued to have difficulty with the newly revised treaty, he complained to Wilson that the senators were being stubborn by denying him a quorum for a vote.[73] Bryan urged the president to bring pressure on the Senate in the form of a message.[74] Wilson did not send any message, but he did speak to Senator William J. Stone, the Senate majority leader, asking him to bring pressure upon his Democratic colleagues.[75]

The Senate delay on the Bryan-Chamorro Treaty presented another problem for the secretary of state. After it was signed in August 1914, the Nicaraguan government, unable to understand the delay, began to pressure Bryan. He found himself caught between the persistence of the Nicaraguan government and the stubbornness of the Senate. Since the Senate remained intransigent, Bryan had no other recourse but to find an excuse for the Nicaraguan government. He told Díaz that immediate action was impossible, because the Senate had been in session for over a year and wanted to adjourn as soon as possible. Bryan conveyed to the Nicaraguan president that if he continued to push the treaty now, it would be defeated. He urged Díaz to be patient, and if all went well, the treaty would probably pass in the next Senate session.[76]

The autumn of 1914 was a troubling time for Bryan, as he so desperately sought financial aid for Nicaragua, fearing the government could fall anytime and chaos would prevail. However, all the secretary of state could do was wait until January 1915 and hope that the Senate would finally act positively on the treaty.

In January 1915, Senator Stone again presented the Bryan-Chamorro Treaty to the Senate Foreign Relations Committee. Hearings were held and experts testified to the pros and cons of the treaty. One of those who testified was Paul Fuller, a member of the New York law firm of Coudert Brothers, a leading Roman Catholic layman, and an authority on Latin American affairs. He immediately denounced the treaty on the grounds that it would strengthen the position of the Díaz government during the next election, and in Fuller's opinion, that government did not represent the majority of the people.[77] He called for a full investigation of the Nicaraguan government and its relations with the people before taking action on the treaty.[78]

Bryan wasted little time in condemning the Fuller proposal, claiming that it would completely destabilize the Nicaraguan government. It would suggest that the United States had no confidence in Díaz and would only encourage revolution by the opposition. Bryan was not opposed to an investigation as to whether Díaz had the support of his people, but he wanted to conduct that inquiry after the treaty was passed.[79]

Bryan wrote Wilson concerning the Fuller proposal and included a personal appraisal of the Díaz government. The secretary of state praised both Díaz and his minister, Emiliano Chamorro. Bryan spoke of Chamorro as a true representative of his people, unselfish, honest, and highly intelligent.[80]

The Bryan-Chamorro Treaty was finally ratified in February 1916, eight months after Bryan resigned as secretary of state. We shall discuss the ratification in chapter 10.

The opposition to the Nicaraguan treaty and its numerous revisions (it was drawn up in February 1913 by Knox, revised with the provisions of the Platt Amendment in July 1913 by Bryan, and again revised in August 1914, and signed as the Bryan-Chamorro Treaty) came not only from the Senate, but also from the majority of Central American states.[81] The two most vociferous opponents of the treaty were Costa Rica and El Salvador. In April 1913, when Costa Rica first learned of the American-Nicaraguan convention, it sent a note of protest to the State Department, asserting that the government of Nicaragua had no right to make the treaty with the United States without first consulting with Costa Rica.[82] It supported its case by referring to an old boundary treaty made between Nicaragua and Costa Rica on April 15, 1858, concerning the use of the San Juan River, which formed part of the dividing line between the two countries.[83] Article Eight stipulated that Nicaragua had to consult with Costa Rica on the use of the San Juan River. Both countries had fought over the terms of this treaty, and on March 22, 1888, President Grover Cleveland acted as an arbitrator, declaring the treaty valid.[84] Costa Rica argued that if the United States built the canal in Nicaragua, it would have to use the San Juan River, and no canal could be built without Costa Rica's consent.[85]

Chamorro defended his country's actions by arguing that the Bryan treaty was not a final canal treaty, but only an option stating what rights the United States might exercise in the event the canal would be built.[86] Evidently, Chamorro had recognized the difficulties his country would have in circumventing the 1858 treaty with Costa Rica.

The use of the San Juan River was only one argument Costa Rica made against the Bryan treaty. It also complained about the terms of the Platt Amendment before they were eliminated in the final revision. These terms would not only permit the United States to intervene in Nicaragua but would also threaten Costa Rica's sovereignty, since the two countries bordered each other.[87]

El Salvador also protested the Nicaraguan treaty. In October 1913, El Salvador's minister to the United States, Francisco Dueñas, wrote Bryan that the Gulf of Fonseca could not be used by the United States for a naval base because of its geographical situation.[88] He declared that it was a territorial bay whose waters were within the jurisdiction of the bordering sates of El Salvador, Honduras, and Nicaragua. All three countries had joint control over the area, and if one of them objected, no naval base could be built.[89] Bryan denied the joint ownership interpretation, insisting that the Gulf of Fonseca belonged to them individually, allowing Nicaragua the right to make the concession.[90] El Salvador based its claim on the treaty of April 10, 1884, between the three countries, dividing the Gulf of Fonseca among them.[91] Bryan, on the other hand, claimed that the treaty was invalid since Honduras never ratified it, and if the treaty were valid, its

interpretation implied that Nicaragua, El Salvador, and Honduras claimed ownership over its own areas.[92] The minister of El Salvador denied Bryan's interpretation, and insisted that the treaty was made to delineate boundaries, but it did not
imply that each country owned a part. He agreed with Bryan that the treaty had
never become law, but insisted that it still recognized the Gulf of Fonseca as
jointly owned.[93]

El Salvador also protested the Platt Amendment provisions of the Bryan
treaty, claiming that it would nullify the treaties of the Washington Conference of
1907, which were made for the purpose of strengthening the relations among the
Central American states and promoting their common interests. Nicaragua's
plight now became the common interest of all the Central American states, and if
the United States held dominant influence here, all Central America would be in
jeopardy of American encroachment.[94]

President Carlos Meléndez of El Salvador protested the Bryan treaty in a
telegram sent to Senator Smith. He emphasized that El Salvador wanted no part
of the treaty and that Bryan had suppressed facts pertaining to El Salvador's
opposition. The telegram was read to the members of the Senate Foreign Relations
Committee and no doubt influenced its decision to kill the treaty with the Platt
Amendment provisions.[95]

As early as July 1913, Bryan had realized that other Central American states
might oppose his Nicaraguan treaty. Thus, when the terms of the treaty agreement
were revealed, he attempted to mitigate the forthcoming criticism by offering
Honduras and El Salvador similar arrangements.[96] However, both countries
refused to negotiate with the secretary of state, since any such agreement would
defeat their main purpose—the desire to form a union of the five Central
American states.[97] The hope of strengthening the ties among themselves and of
lessening the influence of the United States in Central America was the main
reason for their opposition to any such arrangement.[98]

El Salvador called a meeting in September 1913, inviting the governments of
Costa Rica, Guatemala, and Honduras to send representatives to discuss the
Nicaraguan treaty.[99] No formal meeting took place because Costa Rica refused to
attend unless Nicaragua received an invitation. Apparently, unity was only a
theoretical concept and had a long way to go before becoming a reality.[100] Nonetheless, the idea of such a meeting frightened Bryan, and he attempted to dis-
courage the governments of Guatemala and Honduras from attending. He felt that
since the treaty had not been approved, there was no reason for any such
meeting.[101]

In conclusion, it can be said that Bryan's actions toward Nicaragua were
similar to those of the Taft administration. He not only supported the Knox treaty,
but also revised it in July 1913 to include the terms of the Platt Amendment,
which he had opposed so vociferously in 1901. When he was unable to get the
money Nicaragua needed by means of the treaty, he turned to the same bankers
who worked with the Taft-Knox administration. It was true that Bryan remained
unhappy over the terms of the loan, but nevertheless, he approved it, especially

after being informed by the Division of Latin American Affairs that the loan was necessary for economic stability. He continued to defend the terms of the Platt Amendment and the loan as late as July 1914 before the Senate Foreign Relations Committee. However, the Platt Amendment terms were precluded from his treaty when it became evident that the treaty would not be considered with them. Bryan, in the midst of his fight to have the treaty ratified, ignored the protests of the Central American states against it. In regard to American policy toward Nicaragua, Bryan not only practiced the "dollar diplomacy" of the Taft administration but also endangered the friendship and trust between the United States and Central America, the two very principles he had so often stressed before becoming secretary of state.

NOTES

1. John Edwin Fagg, *Latin America: A General History* (New York: Macmillan, 1977), pp. 611-612.

2. Ibid., pp. 412-413.

3. Ibid., p. 612.

4. Ibid.

5. Ibid., pp. 612-613.

6. J. Fred Rippy, *The Caribbean Danger Zone* (New York: G. P. Putnam's Sons, 1940), p. 169; Dana G. Munro, *Intervention and Dollar Diplomacy in the Caribbean, 1900-1921* (Princeton, N.J.: Princeton University Press, 1964), p. 163.

7. Munro, *Intervention and Dollar Diplomacy in the Caribbean*, p. 167.

8. Ibid., p. 186.

9. Issac J. Cox, *Nicaragua and the United States*, vol. 10, no. 7 (Boston: World Peace Foundation Pamphlets, 1927), p. 710.

10. Ibid., p. 711.

11. Munro, *Intervention and Dollar Diplomacy in the Caribbean*, p. 187.

12. Cox, *Nicaragua and the United States*, p. 712.

13. Ibid.

14. Ibid., p. 714.

15. Ibid.; Arthur S. Link, *Wilson: The New Freedom* (Princeton, N.J.: Princeton University Press, 1956), p. 331.

16. Cox, *Nicaragua and the United States*, p. 716.

17. Rippy, *The Caribbean Danger Zone*, p. 178.

18. Munro, *Intervention and Dollar Diplomacy in the Caribbean*, p. 205.

19. Cox, *Nicaragua and the United States*, p. 718.

20. Link, *Wilson: The New Freedom*, p. 332.

21. Ibid.

22. Rippy, *The Caribbean Danger Zone*, p. 180; *Commoner*, January 7, 1910.

23. Mena to Wilson, March 5, 1913, State Department Papers, National Archives.

24. Ibid.

25. Doyle to the Secretary of State, March 25, 1913, State Department Papers, National Archives.

26. Ibid.; Rippy, *The Caribbean Danger Zone*, p. 17.

27. Rippy, *The Caribbean Danger Zone*, p. 180.

28. Selig Adler, "Bryan and Wilsonian Caribbean Penetration," *Hispanic American Historical Review* 20 (May 1940): 206; Bryan to Wilson, May 24, 1913, Bryan Papers, Library of Congress.

29. Adler, "Bryan and Wilsonian Caribbean Penetration," p. 206.

30. Bryan to Wilson, May 24, 1913, Bryan Papers, Library of Congress.

31. Ibid.

32. Louis W. Koenig, *Bryan: A Political Biography of William Jennings Bryan* (New York: G. P. Putnam's Sons, 1971), p. 515.

33. Ibid.

34. Ibid.

35. Wilson to Bryan, June 19, 1913, Bryan-Wilson Correspondence, National Archives.

36. *New York Times*, July 20, 1913; Adler, "Bryan and Wilsonian Caribbean Penetration," p. 207.

37. *New York Times*, July 20, 1913.

38. Ibid.

39. *New York Times*, July 21, 1913.

40. Ibid.

41. Ibid.

42. Ibid., July 20, 1913.

43. Ibid., July 22, 1913.

44. Ibid.

45. Ibid., July 27, 1913.

46. Bryan to Wilson, July 31, 1913, Bryan-Wilson Correspondence, National Archives.

47. *New York Times*, August 3, 1913.

48. Ibid., August 5, 1913.

49. Acting Counselor for Secretary of John B. Moore to the Secretary of War, May 22, 1913, State Department Papers, National Archives.

50. The Legation of Nicaragua to the Department of State, July 15, 1913, *Papers Relating to the Foreign Relations of the United States, 1913* (Washington, D.C.: U.S. Government Printing Office, 1920), pp. 1043-1045.

51. Statement of the features of the loan contracts, October 20, 1913, *Foreign Relations, 1913*, pp. 1061-1063.

52. Ibid.

53. Ibid.

54. Secretary of State to Brown Brothers and Company and J. and W. Seligman and Company, October 6, 1913, *Foreign Relations, 1913*, pp. 1056-1057.

55. Secretary of State to Brown Brothers and Company and J. and W. Seligman and Company, January 13, 1914, *Papers Relating to the Foreign Relations of the United States, 1914* (Washington, D.C.: U.S. Government Printing Office, 1922), pp. 944-945.

56. Adler, "Bryan and Wilsonian Caribbean Penetration," p. 203.

57. Judge Otto Schoenrich to Boaz W. Long, January 17, 1914, State Department Papers, National Archives; Boaz W. Long to Bryan, February 6, 1914, State Department Papers, National Archives.

58. Bryan to Wilson, January 23, 1914, Bryan Papers, Library of Congress.

59. Ibid., January 29, 1914.

60. Ibid.

61. Ibid., January 23, 1914.

62. Minister of Nicaragua to the Secretary of State, February 12, 1914, *Foreign Relations, 1914*, pp. 953-954.

63. *New York Times*, June 18, 1914; Munro, *Intervention and Dollar Diplomacy in the Carribean*, p. 399.

64. *New York Times*, June 19, 1914.

65. Ibid., June 23, 1914.

66. Ibid.

67. Ibid., June 24, 1914.

68. Ibid.

69. Chamorro to the State Department, July 21, 1914, State Department Papers, National Archives.

70. Ibid.

71. *New York Times*, August 6, 1914.

72. Ibid., June 18, 1914; June 24, 1914.

73. Bryan to Wilson, September 30, 1914, Bryan-Wilson Correspondence, National Archives.

74. Ibid.

75. Wilson to Bryan, October 1, 1914, Bryan-Wilson Correspondence, National Archives.

76. Secretary of State to Minister Jefferson, October 1, 1914, *Foreign Relations, 1914*, p. 948.

77. Arthur S. Link, *Woodrow Wilson and the Progressive Era, 1910-1917* (New York: Harper, 1954), p. 129; Bryan to Wilson, January 12, 1915, Bryan-Wilson Correspondence, National Archives.

78. Bryan to Wilson, January 22, 1915, Bryan-Wilson Correspondence, National Archives.

79. Ibid.

80. Ibid.

81. For the early hostility by the Central American states toward the Nicaraguan treaty, see *Foreign Relations of the United States, 1913*, pp. 1021-1034.

82. Minister of Costa Rica to the Secretary of State, April 17, 1913, *Foreign Relations, 1913*, pp. 1022-1023.

83. Ibid; *New York Times*, July 21, 1913.

84. Minister of Costa Rica to the Secretary of State, April 17, 1913, *Foreign Relations, 1913*, pp. 1022-1023.

85. *New York Times*, July 21, 1913.

86. Minister of Nicaragua to the Secretary of State, June 5, 1913, *Foreign Relations, 1913*, pp. 1023-1024.

87. Minister of Costa Rica to the Secretary of State, July 7, 1914, *Foreign Relations, 1914*, p. 959.

88. Minister of El Salvador to the Secretary of State, October 21, 1913, *Foreign Relations, 1913*, p. 1027.

89. Secretary of State to the Minister of El Salvador, February 18, 1914, *Foreign Relations, 1914*, pp. 954-956.

90. Ibid.

91. Minister of El Salvador to the Secretary of State, March 11, 1914, *Foreign Relations, 1914*, p. 57.

92. Secretary of State to the Minister of El Salvador, February 18, 1914, *Foreign Relations, 1914*, pp. 954-956.

93. Minister of El Salvador to the Secretary of State, March 11, 1914, *Foreign Relations, 1914*, p. 957.

94. Chargé d'Affaires of El Salvador to the Secretary of State, July 8, 1914, *Foreign Relations, 1914*, p. 960.

95. *New York Times*, July 9, 1914.

96. Ibid., July 21, 1913.

97. Ibid.

98. Ibid.

99. Bryan to Wilson, September 23, 1913, Bryan-Wilson Correspondence, National Archives.

100. Ibid.

101. Ibid.; Wilson to Bryan, September 25, 1913, Bryan-Wilson Correspondence, National Archives.

5

Haiti

Of all the countries in the Caribbean in the early twentieth century, Haiti appeared the most explosive. Here revolutions occurred so frequently, that before one government could establish itself, it was overthrown. In order to understand the chaotic conditions reigning in Haiti, it is necessary to briefly view its history and to discuss its social and political characteristics prior to 1913.

HAITI BEFORE BRYAN

Haiti occupies the western third of the Caribbean island of Hispaniola (the remainder of the island is occupied by the Dominican Republic), and, after the United States, it is the second oldest independent country in the Western Hemisphere and the world's oldest black republic. The island was discovered by Christopher Columbus in 1492 and became part of the Spanish empire until the middle of the seventeenth century, when French colonists, importing African slaves, developed sugar plantations in the north. Under French rule from 1697, Haiti (then called Saint-Domingue) became one of the world's largest sugar and coffee producers.

Inspired by the French Revolution of 1789, Toussaint L'Ouverture led his fellow slaves in a rebellion in 1791 that ended slavery on the island.[1] However, Toussaint did not declare Saint-Domingue an independent country, as he waited to see how the French would react. It should be noted that Toussaint was more concerned about the institution of slavery than independence. The French did nothing for more than ten years, because it was occupied with its own "reign of terror" and could not be concerned about its colonies. From 1792 to 1795, political chaos in France consumed the nation, as French leaders hardly had time to settle in office before they were sent to their deaths by the guillotine. Finally, in 1802, Napoleon I, France's first emperor, sent his brother-in-law, General Charles

Leclerc, with 20,000 French soldiers to restore French rule in Saint Domingue.[2] Leclerc's expedition occurred during the Treaty of Amiens—a treaty between Great Britain and France in 1802, allowing for a brief peace, during which Napoleon tried to restore France's former colonial empire in America. He hoped to fortify Louisiana and re-establish slavery the sugar business in Saint Domingue.[3] At first it looked like the French would succeed after Toussaint was captured and sent to France, where he eventually died in a French jail. However, Jean Jacques Dessalines continued the rebellion and succeeded with the help of an outbreak of yellow fever, which helped to defeat the French forces.[4] In 1803, Napoleon once again found himself at war with England and all hope of reclaiming France's empire in the new world vanished. By 1804, the French had sold the whole Louisiana territory to the United States, and Saint Domingue had declared its independence and changed its name to Haiti.[5] In 1820, Jean Pierre Boyer united the entire island of Hispaniola, which continued to be called Haiti. Finally, in 1844, the Spanish-speaking eastern part seceded from Haiti and called itself the Dominican Republic.[6]

Throughout most of the nineteenth and into the twentieth century Haiti had been ruled mostly by dictators—former army commanders whose followers put them in power. Nearly all of the people were illiterate; ninety-five percent of the population were of the working class or so-called black peasants. They spoke a dialect called *patois*, a mixture of French, Spanish, and African, and practiced voodoo.[7] The other five percent were the so-called elite, oriented toward Europe and mostly Catholic. They were mainly mulattoes, living mostly in Port-Au-Prince, the capital and chief urban center.[8] The elite and blacks had little contact with each other; the former had little understanding of the social and economic problems of the black peasants. The lack of rapport between these two groups, the high illiteracy rate among the majority of the people, and an almost continuous history of violence since Haiti's independence, gave little hope for stability when Bryan took office in March 1913. In fact, revolutions became more frequent after 1913 as insurgent armies fought for the highest bidder. Many of these armed men knew no other trade except warfare. The majority were *cacos*, peasants living along the northern part of the frontier dividing Haiti from the Dominican Republic.[9] After a successful revolution, the *cacos* were paid and sent home to await a new uprising.[10]

In spite of the instability in Haiti, the United States paid scant attention to the Caribbean island after its independence. It did not recognize the Republic of Haiti until 1864, focusing more on Cuba, Panama, the Dominican Republic, and Nicaragua until spring 1913.[11]

BRYAN'S HAITIAN POLICY

Bryan was one of the few people in Washington who paid any attention to the political disorders in Haiti when he became secretary of state in March 1913. It was not so much the political chaos that bothered him, but the fact that in Haiti, French and German financial influence prevailed, and continued disorder could bring foreign intervention on a large scale.[12] Foreign investment was conspicuous in many of the Caribbean republics, but in Haiti, in 1913, it exceeded that of the United States.[13] The French were the chief creditors and best customers for Haiti's exports.[14] The Germans owned the important public utilities, and German merchants frequently financed the numerous revolutions.[15] In fact, the German government was suspected by the U.S. State Department of using the influence of their merchants to obtain a naval base and coaling station in the harbor of the Mole St. Nicholas, located on the northwestern part of the island.[16]

American financial interests in Haiti were small in 1913. Four New York banks paid $200,000 for 40 percent of the stock in the Haitian National Bank, the remainder of which was in the hands of the Germans and French. Americans held less than half of the stock in the Haitian National Railroad; the rest belonged to the Ethelburga Syndicate of London. There was some American interest in the Haitian Central Railroad, but the majority of the stock was controlled by the Germans.[17] The Grace Syndicate, an American concern, had acquired a concession to build a railroad from the Haitian capital, Port-au-Prince, to Cap Haïtien on the northern coast.[18] The French and German financial interests had been in Haiti much longer than their American counterparts. Link, the Wilsonian historian estimated that total American investment in Haiti was less than $15 million—a good reason for lack of U.S. interest in this Caribbean nation.[19]

Bryan's concern that the dominance of French and German financial interests in Haiti would eventually lead to their political control was reinforced by Boaz W. Long and his two assistants, J. H. Stabler and E. Bell, from the Division of Latin American Affairs. These experts on Latin American affairs worked with Roger L. Farnham, the chief spokesman for American business in Haiti. They made certain that Bryan understood the importance of supporting American business over foreign competition. Long told Bryan that economic control of Haiti would give the United States more input into Haitian politics. If Bryan would support Farnham and American business in Haiti, then the secretary of state would never have to worry about foreign military or political intervention in that country or any other Latin American nation.[20] Long and his associates worked on Bryan's fear of foreign intervention, just as they did in the Nicaraguan case and elsewhere. For example, in May 1913, Bell warned Bryan that the French had designs on Haiti and were sending their gunboat *Descartes* there to protect French financial interests against possible political disorder.[21]

In June 1913, Bryan learned that the German government was interested in obtaining a naval base in the harbor of the Mole St. Nicholas. He wrote Wilson that the United States should press the Haitian government into selling the Mole St. Nicholas to the United States.[22] He desired a strip of land about twenty miles wide, measured from the center of the harbor. It would extend to a point ten miles beyond the eastern end of the harbor so as to give the United States not only the harbor, but plentiful land surrounding it to protect the harbor from attack.[23]

Bryan was aware that the Mole St. Nicholas is located on the northwestern part of the island and is directly across the Windward Passage and the American naval base at Guantánamo Bay in Cuba, making its possession strategically important for the United States.[24] Though Bryan was unable to secure this area in 1913, he did receive assurances from the Haitian government that the harbor would not be sold to a European power.[25]

In May 1913, only two months after Bryan had taken office, the Haitian president Tancrède Auguste presumably died of poisoning, and his successor Michel Oreste was elected. The United States, as a matter of course, immediately recognized the new Haitian president.[26] However, Oreste was not in office very long, as a new revolution broke out in January 1914. The State Department received reports of the new revolution from the American minister and American financial agents. It was the financial interests, in particular, that put increasing pressure on Bryan, warning of imminent disaster if the U.S. government did nothing to counter the revolt.[27] It was Farnham, the vice-president of the National Bank in Haiti, who pushed Bryan into taking action against the rebel forces that threatened the Oreste government. He sent the following telegram to the secretary of state in January 1914: "The political situation is very serious. Rebels are in possession of Letion and Bahon. They have notified us to discontinue the trains to Bahon as they will not be responsible of the consequences."[28] Farnham wanted American protection against the rebels, since the current Haitian government appeared incapable of dealing with the revolution.[29] Bryan responded by sending the cruiser *Nashville* to Port-au-Prince to afford whatever protection that might be necessary.[30]

Farnham expertly pushed the right buttons to get Bryan's cooperation so quickly. He warned the secretary of state that French and German interests were behind the current revolution and that they would attempt to dominate any new government formed. He declared that it was necessary for the United States to intervene, not only to protect American financial interests (Bryan, unlike Long, had little interest in just doing that), but also to maintain its own political interest. Bryan had no desire to see Haiti become a colony of either France or Germany.[31] Thus, the secretary of state sent the cruiser, and then sent a message to the American minister, Madison Smith, threatening to take further action against the rebels if they did not respect American property and life. He also insisted that all obligations to American financial interests, including the Haitian National Bank, had to be respected.[32]

In January 1914, the Oreste government fell, but there was no immediate indication of what rebel leader would emerge as victor. In fact, the fighting grew worse as the rebels fought among themselves, and destruction of property became prevalent. Farnham continued to urge the dispatch of more American forces. He wrote to Bryan: "The situation has grown worse. The situation is very much complicated by the revolution's leaders fighting each other."[33] The two leaders that were seeking power were Oreste Zamor and General Davilmar Theodore. By February 3, 1914, Zamor won, and six days later, he became the new president of

Haiti.[34]

Though Zamor was named president, Bryan refused to recognize him. This decision was influenced by Long, who was following the advice of Farnham. Long had written Bryan that Farnham and Elbert F. Baldwin, the spokesman for the Outlook Company (Baldwin had financial interests in the customs houses) feared that the Zamor government was incapable of protecting their interests, since the new government, in their opinion, would last only a few weeks. They warned that further political instability would follow the fall of the new government, and this would invite German and French intervention.[35]

The fighting finally ended in late February 1914, with Zamor still in command, and Bryan again had to make a decision on recognition. The secretary of state, realizing that political disorder could occur at any moment, wanted to make recognition contingent upon American control of the customs and acquisition of the harbor Mole St. Nicholas.[36] Stabler influenced Bryan's decision; he wrote the secretary of state that the United States should withhold recognition until it received assurances from the Haitian government that Zamor would allow American control of the customs and give the United States the Mole St. Nicholas.[37] The Zamor government, however, declared that it could not negotiate any deal with the United States until it was first recognized as the legitimate government of Haiti.[38] On March 2, 1914, Bryan, against the advice of Stabler, recognized the Zamor government, hoping that the new Haitian president would now agree to the demands of the American government.[39]

Though the American plan to control the Haitian customs was never implemented in 1914, it, nonetheless, caused furor and anxiety in France and Germany. On the other hand, rumors spread of financial agreements between the two European governments and the Haitians. Bryan was very concerned about these rumors, and when he investigated them, both the French and German governments were quick to deny any deals made between them and the Haitians. For instance, in May 1914, the German government disclaimed the accusation of permitting a German financial syndicate to offer to finance the poverty-stricken Haitian government in exchange for a coaling station and other concessions.[40] Bryan also was very worried that the German and French governments would seize the Haitian custom houses in order to acquire the necessary funds to pay their nationals—a point vigorously denied by both European governments.[41]

Though both the German and French governments denied any interest in the Haitian customs houses, they were aware that Bryan was seeking U.S. control of them. Both European governments made clear to Bryan that they would oppose American control of customs; however, they did propose a joint control arrangement with the United States where representation of each of the three governments would be in proportion to the amount of claims held by their nationals.[42] It seemed like an equitable arrangement, but Bryan opposed it, and for good reason. The secretary of state was informed by his staff that U.S. representation would be minimal, since it only accounted for 5 percent of the total amount to be collected.[43]

In late June 1914, a new revolution occurred. Like the previous ones, the fighting caused much destruction, interruption of train service and communica-tion, and fear among American financial interests that their property would be destroyed.[44] Farnham went to Washington to confer with Bryan on what steps should be taken to ensure financial stability in the midst of the new revolt. He had the secretary of state's full attention when he declared that French and German interests in Haiti were working with their governments to take control of the Haitian government. He appealed to the secretary of state that immediate action was needed and proposed what became known as the Farnham Plan.[45] Bryan accepted the plan without hesitation and sent a draft to the new American minister in Haiti, Arthur Bailly-Blanchard. It was quickly sent to the Zamor government for approval.[46] The plan was nothing more than convention between the United States and Haiti that would: (1) empower the president of the United States to appoint a financial adviser to improve Haiti's finances and strengthen its credit; (2) provide for the payment of all customs duties to a General Receivership; (3) ensure that the money collected by the General Receiver would be put toward the salaries of the General Receiver and his assistants, to the interest and sinking fund of the public debt of Haiti, and to the Haitian government for current expenses; (4) prevent further increase in the Haitian public debt without American consent; and (5) give the United States the right to prevent any interference with the operation of the receivership.[47]

Charles Zamor, the brother of the Haitian president, accepted the Farnham Plan, but only on condition that it would be made to appear that it was being forced upon his government. He wanted the American navy to occupy Port-au-Prince and threaten bombardment if the plan was not accepted. The Haitian people had to be convinced that he was not a puppet of the United States or his government's position would be gravely endangered.[48] Bryan refused to make any such agreement with Zamor: The Haitian government had either to accept or reject the plan. President Zamor disliked the Farnham Plan but saw it as an opportunity to stay in power with American support. However, he could not appear to be an United States puppet or he would lose any support he had among his people, as well as the backing of the Germans and the French who opposed the plan. Thus, if the Americans refused to force the plan on him, he had no recourse but to reject it.[49]

The revolution that began in June 1914 grew worse by July, and Bryan, espec-ially after the Farnham Plan was rejected, decided to increase American naval forces in the Caribbean.[50] Franklin Roosevelt, assistant secretary of the navy, ordered 750 marines sent to Guantánamo, Cuba, to prepare for action in Haiti.[51] The intention was not only to protect American citizens and property in Haiti, but to deter any actions the Germans or French might take in regard to the recent revolution.[52] The French and German governments continued to press the Haitian government for payment of debts owed their nationals and had threatened to seize the Haitian customs.[53] These European governments also distrusted American intentions; on July 15, the German minister in Port-au-Prince telegraphed the German consul at Cap Haïtien, asking whether American soldiers had taken control of the customs house there.[54]

Bryan's position on the role of German and French financial interests in the development of Haiti was most interesting. Actually, he had nothing against their involvement in Haitian financial ventures that would lead to the economic growth of Haiti. His major concern was that this would lead to a political takeover of Haiti by the German and French governments.[55] The secretary of state was a firm believer in the principles of the Monroe Doctrine and was opposed to any foreign power that might gain political control of any nation in the western hemisphere. This would endanger Latin American independence and threaten the sovereign position of the United States.[56] In August 1914, Bryan's fear of German and French collusion in Haiti subsided considerably because of the outbreak of World War I, with Germany and France on opposing sides.[57]

The Haitian revolution that began in June 1914 finally ended in October, after four months of continuous fighting. President Oreste Zamor and his followers were ousted from power, and Davilmar Theodore emerged as the new head of state.[58] Once again, Bryan refused to recognize the new government. He demanded assurances that the Theodore government could control the country; he again attempted to implement a plan for financial control of the country.[59] Bryan asked Theodore to send a three-man commission to Washington with the powers to negotiate a customs convention between the United States and Haiti in accordance with the Farnham Plan of the previous July. Bryan specifically wanted to do the following: (1) settle all questions outstanding between the American railroad and the government of Haiti; (2) solve all problems between the government of Haiti and the bank; (3) provide for protection of American interests; (4) agree that Haiti would never lease any of its territory to a foreign nation except the United States.[60] If the Haitian government complied with these provisions, recognition would be forthcoming. There was little doubt that these proposals favored American financial interests—Bryan and Farnham had consulted on these matters previously when the latter was in Washington. Nonetheless, the most startling part of Bryan's plan was that he wanted to name the three Haitian commissioners that would represent their country in Washington.[61] If the secretary of state had his way, there would be no true negotiations or discussion of these terms, but the Haitian government would have to accept them as dictated Bryan. Nonetheless, President Theodore refused to consider any plan until the United States first recognized his government. The Haitian president was regularly elected by the National Assembly on November 13, 1914.[62]

Throughout the remainder of November, both Bryan and Theodore continued to argue their positions on recognition. Bryan refused to yield—an agreement must be formulated, especially on control of the customs. Theodore continued to insist that before any negotiations could be considered, recognition must be granted. Actually, Theodore was in no position to concede to Bryan's demands. Nationalistic opinion prevailed in both the Haitian public and Senate against customs control by the United States.[63]

On December 12, 1914, Theodore offered Bryan a substitute plan favoring

American financial interests. It gave prospecting rights to American miners, with the Haitian government paying the mining engineer's salaries; the engineers could exploit the mines for twenty years.[64] Bryan rejected this proposal stating: "While we desire to encourage in every proper way American investments in Haiti, we believe that this can be better done by contributing to stability and order than by favoring special concessions to Americans."[65]

As much as Bryan wanted a customs convention tied to recognition, he now realized that this would be impossible to obtain, due to the intense hostility in the Haitian Congress against any such agreement.[66] Therefore, he separated recognition from the customs convention; recognition now would be considered on its own merits. He wrote Blanchard the following: "Recognition will be considered on its merits and that recognition will be granted whenever this government is satisfied that there is in Haiti a government capable of maintaining order and meeting the country's obligations to outside nations. Such a government is impossible, however, unless it rests upon the consent of the governed and gives expression to the will of the people."[67] Bryan stressed financial stability and demanded information on the fiscal plans of the Haitian government before recognition could be considered.[68]

Aside from wanting recognition, Theodore desired a loan, but the bankers had refused to consider any loan until an arrangement was made for repayment. Both Bryan and the American bankers were skeptical of Haiti's ability to meet its financial obligations. If the customs convention had been accepted, there would have been no difficulty in obtaining financial help.[69]

In December 1914, while Theodore continued to argue for financial aid, threatening to remove funds his government needed, Bryan and American representatives of the National Bank, decided to remove $500,000 in gold and have it transported to New York on the gunboat *Machias*.[70] The secretary of state defended his actions by criticizing the instability of the Theodore government and stressing the threat it presented to American financial interests.[71] This action was made more intolerable to the Haitian government, because a large number of marines were used to escort the gold; it protested vehemently, threatening to retaliate by removing the rest of the funds in the bank.[72]

By January 1915, U.S.-Haitian relations had deteriorated considerably. Bryan wrote Wilson about the gravity of the Haitian situation and gave his opinion on what should be done. Bryan, who in the past held little sympathy for bankers, told the president that the United State must defend the National Bank against any attempt by the Theodore government to remove the bank's funds.[73] Bryan also informed Wilson that a new revolution had begun, and in his opinion, there would never be any peace in Haiti unless the Wilson Plan, already used in the Dominican Republic, was implemented in Haiti. The Wilson Plan, which will be discussed in more detail in the next chapter, called for an end to the fighting, an appointment of a provisional president who was agreeable to all, and the holding of free elections, supervised by a two-man commission from the United States.[74] Wilson wasted little time in agreeing with Bryan, and the secretary of state recommended to the president that ex-governor of New Jersey, James Fort, and Charles Cogswell Smith be sent to Haiti. They were successful in getting the plan implemented in the Dominican Republic, and hopefully, they would be able to do the same in Haiti.[75]

The Theodore government, weakened from lack of money, lost the loyalty of its military supporters when it could not pay their salaries. In December 1914, Theodore appointed General Vilbrun Guillaume Sam as leader of the northern army. Sam turned against his president and led a new revolt.[76] By the middle of January 1915, the fighting had spread throughout the country, causing great loss of life and destruction of property. Bryan quickly asked the Navy Department to send a cruiser to Cap Haïtien for the protection of American life and property.[77]

From January to February 1915, Bryan made preparations to have the Wilson Plan implemented in Haiti. He informed his minister to Haiti, Bailly-Blanchard, of the plan. Blanchard told Bryan that the plan would not work—elections in Haiti, unlike the Dominican Republic, were not popularly conducted. They were part of the military system where the victorious general was always appointed to the presidency by the Congress.[78] Blanchard wanted Bryan to delay the arrival of the commission until Sam, victor of the revolution, could take the oath of office.[79] Bryan refused, however, to take Blanchard's advice; he did not want to delay the mission. He told Wilson that the sooner the commissioners arrived in Haiti, the faster they could gather important information on the new government—information that would determine whether State Department recognition would be forthcoming. The secretary of state had told Wilson that he disagreed with Blanchard's assessment and that, in his opinion, the Wilson Plan had an excellent opportunity of succeeding if the United States demanded its immediate adoption. He had also informed Wilson that he still wanted control of the Haitian customs, but he would not make it an absolute condition of recognition, if the Wilson Plan was adopted.[80]

When Fort and Smith arrived in Haiti on March 5, they met with President Sam. He was very gracious to his American hosts, but he refused to consider accepting the Wilson Plan until his government was first recognized.[81] Sam wanted U.S. recognition badly, knowing that with it came the financial support he would need to stay in power. He also knew that Blanchard had opposed the Fort and Smith mission to Haiti and had favored recognition of his government. He decided to allow Blanchard to try and secure recognition for him. On the other hand, when Fort and Smith sent their report to Bryan, they strongly recommended that recognition be withheld until the Wilson Plan was accepted.[82]

The Haitian situation was in diplomatic turmoil; Bryan had to decide whether to listen to his minister to Haiti, Blanchard, who had a firm grasp of the situation or to take the advice of his commissioners, Fort and Smith, who had achieved success in the Dominican Republic. The secretary of state made his decision in favor Fort and Smith. He desperately wanted to bring stability to Haiti and believed that the Wilson Plan would work there.[83] Blanchard's continued insistence that the Wilson Plan was inoperable in Haiti and on recognition of the

Sam government immediately caused problems with Bryan.[84] Throughout the month of March, Blanchard used every means he could think of to get his government to recognize the Haitian government. He had even informed Bryan that both the German and Italian governments had already recognized Sam and that the French would soon follow.[85] Blanchard argued that Sam appeared to have established a more stable government and had access to more money, since both the German and French financial interests supported him. It was Blanchard's contention that if the United States continued to deny the Sam government recognition, American business interests would find itself at a competitive disadvantage in Haiti.[86]

Working in Blanchard's favor was a rumor that French and German financial interests were cooperating, once again, to secure the Mole St. Nicholas. A French company was supposed to have paid the new Haitian government $1 million for this concession.[87] This was a rumor that might easily be ignored, since France and Germany were fighting each other in World War I at this time. However, it was not impossible for the financial interests of two warring countries to cooperate in Haiti when it could prevent the United States from establishing financial dominance.

Though Bryan believed that such a German-French conspiracy existed, he still refused to recognize the Sam government.[88] He wrote Wilson in March 1915 that to grant the Sam government recognition would not guarantee the adoption of the Wilson Plan. He also warned the president of collusion between the French and German financial interests and of the need to support American business groups in Haiti. He especially mentioned to the president how important it was to keep control of American interests in the National Bank, declaring that the American bankers could dispose of their stock in the bank without loss, but that would be against the best interests of the United States.[89] Bryan also stressed the importance for the United States to acquire an agreement on the Mole St. Nicholas. He told Wilson that if immediate action was not taken, the Mole would probably be bought by France or Germany.[90]

Bryan continued to badger Wilson with his belief in a foreign conspiracy that was aimed at the United States. He wrote the president in April 1915 that foreign capitalists were in control of the Haitian government and were discriminating against American interests.[91] He told the president that he would seriously consider using military intervention in Haiti to protect American interests if needed. He revived his customs control plan but added an alternative to it. He stated that "the Haitians might be allowed to choose between a resident adviser such as the Dutch maintain in Java, and a customs convention."[92] Bryan wanted this sent to Haiti in the form of an ultimatum, and if it was not accepted, it would be imposed by force. However, Bryan wanted to send one more envoy to Haiti before resorting to the ultimatum.[93]

In May 1915, with the president's full support of his Haitian policy, Bryan sent Paul Fuller, Jr., the son of Wilson's special envoy to Mexico, to propose the following agreement to the Sam government: President Sam would agree to receive an adviser, an American minister plenipotentiary; he would also make no agreements with any European power concerning the Mole St. Nicholas; no mention was made of a customs collectorship. The United States, in return, would not only extend formal recognition, but would also assist in preventing further insurrections.[94] These terms were embodied in a draft treaty by Fuller and submitted to the Sam government on May 22, 1915. Sam, however, refused to discuss the Fuller proposals until the United States first recognized his government. Bryan suspended all negotiations on June 5, 1915, just four days before he resigned his office over the *Lusitania* crisis.[95]

Bryan's policy toward Haiti was primarily determined from fear—fear that both German and French financial interests would completely dominate and lead eventually to European political control. As early as April 1913, Bryan wanted possession of the Mole St. Nicholas to prevent it from falling into the hands of France or Germany. When three major Haitian revolutions occurred during Bryan's term of office, he sent ships to Haiti not only to protect American lives and property, but also to warn the French and Germans, whom he feared would make use of the revolutions to seize control of the customs. Bryan supported the Farnham Plan, which called for control of the Haitian customs, not so much because he was an ardent advocate of American business, but because he was led to believe by Bell, Stabler, and Long of the Division of Latin American Affairs that this was the only way to counter French and German pecuniary interests. Bryan opposed the French-German recommendation for joint control of the Haitian customs in proportion to the amount of investment of each country, since it would be to the disadvantage of the United States. When the European war began in August 1914, with the Germans and French on opposite sides, collusion appeared less feasible to Bryan, but he was still not entirely convinced that these two warring governments were not involved in a conspiracy to gain control of the Mole St. Nicholas and to manipulate the Haitian government. His obsession with the conspiracy plot grew to desperation, and from April to June 1915, he became an outright imperialist, threatening to use the navy if the Haitian government would not agree to a financial convention. The Fuller mission, in May 1915, was the last peaceful attempt to impose American financial control over Haiti. Bryan resigned in June 1915, and full scale intervention occurred the following month. We shall deal with Bryan's attitude toward this intervention in chapter 10.

NOTES

1. John Edwin Fagg, *Latin America: A General History* (New York: Macmillan, 1977), p. 311.

2. Ibid.

3. Ibid.

4. Ibid., p. 355.

5. Ibid.

6. Ibid., p. 414.

7. Dana G. Munro, *Intervention and Dollar Diplomacy in the Caribbean, 1900-1921* (Princeton, N.J.: Princeton University Press, 1964), p. 327.

8. Ibid., p. 328.

9. Ibid., p. 330.

10. Ibid.

11. Arthur S. Link, *Wilson: The Struggle for Neutrality, 1914-1915* (Princeton, N.J.: Princeton University Press, 1960), p. 517.

12. Munro, *Intervention and Dollar Diplomacy in the Caribbean*, p. 326.

13. Ibid., p. 331.

14. Ibid., p. 326.

15. Ibid.

16. Ibid.

17. Ibid., pp. 331-332.

18. Link, *Wilson: The Struggle for Neutrality*, p. 517.

19. Ibid.

20. Munro, *Intervention and Dollar Diplomacy in the Caribbean*, p. 332.

21. E. Bell to the Secretary of State, May 5, 1913, State Department Papers, National Archives.

22. Bryan to Wilson, June 20, 1913, Bryan-Wilson Correspondence, National Archives.

23. Ibid.

24. Selig Adler, "Bryan and Wilsonian Caribbean Penetration," *Hispanic American Historical Review* 20 (May 1940): 221.

25. Ibid., p. 222.

26. Link, *Wilson: The Struggle for Neutrality*, p. 517; American Minister to the Secretary of State, May 5, 1913, *Papers Relating to the Foreign Relations of the United States, 1913* (Washington, D.C.: U.S. Government Printing Office, 1920), p. 574.

27. Huttlinger and Struller of New York City to the Secretary of State, January 5, 1914, State Department Papers, National Archives.

28. Roger L. Farnham to the Secretary of State, January 20, 1914, State Department Papers, National Archives.

29. Ibid.

30. Bryan to Madison Smith, January 14, 1914, State Department Papers, National Archives.

31. Roger L. Farnham to the Secretary of State, January 24, 1914, State Department Papers, National Archives.

32. Bryan to Madison Smith, January 25, 1914, State Department Papers, National Archives.

33. Roger L. Farnham to the Secretary of State, February 2, 1914, State Department Papers, National Archives.

34. Madison Smith to the Secretary of State, February 9, 1914, State Department Papers, National Archives.

35. Boaz W. Long to the Secretary of State, January 28, 1914, State Department Papers, National Archives; Roger L. Farnham to the Secretary of State, February 13, 1914, State Department Papers, National Archives; Bryan to Wilson, February 11, 1914, State Department Papers, National Archives.

36. Secretary of State to Madison Smith, February 26, 1914, State Department Papers, National Archives.

37. J. H. Stabler to the Secretary of State, February 3, 1914, State Department Papers, National Archives.

38. Madison Smith to the Secretary of State, February 28, 1914, State Department Papers, National Archives.

39. Bryan to Madison Smith, March 1, 1914, State Department Papers, National Archives.

40. *New York Times*, May 14, 1914.

41. Ibid.

42. Ibid.

43. Ibid.

44. Roger L. Farnham to the Secretary of State, June 19, 1914, State Department Papers, National Archives.

45. Munro, *Intervention and Dollar Diplomacy in the Caribbean*, p. 337.

46. Bryan to Blanchard, July 2, 1914, *Papers Relating to the Foreign Relations of the United States, 1914* (Washington, D.C.: U.S. Government Printing Office, 1922), pp. 347-350.

47. Ibid.

48. Livingston to the Secretary of State, July 23, 1914, State Department Papers, National Archives.

49. Munro, *Intervention and Dollar Diplomacy in the Caribbean*, p. 339.

50. Bryan to the Secretary of the Navy, July 10, 1914, State Department Papers, National Archives.

51. *New York Times*, July 14, 1914.

52. Ibid., July 15, 1914.

53. Ibid.

54. Livingston to the Secretary of State, July 15, 1914, State Department Papers, National Archives.

55. Munro, *Intervention and Dollar Diplomacy in the Caribbean*, p. 340; Bryan to Wilson, October 28, 1913, Bryan Papers, Library of Congress.

56. Ibid.

57. Munro, *Intervention and Dollar Diplomacy in the Caribbean*, p. 340.

58. Blanchard to the Secretary of State, October 29, 1914, State Department Papers, National Archives.

59. Bryan to Blanchard, November 12, 1914, State Department Papers, National Archives.

60. Ibid.

61. Ibid., November 16, 1914.

62. Blanchard to the Secretary of State, November 18, 1914, State Department Papers, National Archives.

63. Ibid., December 2, 1914.

64. Ibid., December 12, 1914.

65. Bryan to Blanchard, December 19, 1914, State Department Papers, National Archives.

66. Blanchard to the Secretary of State, December 2, 1914, State Department Papers, National Archives.

67. Bryan to Blanchard, December 11, 1914, Bryan Papers, Library of Congress.

68. Ibid.

69. Blanchard to the Secretary of State, December 12, 1914, State Department Papers, National Archives; Munro, *Intervention and Dollar Diplomacy in the Caribbean*, p. 344.

70. Adler, "Bryan and Wilsonian Caribbean Penetration," pp. 223-224.

71. Ibid.

72. Munro, *Intervention and Dollar Diplomacy in the Caribbean*, p. 345; *New York Times*, December 20, 1914; Bryan to Wilson, January 7, 1915, Bryan Papers, Library of Congress.

73. Bryan to Wilson, January 7, 1915, Bryan Papers, Library of Congress; Secretary of State to Minister Blanchard, January 26, 1915, *Papers Relating to the Foreign Relations of the United States, 1915* (Washington D.C.: U.S. Government Printing Office, 1924), p. 506.

74. Bryan to Wilson, January 7, 1915, Bryan Papers, Library of Congress.

75. Bryan to Wilson, January 15, 1915, Bryan-Wilson Correspondence, National Archives.

76. Munro, *Intervention and Dollar Diplomacy in the Caribbean*, p. 346.

77. Bryan to Blanchard, January 16, 1915, State Department Papers, National Archives.

78. Blanchard to the Secretary of State, February 27,.1915, State Department Papers, National Archives; Munro, *Intervention and Dollar Diplomacy in the Caribbean*, p. 347.

79. Bryan to Wilson, February 25, 1915, Bryan-Wilson Correspondence, National Archives; Fort to the Secretary of State, March 9, 1915, State Department Papers, National Archives.

80. Bryan to Wilson, February 25, 1915, Bryan-Wilson Correspondence, National Archives.

81. Ibid., March 23, 1915.

82. Ibid.; Munro, *Intervention and Dollar Diplomacy in the Caribbean*, p. 348.

83. Bryan to Wilson, March 23, 1915, Bryan-Wilson Correspondence, National Archives.

84. Ibid., February 25, 1915.

85. Blanchard to the Secretary of State, March 19, 1915, State Department Papers, National Archives.

86. Munro, *Intervention and Dollar Diplomacy in the Caribbean*, p. 348.

87. Adler, "Bryan and Wilsonian Caribbean Penetration," p. 224.

88. Bryan to Blanchard, March 26, 1915, State Department Papers, National Archives.

89. Bryan to Wilson, March 27, 1915, Bryan Papers, Library of Congress.

90. Ibid.

91. Bryan to Wilson, April 3, 1915, Bryan-Wilson Correspondence, National Archives.

92. Adler, "Bryan and Wilsonian Caribbean Penetration," p. 225.

93. Ibid.

94. Ibid.; *New York Times*, May 4, 1915; Munro, *Intervention and Dollar Diplomacy in the Caribbean*, p. 349.

95. Munro, *Intervention and Dollar Diplomacy in the Caribbean*, p. 350.

6

The Dominican Republic

THE DOMINICAN REPUBLIC BEFORE BRYAN

The Dominican Republic occupies the eastern two-thirds of the Caribbean Island of Hispaniola, located between Cuba and Puerto Rica. Columbus landed on the island in 1492, and the earliest Spanish colony in the Americas was established there. In the early nineteenth century, the Dominican Republic's history was associated with Haiti, its western neighbor. In 1821, a group of Creole planters proclaimed the independence of Santo Domingo and hoped to associate their state with Simon Bolívar's Colombia. However, the Haitian army had different plans for Santo Domingo, and in 1822, it invaded that country and incorporated it into greater Haiti where it remained until it acquired its freedom in 1844.[1] From 1844 to 1905, the country was for the most part ruled by petty dictators who raided the treasury and left the country impoverished. By 1904, several European governments were willing to assist their subjects in collecting about $32 million in bad debts against the Dominican Republic. It was under these conditions that the Roosevelt administration decided to take charge of the Dominican government's finances.[2]

In 1905, the Dominican Republic became the first Caribbean country to experience U.S. financial control when President Theodore Roosevelt, responding to the pleas from Dominican political leaders and wanting to avoid bankruptcy and possible European intervention (the American minister to the Dominican Republic warned the Roosevelt administration that Italian naval forces were threatening intervention to secure debts owed their nationals), established an American receivership of the Dominican customs.[3] The receivership plan was sent to the Senate in 1905 in the form of a protocol between the United States and the Dominican Republic. It called for a receivership controlled by an American agent, appointed by the president of the United States, who would be charged with collecting all customs duties. After paying the current operating expenses of the receivership, the agent would then appropriate about 45 percent of the collected money to the various creditors of the Dominican government; the remainder of the money would be turned over to the Dominican government for current expenses.[4] Though this protocol was submitted to the Senate in 1905, it was not approved until 1907. However, Roosevelt, without Senate approval, implemented the protocol by executive agreement. During the next four years, American financial agents in the Dominican Republic did an excellent job in refinancing the Dominican foreign and domestic debt, and the treasury had plenty of money to pay off all debts owed to foreigners.[5]

The principle that allowed the United States to intervene in Caribbean countries to ensure financial stability was known as the Roosevelt Corollary to the Monroe Doctrine, which has already been discussed in detail in chapter 2. It should be remembered that the Roosevelt Corollary was formulated out of fear—fear that European powers would use the weakened economic state of Latin American governments and failure to pay their debts as an excuse for political intervention. From the time of the Roosevelt Corollary, the United States assumed economic responsibility in the Caribbean, and European creditors did not have to worry about receiving payment of all debts owed them.[6]

The Roosevelt and Taft administrations had good reason to be concerned about the Dominican Republic's ability to pay its debts. Similar to Haiti, the Dominican Republic had experienced numerous political upheavals, as various military leaders sought political power. There were sixteen revolutions in the forty years prior to 1907, and the total Dominican debt amounted to $32 million.[7]

In November 1911 President Ramón Cáceres was assassinated, throwing the Dominican Republic into turmoil. He was succeeded by Don Eladio Victoria who attempted to calm the country but instead had to deal with a major revolution that lasted into 1912. In the autumn of 1912, Taft's secretary of state, Philander Knox, was able to influence the appointment of Monseñor Adolfo A. Nouel, Archbishop of Santo Domingo to the Dominican presidency. Nouel, who was in poor health, did not really want the job and resigned on March 31, 1913, notwithstanding American entreaties to remain as president.[8]

BRYAN AND THE DOMINICAN REPUBLIC

In April 1913, one month after Bryan became secretary of state, José Bordas Valdés was chosen president of the Dominican Republic.[9] The situation remained relatively calm until September when Governor Céspedes of Puerto Plata, an *horacista* (the two principal political parties in the Dominican Republic were the *horacistas* led by Horacio Vásquez and the *jimenistas* led by Juan Isidro Jiménez) began a revolt against the Bordas government after it had leased a railroad line, running from Puerto Plata to the interior of the country, to a *jimenista*. Céspedes had previously controlled the line and had opposed the option given to the *jimenista* bidders. The railroad was used to provide jobs and revenue for the *horacista* party.[10]

Wilson had little time to devote to the numerous revolutions in the Caribbean and paid scant attention to the details unless they affected the security of the United States. He left most of the details to his secretary of state, who like the president believed that democracy was the best political system and that Latin American countries could learn how to implement democratic government. Thus, when the revolt against Bordas occurred, Bryan had immediately condemned Céspedes and his followers, declaring that any change in government should be accomplished by election.[11] The secretary of state demanded political stability and worried that the constant political bickering would threaten American control of the receivership and drain the Dominican treasury, making repayment of debts to German, British, and French merchants impossible. As in Haiti, Bryan was concerned that European governments were looking for a good excuse to intervene in the affairs of Latin American countries.[12]

Shortly after the Céspedes revolt, Bryan declared that he would hold the entire *horacista* party, and especially its leader Vásquez, responsible for any loss of life or property damage to American citizens. To show the rebels that he meant business, he sent the cruiser *Nashville*, stationed in Honduras, to the north shore of Santo Domingo, the area of the Céspedes revolt. He also ordered marines to ensure that there would be no interference with American control of the customs houses, an action which he contended was in the best interests of the Dominican people.[13]

It should be noted that Wilson totally agreed with Bryan's policy regarding the Céspedes uprising. Immediately after his inauguration, the president had made clear that he would have no sympathy for revolutionaries in Latin America who wanted "to seize the power of government to advance their own personal interests or ambition."[14] Both Bryan and Wilson's support of the Bordas government remained unwavering. In fact, the secretary of state wrote to his new minister to the Dominican Republic, James M. Sullivan, to inform the rebels that "this government will employ every legitimate means to assist in the restoration of order and in the prevention of further insurrections, holding itself open at all times to advise with the government in behalf of those who feel that they have a grievance."[15] He revealed that even if the revolution succeeded, the United States would withhold recognition of the de facto government and any money due the Dominican government from the customs collection.[16]

In carrying the secretary of state's message to the rebels, Sullivan was successful in arranging a cease fire between the Bordas government and the followers of Céspedes. Sullivan, delighted over the outcome (Bordas was to remain in power, and Céspedes had to resign as governor of Puerto Plata, though he was allowed to name his successor), predicted that there would be no future revolutions because the United States would continue to oppose them.[17] This was exactly Bryan and Wilson's position, for they were firm believers that all dissidence could be settled peacefully by free elections.[18]

Now that the revolution had ended, Bryan, in November 1913, attempted to prepare the way for free elections to the Dominican Constitutional Convention. He wrote Sullivan asking him for suggestions on how to conduct fair election. The American minister wanted agents, appointed by the State Department, at all principal towns and polling places. He also wanted Bryan to impress upon Bordas that unless the elections were conducted without fraud, the United States would hold new elections.[19] On the basis of these suggestions, Bryan formulated a plan that he thought would be acceptable to all. American commissioners would be sent to the Dominican Republic; they would not be election officials but only informal election inspectors, ensuring free elections by adding their "moral influence."[20]

Boaz W. Long, the chief of the Division of Latin American Affairs, was opposed to Bryan's plan. Until now, Long, whom Bryan depended on directly for guidance in dealing with Caribbean republics, had supported both his Haitian and Nicaraguan policies and had voiced no objection to his Dominican policy. Now, Long wrote Bryan that it did not make any difference whether the commission was formal or informal; it was bound to arouse the hostility of the opposition leaders, who at this point firmly believed that the United States favored the Bordas government and would keep it in power at all costs.[21]

It did not really matter what Long thought about a commission because the Bordas government also rejected the idea. Bordas appreciated the U.S. support, but he had opposed this interference in the Dominican Republic, claiming that it would only make the political situation worse. However, the Dominican president did not see any reason why individual Americans, without title, such as commissioner, could not unofficially supervise the elections.[22] Bryan, after consulting with Long, agreed to Bordas's suggestion, and on December 11, 1913, three members of the State Department and thirty assistants arrived in the Dominican Republic. Sullivan, with Bryan's confidence, was to take charge of the whole operation.[23]

The voting began on December 15, and during the next few days, there were sporadic complaints by the government's opposition. Bryan had insisted that all complaints be investigated immediately, and in cases where voter's rights had been violated, the Bordas government had to call special elections.[24] These complaints were few, and for the most part, the elections appeared to run smoothly and free of corruption. The opposition party seemed to have won a large victory—seventeen of the twenty-four delegates chosen to sit in the Dominican Constitutional Convention on January 15, 1914 were from the opposition.[25]

Beginning in January 1914, Bryan became deeply involved in both the political and financial affairs of the Dominican Republic. In January, he wrote his favorite minister in the Caribbean, Sullivan, that he wanted to revise the Dominican Republic's organic laws and amend its Constitution with the establishment of *habeas corpus*, bail, military conscription, and an electoral law that would make the people responsible for the election of all governors, rather than having them appointed by the central government.[26] This was blatant interference in the Dominican Republic's political system, which neither Bryan nor Wilson seemed to mind. Both men were firm believers that the U.S. system of political democracy and its constitution represented the highest form of government in the world, and it was the duty and obligation of U.S. policy makers to impose that system on others whether they wanted it or not. Bryan saw nothing wrong in teaching these backward and ignorant neighbors how to write good constitutions.[27]

In January 1914, the Dominican government needed a loan badly, as it had mismanaged its finances, and Bryan, realizing the critical situation, agreed to place an additional $20,000 of its percentage of the customs at its disposal.[28] However, the Bordas government needed more than the $20,000, but Bryan refused to consent until a financial agreement was reached between the two countries. The United States, though it controlled the customs, was unable to prevent bankruptcy in the Dominican Republic, since the Bordas government did what it wished with its money. Bryan now decided that it was time to run the country financially and proceeded to formulate a plan calling for the Dominican bonds in the possession of the Guaranty Trust company to be used in payment of long overdue claims and salaries, the doubling of the Dominican government's alcohol and tobacco taxes to increase its revenue, and the invitation of an American financial expert who would act as an adviser—he would adjust government expenditures and have veto power over the budget.[29]

Though the Bordas government accepted the plan, Bryan believed that Wilson should be consulted on the matter. He wrote the president that the financial plan was the only way to ensure economic stability in the Dominican Republic. He realized that this was a major step in the enlargement of U.S. influence but was hard pressed to find an alternate solution.[30] Wilson praised his secretary of state for his understanding of the difficult situation that confronted him and urged Bryan to begin his search for the most qualified person for the position of financial adviser to the Dominican Republic. Bryan hoped to find someone who could speak Spanish and had a knowledge of accounting.[31]

While negotiations for a financial adviser were continuing, a new revolution began in February 1914 in the northern provinces under the leadership of General Desiderio Arias. Arias, a demagogue and smuggler, who had ambitions of being president himself, was befriended by Bordas in 1913 at the expense of alienating members of the president's own party, the *horacistas*. Bordas had removed certain leaders of the *horacistas* as managers of the Central Dominican Railroad and allowed friends of Arias to occupy those positions.[32]   Now, Arias turned against Bordas for two major reason: (1) Arias had discovered that Bordas was planning to run for president in the June elections—the general believed that he had an agreement with Bordas that the president would not run, and he would throw his support to Arias; and (2) Arias vehemently opposed the new financial agreement that Bryan had made with the Bordas government. In his opinion, the appointment of an American financial adviser to the Dominican Republic was a violation of the country's sovereignty.[33]

Sullivan opposed the Arias revolt and urged Bryan to use American military force to "eliminate Arias and his gang."[34] Though Sullivan considered Arias and his supporters as nothing more than outlaws and troublemakers, Bryan was not so quick to dismiss them. He asked Sullivan to confer with Arias, to find out his grievances, and then to emphasize to him that the days of revolution were over.[35]

A meeting was held at Puerto Plata, in March 1914 between the Bordas government and Arias. Here, a tentative agreement was reached in which Bordas would remain in power until June 1914, when the new president would assume office. However, there was still no decision on the exact date of the presidential elections or who would be the candidates.[36] The elections had been set for some time in April, but Bordas began another crisis by calling for elections for April 1, giving Arias and his followers little time to organize.[37] Bordas furthered irritated Arias by removing the governors of Monte Cristi, Puerto Plata, Santiago, and Seibo provinces, all of whom were Arias's supporters.[38] Due to the rash actions by Bordas, Arias continued the revolution, but this time, Bryan did not hesitate in denouncing Arias and his followers, calling them smugglers and outlaws who had to be stopped at all costs.[39]

There was no question that Bryan was influenced by Sullivan in condemning Arias's actions. The tragedy here, as we shall see later in greater detail, was that Sullivan was a New York lawyer, who knew nothing about Caribbean politics, and his major concern was keeping Bordas in power, so as to make sure that the financial plan would be implemented by the Dominican government.[40]

While the fighting in the Dominican Republic continued, Bryan was busily engaged in finding a suitable person to handle the finances of the Dominican government. On April 11, 1914, he wrote Wilson that he had finally found the man who met all his qualifications. Bryan had chosen Charles Johnston, who had sufficient business ability to supervise expenditures; he could speak and write Spanish; and most important, he was in sympathy with the aims of the Democratic administration in the Dominican Republic. Wilson wrote his secretary of state, commending him on his choice of Johnston; unfortunately, the new financial adviser was unable to assume his new responsibilities in June 1914.[41]

The negotiations between the Bordas government and Bryan over the appointment of an American financial adviser were difficult and time consuming. Bordas naturally wanted to yield as little control as possible and not appear as a lackey of the United States. However, he desperately needed the assistance of the State Department in obtaining the funding from the banks and commercial houses in order for his government to continue to operate. Therefore, he had no choice but to accept almost all the demands imposed upon him by the State Department.[42]

In the meantime, the revolution was growing worse, and Sullivan was clamoring for American military intervention to put down the revolt. Bordas's troops were already marching on Puerto Plata, and Sullivan blamed Arias for the continued fighting, as he was trying to prevent the presidential elections from taking place, which he could no longer win.[43] One week later, the American consulate in Puerto Plata also wrote Bryan about the critical situation. He told Bryan that Bordas's troops had blockaded Puerto Plata and had threatened to bombard the town. If the Dominican president were allowed to carry out his plans, he would endanger the lives of Americans and foreign nationals, as well as interfere with the collection of the customs.[44] Bryan was quick to respond, sending the gunboat *Petrel* to reopen the customs houses in Puerto Plata and also to protect both American and foreign interests.[45] But Bryan at this point would go no further—he was unwilling to interfere actively in the fighting. Only in June 1914, when the situation worsened and Bordas began firing on Puerto Plata, did Bryan order the gunboat *Machias* to enter the inner harbor of that port and fire upon the batteries of Bordas. It was done only because American lives and property were endangered and not because the United States had decided to take sides in the revolution.[46]

Bryan next tried to bring the rival leaders to declare an armistice and to find an honest person, not connected to either side, to run the country. A series of meetings between Bordas and his enemies were held aboard the American warships *Washington* and *South Carolina* in the harbor of Puerto Plata, but the mediation failed because Bordas refused to agree to resign from office.[47] In fact, in the middle of June, Bordas held private elections in eight of the twelve Dominican provinces, and since he ran unopposed, he won election unanimously, declaring himself the lawfully elected president of the Dominican Republic.[48]

In the meantime, Arias told the American consul at Puerto Plata that he could gain control of the country, protect American lives and property, and save the United States the trouble and expense of intervention if the State Department would support his movement. Sullivan, however, continued to warn Bryan against dealing with Arias, even as the Bordas government became more overtly corrupt.[49]

By the middle of July, the revolution had spread to the south and was threatening the capital. Foreigners and Americans were leaving the Dominican Republic in great numbers. At this point, Sullivan traveled to Washington to confer with Bryan and Wilson. The American minister had no qualms about using military force and told Bryan that it was the only way to alleviate the worsening conditions. Sullivan asked Bryan to send the 300 marines that were already stationed at Veracruz to the Dominican Republic, but both Bryan and Wilson were still reluctant to use force except to protect American lives and property.[50]

As intervention was put on hold, something had to be done to end the crisis in the Dominican Republic, and Bryan called upon his staff in the State Department to find a solution. Working from a memorandum created by members of the Latin American Affairs division, the president, by August 1914, prepared a plan that became known as the Wilson Plan. This plan would be the last peaceful attempt to restore order in the Dominican Republic without having to resort to military intervention.[51] The plan contained the following elements: (1) It called upon the Dominican leaders of both the government and the opposition to decide upon a provisional president. Bordas, who could not run for office, would then relinquish his authority, and the United States would recognize the provis- ional president. (2) If no agreement was reached between the two sides, the United States would appoint the provisional president. (3) Free elections were to be held at the earliest date under the authority of the provisional president; the United States would send observers to ensure that the elections went smoothly. (4) If the United States was satisfied with the outcome of the elections, it would recognize the new president, but if fraud prevailed, new elections would be held. The plan was entrusted to ex-Governor James F. Fort of New Jersey and Charles Cogswell Smith, who accompanied Sullivan on his return to the Dominican Republic.[52]

On August 6, 1914, about nine days prior to the arrival of the Fort mission, a general armistice was signed between the Bordas government and Arias.[53] On August 15, the Fort mission arrived at Puerta Plata and presented the Wilson Plan to all the Dominican factions, and then proceeded to Santo Domingo for the final conference, where all the leaders were to meet and choose a provisional president. However, on the agreed-upon meeting day, Bordas was conspicuously absent. He sent a message through his envoys that since he was the *de jure* president, he would not resign.[54] The Fort commission sent word to Bordas that he should immediately resign or American troops would land to support a new provisional president. Both Bryan and Wilson, on hearing of Bordas opposition to their plan, told the Fort commission to (1) "Yield nothing; insist upon full and literal compliance with plan. (2) Time limit left to judgment of the commission, but should be short. (3) Bordas should be given distinctly to understand that the U.S. means business. This government will not brook refusal, changes of purpose, or unreasonable delay."[55] On August 25, Bordas, having no choice, finally resigned from the presidency, and after some debate, the Dominican leaders chose, on August 27, Doctor Ramón Báez as the new provisional president of the Dominican Republic. Báez agreed to abide by the provisions of the Wilson Plan, and he was immediately recognized by the United States.[56]

The presidential election that was originally set for April 1914, then changed to June 1914, but then again postponed because of the revolution, was now moved to October 1914. The two principal candidates were Juan Isidro Jiménez and Horacio Vásquez, the nominal leaders of their parties.[57] The election began on October 25 and lasted about three days, with two American observers at each polling place. When the balloting ended, Jiménez was the winner with a total of 40,076 votes to Vásquez's 39,632 votes. Jiménez won seven of the twelve provinces.[58] When Bryan heard that the election had been conducted fairly, he was overjoyed; he saw no reason why the Dominican Congress would not approve it.[59] Both Fort and Smith were optimistic about the new Jiménez government, with Fort declaring that "Jiménez's election seemed to give general satisfaction, and there was nothing to indicate that the defeated factions would resort to arms."[60] On December 5, Jiménez was officially declared president of the Dominican Republic by the National Congress, and on the following day, he took the oath of office.[61]

Though the president had been elected, and optimistic forecasts came from Sullivan and commissioners Fort and Smith concerning the political situation, the problems confronting the new Dominican government were just beginning. The blame for these ongoing problems can be placed squarely on the U.S. government and specifically on Secretary of State Bryan; it was he who attempted to continue the past policies of interference in the Dominican government.[62]

Bryan, only one week after the new Jiménez government took office, warned that the new government would have to honor the financial agreement made with the previous Bordas government. It must recognize Charles Johnston as the official financial adviser, with the title of Comptroller of Finances of the Dominican Republic, whose duties were to prepare the Dominican budget and to approve and countersign any payments made by the new government. The secretary of state also wanted to replace the regular Dominican army with an American trained constabulary.[63] Jiménez reluctantly agreed to these arrangements; he realized that he would lose support at home by yielding to these American demands, which he believed were unnecessary interference in his government. However, he really did not have much choice, since he needed American support to remain in power in a still unstable environment.[64]

Though Jiménez ingratiated himself to the United States by accepting the financial plan, the Dominican Congress, the majority of which was composed of *horacistas* and loyal supporters of Arias, who was now minister of war, rejected it outright. The new minister of war had always been very critical of the United States financial plan. He first opposed it in January 1914, when it was first proposed and accepted by his rival Bordas. To Arias, American influence was already too prevalent in the affairs of the Dominican Republic.[65]

From January to June 1915, Jiménez found himself threatened by a hostile congress opposed to the appointment of Charles Johnston and the United States government, which insisted that Johnston had to remain (Johnston had been appointed on June 1, 1914). The Dominican president decided to retain Johnston, and it was issue that brought about continuing political chaos and more United States interference.

It was Sullivan, an ardent supporter of Jiménez, who warned Bryan, as early as January 1915, that Arias was threatening to rebel again. The secretary of state lost no time in replying that the State Department was firmly behind the Jiménez government and that no revolts would be tolerated.[66]

Bryan really did not want Arias in Jiménez's cabinet. Unfortunately, the secretary of state did not understand the importance of having different political parties represented in the cabinet, so that their political views could be heard, rather than having them fight it out on the battlefield. Bryan listened too much to Sullivan when it came to dealing with Arias. Sullivan had always despised Arias and depicted him as a troublemaker, and this was what Bryan had come to believe. He especially worried that Arias would use his position as minister of war to incite the soldiers to revolt, and he told Jiménez that he should expel Arias from the cabinet and banish him from the country. The secretary of state was not interested in dissent when it was directed toward what he thought was in the best interests of the Dominican government, which in this case was the imposition of the financial plan and loyalty to Jiménez who supported that plan. Bryan told

Jiménez that he should not be concerned about revolution if he fired Arias. He declared that the United States "would use whatever means necessary to maintain order."[67]

In April 1915, Bryan, once again, meddled in the internal affairs of the Dominican government. The Dominican Congress, angry over the close relationship of Jiménez to the U.S. government, was threatening to impeach him. Bryan immediately came to Jiménez's support by refusing to recognize the right of that Congress to impeach. He sent the following message to Sullivan: "You may say to President Jiménez and those connected with the plot that this Government will not permit any attack to be made upon President Jiménez for acting in good faith toward the United States."[68] Bryan went further than he had ever gone before in supporting Jiménez by declaring that he would compel, though he did not make known the means, the plotters to respect the new government.[69]

Bryan was treating Jiménez's opponents like children who did not know what was good for them. He was causing more problems for the Dominican president than he realized when he continued to insist that they accept the financial plan as constituted. However, Arias had enough of Bryan's preaching and threats, and in April, he challenged both the United States and Jiménez by beginning another revolution. Most of the country seemed sympathetic toward Arias, and a worried Jiménez realizing this, attempted to compromise with Bryan on the status of Charles Johnston. An agreement was worked out in late May, where Johnston would not have a separate office or title; instead, the receivership's functions would be enlarged, and he would be assigned to that body as a special adviser.[70] Several weeks after this compromise, Bryan resigned from office with Arias and his followers still dissatisfied.

THE CORRUPTION OF JAMES M. SULLIVAN

In viewing Bryan's policy toward the Dominican Republic, one cannot overlook his ministerial choice, James M. Sullivan. Sullivan and Bryan consulted frequently, with the former playing an important role in U.S.-Dominican policy. However, as it turned out, the Sullivan appointment caused much embarrassment to Bryan after a Senate investigating committee uncovered corruption and scandal committed during the American minister's appointment.

James M. Sullivan fitted perfectly the phrase "deserving Democrat," the words used by Bryan to describe his diplomatic appointments. Sullivan, previous to his appointment, was a fight promoter, a New York lawyer with offices in Park Row, and extremely prominent in Irish-Democratic politics. In the presidential campaign of 1912, he played an important role as a Democratic club organizer.[71] He was not well known to Bryan in 1913, and though Bryan approved of Sullivan's appointment and defended his minister amid much criticism, he was not the driving force behind his appointment. The Sullivan choice was engineered by financial interests in the Dominican Republic and supported by prominent

American politicians. William C. Beer, a friend of Samuel Jarvis, who was the organizer of Banco Nacional in the Dominican Republic, was said to have influenced the appointment of Sullivan.[72] The Banco Nacional and the National City Bank, both American controlled, were competitors for Dominican government loans and contracts. In January 1913, the National City Bank secured a loan for the Dominican government, and Banco Nacional argued that Minister William W. Russell, the presiding American minister at the time, favored the National City Bank, and he had persuaded the Dominican government to do business with that bank.[73] Beer and Jarvis hoped that Sullivan would work on behalf of Banco Nacional.[74]

Though Beer had recommended Sullivan, his appointment was ardently supported by Senator James A. O'Gorman of New York and Joseph Tumulty, private secretary to President Wilson. These men believed that Sullivan had earned a diplomatic post for his loyalty to the Democratic party; Sullivan himself contended that he needed the position for the money, in order to pay off his debts.[75] Bryan was influenced by O'Gorman who convinced him that Sullivan would be the perfect individual for the post.[76] The secretary of state, at the time, was well aware of the competition between the two banking groups and made it clear to both Wilson and O'Gorman that he was looking for an impartial minister; he had condemned Russell for favoring the National City Bank.[77] As early as June 1913, he had supported Sullivan, believing that he was the best person for the ministerial appointment. Approximately a month later, Sullivan's nomination was officially announced and was finally confirmed by the Senate on August 12, 1913.[78]

Sullivan arrived in the Dominican Republic in September 1913, and it took only three months before Bryan had to come to his aid. A story came out in December 1913, that Sullivan had secured a position for his cousin, Timothy Sullivan, a building contractor, in the Dominican government. When a bridge was blown up between Puerto Plata and Santiago, Timothy Sullivan was given the contract by the Bordas government to rebuild it.[79] Bryan denied that any favoritism had been shown to Sullivan's cousin; he declared that since there was no engineer available, Sullivan was asked to work as a favor to the Dominican government without payment. As far as Bryan was concerned, Sullivan's cousin was not officially connected in any way with the Dominican government.[80]

Sullivan's chief enemy in the Dominican Republic was Walker W. Vick, general-receiver of the customs. Vick was critical of Sullivan for his favoritism toward certain financial interests and his ardent support for the provisional government. Vick believed that Sullivan should have taken a neutral position as a representative of the United States and was not shy about telling him so.[81] In April 1914, Vick, at the request of his superior, the secretary of war, informed Bryan of the complaints against the American minister. He criticized Sullivan for his close relations with the Banco Nacional and for his association with Frank J. R. Mitchell, its president. Vick also told Bryan that Sullivan publicly declared that he was the "second choice" of the late Samuel M. Jarvis, former head of the Banco Nacional, for his post, and he complained, to the secretary of state, that

Timothy Sullivan had received a special loan of $1,000 from the Banco Nacional, which was endorsed by the American minister.[82]

As soon as Bryan read the report, he immediately informed his minister about Vick's accusations. Within ten days an indignant Sullivan demanded a full investigation of Vicks's charges. The American minister professed his innocence of any collusion with the Banco Nacional and declared that a thorough investigation would not only clear him, but mute any criticism aimed at the Wilson administration regarding his appointment.[83] Sullivan also believed that an inquiry would provide a standard, comparing the performances of the Wilson administration with its predecessors not only in the Dominican Republic, but throughout Latin America. He was certain that if corruption existed, it was due to the practices of past administrations and not the responsibility of the current government.[84]

Bryan, pleased with Sullivan's desire for vindication, asked Fort, who had gone to the Dominican Republic in August 1914 to deliver the Wilson Plan, to begin an investigation into the charges made by Vick. During his short stay, Fort found nothing to suggest that Sullivan was directly implicated in any collusion or corruption, and Bryan, as a result of this cursory inquiry, completely exonerated Sullivan from any wrongdoing in October 1914.[85]

In December 1914, the editor of the *New York World*, after a lengthy investigation of the Sullivan affair, repudiated the brief Fort inquiry, criticized Bryan for his unqualified support of his minister, and published a series of articles linking Sullivan to special financial interests, including the Banco Nacional.[86] Two days after the *New York World*'s revelation, Wilson ordered an official investigation into the Sullivan affair; he appointed Senator James D. Phelan of California, to head a special investigating committee.[87] The hearings began on January 12, 1915, at the Waldorf Astoria in New York with Vick, who had resigned his post in July 1914, as the first witness to testify. Vick told the committee that Bryan had superficially investigated his charges of Sullivan's close connections to the Banco Nacional. He also declared that Sullivan had favored the Banco Nacional by moving the receiver's funds into its vaults. Vick told the committee that William Beer was the driving force behind Sullivan's appointment and that he was good friends with the late Jarvis, the former president of the Banco Nacional.[88]

Sullivan, who was in the Dominican Republic when the Phelan investigation began, cabled Bryan claiming that he was innocent of these charges. He denied that he favored the Banco Nacional and that Beer had influenced his appointment. He had also denounced other charges that he had obtained contracts, from the Dominican government, for both his cousin Timothy and James K McGuire, an intimate friend.[89]

As the investigation probed deeper, Bryan also became a target of criticism. W. E. Pulliam, former general-receiver under the Roosevelt and Taft administrations, claimed that Bryan might have been responsible for the favoritism shown the Banco Nacional. Pulliam declared that Bryan disliked Banco Nacional's rival,

National City Bank, because he believed that it represented a powerful trust that he wanted to destroy. Pulliam's accusation could not be proven, since the former general-receiver was an ardent supporter of the National City Bank.[90]

The turning point of the investigation for Bryan came on January 22. Until this time, he had supported Sullivan against all charges. However, on that day, John G. Gray, Bryan's close friend and one of the people who had recommended Sullivan, testified before the Phelan commission. He had submitted a letter written to him by Sullivan in January 1914, which proved embarrassing to the Wilson administration and forced Bryan to ask for Sullivan's resignation.[91] This letter presented Sullivan's explanation for the instability in the Dominican Republic. He denounced the Dominican people as immoral and incapable of self-government, while praising the Catholic Church as the great moral force in the land. However, according to Sullivan, the church was powerless to change the deteriorated situation, since it was stripped of all political power and was constantly on the defensive. In this letter, he proposed that the United States intervene on behalf of the church to strengthen it by ending the discrimination against it and to ensure that it would receive proper funding.[92] This letter was published in the Dominican press, causing much furor, and by April, 1915, Wilson firmly believed that Sullivan could no longer be retained. Bryan concurred, issuing the following statement: "I feel that this is the only conclusion that can be reached unless we intend to discard the rules that govern diplomatic relations."[93] However, Wilson decided to leave Sullivan in place until after the Phelan commission had completed its investigation.[94]

In the meantime, the Phelan committee, after adjourning in New York on January 28, 1915, met in early February in Washington. It was decided there to withhold a final report until Senator Phelan could personally obtain information in the Dominican Republic.[95]

Although the Phelan report was made public on July 27, 1915, Sullivan had already been recalled in late June. On July 6, his resignation was officially requested by the State Department; he formally resigned on July 24, three days before the Phelan findings were published.[96]

The Phelan report upheld many of the charges against Sullivan. It claimed that his appointment was influenced by Beer and the Banco Nacional and that the Banco Nacional was interested in obtaining the customs receipts. It showed that Sullivan had known Beer as early as 1904 and had accepted business from him. Though the report exonerated Sullivan from taking graft from James K. McGuire, a building contractor, it pointed out that McGuire had been very active in obtaining Sullivan's appointment. McGuire had been a former mayor of Syracuse who was influential in New York politics. The report exonerated Bryan from having any favoritism toward the Banco Nacional—he did not know of Beer's close relationship with Jarvis when Beer talked with him in favor of Sullivan. Finally, the report criticized Sullivan for his letter to Gray degrading the Dominican people—it emphasized that this letter impaired Sullivan's usefulness, a point on which Bryan and Wilson both concurred the previous April, and made it impossible for him to retain his ministerial position.[97]

To conclude, Bryan, in the Dominican Republic, had refused to accept the validity of revolution and attempted to increase American control over Dominican finances. In September 1913, he supported the Bordas government against the revolution initiated by Céspedes. He urged free elections to the Dominican Constitutional Conventional in December 1913, sending a special commission to supervise the elections. In January 1914, he attempted to appoint a financial adviser to the Dominican government with veto power over Dominican spending. Opposition to President Bordas's acceptance of this plan and fear that the president wanted to remain in power paved the way for a new revolution led by Arias and his followers in March 1914. The fighting ended in August 1914, with the implementation of the Wilson Plan, which promised free elections, among other things. Jiménez was elected in October 1914 but the situation had not improved because Bryan continued his insistence on a financial adviser, while supporting Jiménez, who accepted the financial plan against all opposition.

James M. Sullivan, American minister to the Dominican Republic, influenced Bryan's Dominican policy. Sullivan clamored for supervised elections, insisted upon stability, and gave unqualified support to the Bordas and Jiménez governments. It was Sullivan who had caused Bryan considerable embarrassment when an investigation, begun in April and terminated in July 1915, proved Sullivan an incompetent choice.

NOTES

1. John Edwin Fagg, *Latin America: A General History* (New York: Macmillan, 1977), pp. 414-415.

2. Ibid., pp. 590-591.

3. Samuel Flagg Bemis, *The Latin American Policy of the United States* (New York: Harcourt, Brace and Company, 1943), p. 154.

4. Ibid., p. 156.

5. Arthur S. Link, *Wilson: The Struggle for Neutrality, 1914-1915* (Princeton, N.J.: Princeton University Press, 1960), p. 496.

6. Bemis, *The Latin American Policy of the United States*, p. 157.

7. Ray Stannard Baker, *Woodrow Wilson: Life and Letters*, vol. 4 (Garden City, N.Y.: Doubleday, Page and Company, 1927), p. 441; Bemis, *The Latin American Policy of the United States*, p. 154.

8. Link, *Wilson: The Struggle for Neutrality*, p. 496.

9. Curtis to the Secretary of State, April 14, 1913, *Papers Relating to the Foreign Relations of the United States, 1913* (Washington, D.C.: U.S. Government Printing Office,1920), p. 423.

10. Dana G. Munro, *Intervention and Dollar Diplomacy in the Caribbean, 1900-1921* (Princeton, N.J.: Princeton University Press, 1964), p. 277.

11. Link, *Wilson: The Struggle for Neutrality*, pp. 497-498.

12. Munro, *Intervention and Dollar Diplomacy in the Caribbean*, p. 277; Bemis, *The Latin American Policy of the United States*, pp. 190-191.

13. Bryan to Curtis, September 4, 1913, *Foreign Relations, 1913*, p. 425; *New York Times*, September 13, 1913.

14. Link, *Wilson: The Struggle for Neutrality*, p. 497.

15. Secretary of State to the American Minister, September 9, 1913, *Foreign Relations, 1913*, pp. 425-426.

16. Secretary of State to the American Consul at Santiago de Cuba, September 12, 1913, *Foreign Relations, 1913*, p. 427.

17. American Minister to the Secretary of State, September 19, 1913, *Foreign Relations, 1913*, p. 428.

18. *New York Times*, October 9, 1913; Munro, *Intervention and Dollar Diplomacy in the Caribbean*, p. 279.

19. The Secretary of State to the American Minister, November 21, 1913, *Foreign Relations, 1913*, p. 435; American Minister to the Secretary of State, November 22, 1913, *Foreign Relations, 1913*, pp. 435-436.

20. Bryan to Wilson, December 1, 1913, Bryan Papers, Library of Congress; Secretary of State to the American Minister, November 24, 1913, *Foreign Relations, 1913*, p. 436.

21. Long to Bryan, December 4, 1913, State Department Papers, National Archives.

22. American Minister to the Secretary of State, December 5, 1913, *Foreign Relations, 1913*, pp. 440-441.

23. Secretary of State to the American Minister, December 10, 1913, *Foreign Relations, 1913*, p. 446; *New York Times*, December 9, 1913.

24. The American Minister to the Secretary of State, December 17, 1913, *Foreign Relations, 1913*, p. 447; Secretary of State to the American Minister, December 18, 1913, *Foreign Relations, 1913*, p. 448.

25. American Minister to the Secretary of State, December 23, 1913, *Foreign Relations, 1913*, pp. 453-454; *New York Times*, January 2, 1914.

26. Secretary of State to the American Minister, January 18, 1914, *Papers Relating to the Foreign Relations of the United States, 1914* (Washington, D.C.: U.S. Government Printing Office, 1922), p. 198.

27. Link, *Wilson: The Struggle for Neutrality*, p. 497.

28. Secretary of State to the American Minister, January 12, 1914, *Foreign Relations, 1914*, pp. 197-198.

29. Acting Secretary of State to the American Minister, January 26, 1914, *Foreign Relations, 1914*, p. 199-200.

30. Bryan to Wilson, January 27, 1914, Bryan Papers, Library of Congress.

31. Bryan to Wilson, February 5, 1914, Bryan-Wilson Correspondence, National Archives.

32. Link, *Wilson: The Struggle for Neutrality*, p. 500.

33. American Minister to the Secretary of State, February 12, 1914, *Foreign Relations, 1914*, pp. 206-207; Munro, *Intervention and Dollar Diplomacy in the Caribbean*, p. 285.

34. American Minister to the Secretary of State, February 12, 1914, *Foreign Relations, 1914*, pp. 206-207.

35. Bryan to Wilson, February 26, 1914, Bryan Papers, Library of Congress.

36. Munro, *Intervention and Dollar Diplomacy in the Caribbean*, pp. 287-288.

37. American Minister to the Secretary of State, March 15, 1914, *Foreign Relations, 1914*, p. 217; Munro, *Intervention and Dollar Diplomacy in the Caribbean*, pp. 287-288.

38. Munro, *Intervention and Dollar Diplomacy in the Caribbean*, p. 288.

39. Secretary of State to the American Minister, April 4, 1914, *Foreign Relations, 1914*, pp. 223-224.

40. Munro, *Intervention and Dollar Diplomacy in the Caribbean*, p. 288.

41. Bryan to Wilson, April 11, 1914, Bryan Papers, Library of Congress; Secretary of State to the Chargé d'Affaires, June 1, 1914, *Foreign Relations, 1914*, pp. 235-236.

42. For negotiations on this point, see Minister Sullivan to the Secretary of State, January 12, 1914, *Foreign Relations, 1914*, p. 197.

43. American Minister to the Secretary of State, April 21, 1914, *Foreign Relations, 1914*, p. 228.

44. American Consulate to the Secretary of State, April 29, 1914, *Foreign Relations, 1914*, p. 229; American Minister to the Secretary of State, April 30, 1914, *Foreign Relations, 1914*, p. 229.

45. Secretary of State to the American Minister, May 5, 1914, *Foreign Relations, 1914*, pp. 229-230.

46. *New York Times*, June 29, 1914.

47. Link, *Wilson: The Struggle for Neutrality*, pp. 510-511.

48. Ibid., p. 511.

49. Ibid., p. 507.

50. *New York Times*, July 19, 1914.

51. Plan of President Wilson, August 1, 1914, *Foreign Relations, 1914*, pp. 247-248.

52. Ibid.; Munro, *Intervention and Dollar Diplomacy in the Caribbean*, p. 292.

53. Munro, *Intervention and Dollar Diplomacy in the Caribbean*, p. 292.

54. Link, *Wilson: The Struggle for Neutrality*, p. 515.

55. Ibid.

56. Fort to the Secretary of State, August 25, 1914, *Foreign Relations, 1914*, p. 249; Chargé d'Affaires to the Secretary of State, August 28, 1914, *Foreign Relations, 1914*, p. 249.

57. Munro, *Intervention and Dollar Diplomacy in the Caribbean*, pp. 293-294.

58. Ibid.; Chargé d'Affaires to the Secretary of State, November 18, 1914, *Foreign Relations, 1914*, p. 256.

59. Secretary of State to the Chargé d'Affaires, November 25, 1914, *Foreign Relations, 1914*, p. 257.

60. *New York Times*, November 25, 1914.

61. Ibid., December 6, 1914; American Minister to the Secretary of State, December 5, 1914, *Foreign Relations, 1914*, p. 258.

62. Sumner Welles, *Naboth's Vineyard: The Dominican Republic, 1844-1924*, vol. 2 (New York: P. P. Appel, 1966), p. 748.

63. Secretary of State to the American Minister, December 14, 1914, *Foreign Relations, 1914*, pp. 260-261.

64. Welles, *Naboth's Vineyard*, p. 748.

65. Ibid., p. 749.

66. American Minister to the Secretary of State, January 9, 1915, *Papers Relating to the Foreign Relations of the United States, 1915* (Washington, D.C.: U.S. Government Printing Office, 1924), p. 279; Secretary of State to the American Minister, January 12, 1915, *Foreign Relations, 1915*, pp. 279-280.

67. Bryan to Wilson, January 15, 1915, Bryan-Wilson Correspondence, National Archives.

68. Welles, *Naboth's Vineyard*, p. 752; Secretary of State to the American Minister, April 9, 1915, *Foreign Relations, 1915*, pp. 283-284.

69. Ibid.

70. Department of State to the Dominican legation, June 8, 1915, *Foreign Relations, 1915*, pp. 311-313; Selig Adler, "Bryan and Wilsonian Caribbean Penetration," *Hispanic American Historical Review* 20 (May 1940): 220.

71. Arthur S. Link, *Wilson: The New Freedom* (Princeton, N.J.: Princeton University Press, 1956), p. 107; *New York Times*, July 23, 1913.

72. *New York World*, December 7, 1914.

73. Munro, *Intervention and Dollar Diplomacy in the Caribbean*, pp. 266-267.

74. *New York World*, December 7, 1914.

75. Ibid; Munro, *Intervention and Dollar Diplomacy in the Caribbean*, p. 275.

76. Bryan to Wilson, June 9, 1913, Bryan-Wilson Correspondence, National Archives.

77. Ibid.

78. Ibid; *New York World*, December 7, 1914.

79. *New York Times*, December 12, 1913.

80. Ibid.

81. Walker W. Vick to Bryan, April 14, 1914, Bryan-Wilson Correspondence, National Archives.

82. Ibid.

83. Sullivan to Bryan, April 25, 1914, Bryan Papers, Library of Congress.

84. Ibid.

85. *New York Times*, October 1, 1914.

86. *New York World*, December 7, 1914.

87. *New York Times*, December 9, 1914; December 27, 1914.

88. Ibid., January 13, 1915.

89. *New York World*, January 13, 1915.

90. *New York Times*, January 15, 1915.

91. Ibid., January 23, 1915.

92. James M. Sullivan to John G. Gray, January 31, 1914, Bryan-Wilson Correspondence, National Archives.

93. Bryan to Wilson, April 2, 1915, Bryan-Wilson Correspondence, National Archives.

94. Wilson to Bryan, April 3, 1915, Bryan-Wilson Correspondence, National Archives.

95. *New York Times*, January 29, 1915; February 17, 1915.

96. Ibid., June 22, 1915; July 24, 1915.

97. Ibid., July 28, 1915.

7

Mexico

Mexico is the largest Spanish-speaking country and the second-largest Roman Catholic nation in the world. It covers an area from the 14th to the 32nd parallel north of the equator in southern North American. The only Latin American countries larger in area are Brazil and Argentina. The United States borders Mexico to the north, with Guatemala and Belize to the southeast, the Gulf of Mexico and the Caribbean Sea to the east and the Pacific Ocean to the west and south.

MEXICO FROM HERNÁN CORTÉS TO PORFIRIO DÍAZ

Hernán Cortés officially conquered New Spain, as it was called then, when he subdued the Aztec nation in the year 1521. Spain ruled Mexico for 300 years until it became independent in 1821. From 1823 to 1855, Mexico, for the most part, was ruled by General Antonio Lopez de Santa Anna, and its relationship with the United States was hostile. Texas, a part of Mexico and settled by U.S. citizens, declared its independence from Mexico in March 1836. By 1845, Texas became part of the United States, and a year later Mexico and the United States went to war. The disunited Mexicans were routed, and in the peace treaty of Guadalupe Hidalgo, Mexico lost more than half of its territory, including the area of the present U.S. states of California, New Mexico, and southern Arizona. After Santa Anna, Mexican liberals and conservatives fought for control of the Mexican government. The liberals, under the leadership of Benito Juarez seized power in 1857. However, by 1862, the conservatives, with the aid of Napoleon III of France, made the Austrian prince Maximilian emperor of Mexico. The United States, involved in the Civil War, was too busy to do much about what was going on in Mexico. However, when the Civil War ended, the American government made it clear to Napoleon III that his troops were not welcomed there. By 1867, the French withdrew their troops, Maximilian was captured and shot, and Juarez led Mexico until his death in 1872.[1]

THE ERA OF PORFIRIO DÍAZ

Juarez's liberal successors faltered, and in 1876, General Porfirio Díaz seized power. Díaz governed Mexico until its revolution in 1911, serving as president from 1877 to 1880 and 1884 to 1911. During this period, a new Mexico emerged. Díaz established order and a workable government. There were no more civil wars, and banditry disappeared from the countryside.[2] The new president created a political apparatus that remained completely loyal to him. Each state of the Mexican republic contained a machine of the Liberal party that directly reported to the president. The legislatures were filled with obedient politicians who depended upon Díaz not only for their positions, but also for their economic life and freedom. The judiciary, which was also expected to be independent of the president, was filled with obedient judges who did his bidding. Provisional governors obeyed the law emanating from Mexico City, and the army, ardent supporters of the president, became professionalized. The *rurales*, a militarized police force of several thousand, ensured order throughout the country. During Díaz's long reign, the Mexican government welcomed foreign investment from all over the world, especially from Great Britain and the United States. All obstacles to commerce such as state tariff barriers and taxes on production were either modified or abolished in order to encourage foreign investment.[3] Exports and national income increased; new highways, railroads, and telegraph lines crossed Mexico and new industries spread throughout the countryside. Foreign investment and technology had revived the mining industry and created major oil fields in and around Veracruz.

Díaz's Mexico, however, contained the roots of its own destruction. The urban and rural masses remained impoverished, and Mexicans of all classes despised the increasing foreign and economic dominance. The direct cause of the revolt was Díaz's monopoly of political power. In 1908, in order to refute charges about the autocratic nature of his rule, he held an interview with American journalist James Creelman. The president declared that Mexico would be ready for free elections in 1910 and that he would not be a candidate.[4] After the publication of the interview, discontented politicians began to organize around an eccentric northern landowner, Francisco Madero, who had the resources, contacts, and time to organize an effective political movement. However, Díaz had no intention of stepping down, even as he approached his eightieth birthday. At first, the president tried to reason with Madero but found him to be a lunatic who insisted upon staying in the race. Madero's campaign slogan stated "effective suffrage and no re-election." As the election neared, Díaz had enough of Madero and had him jailed in San Luis Potosí. Nonetheless, the rigged election went on as scheduled, and Díaz won by a landslide. After Madero was released from prison, he fled to the United States and called upon the Mexican people to rise up against Díaz.[5]

THE BEGINNING OF THE MEXICAN REVOLUTION

The Mexican Revolution, beginning in 1911, was one of the great social upheavals of the twentieth century. Though it began about two years before the Wilson administration took office, U.S. involvement in the revolution really started with the inauguration of Woodrow Wilson in March 1913. It was his administration that formulated U.S. policy toward Mexico from 1913 to 1920, and it was primarily the president who played the leading role. Bryan, as Wilson's secretary of state, did not assume the dominant role he had played in Nicaragua, Haiti, and the Dominican Republic, but nevertheless aided Wilson during the Mexican crisis until he retired in June 1915. Bryan contributed to, and differed with, the president on many of the important issues.

Bryan had been an ardent supporter of Díaz as early as 1901. At first, it might seem strange that Bryan, an ardent supporter of democracy and free elections could speak favorably of the dictator Díaz. However, in March 1901, he remarked on the magnificent economic progress Mexico was making under the Díaz government. He wrote that Americans and foreigners residing in Mexico were being treated fairly. They owned large tracts of land as well as most of the oil business. According to Bryan, this investment by foreign and American capitalists was making Mexico one of the richest countries in Latin America.[6] Bryan hoped that Díaz would continue in power and if he should die (he was in his seventies in 1900), he was certain that a successor would be chosen without violence.[7] He believed that Mexico's proximity made it impossible for the United States not to take an active interest in its affairs. In 1901, Bryan declared that "the Republic of Mexico is closely bound to us by political interests as well as by location, and her welfare must always be a matter of deep concern to our people."[8]

Events in Mexico occurred rapidly after Díaz was overthrown in 1911. Francisco Madero, a mystic and a dreamer, was the leading contender for the presidency. As Madero made his way to the capital by slow train, numerous people greeted him on the way as a messiah. When Díaz, first met Madero, he really thought he was quite mad. Madero was an educated aristocrat who truly believed that he received guidance from the spirits of the dead. He had little experience in world affairs and absolutely no knowledge of how government should function. In October 1911 the caretaker government that followed Díaz held the most honest elections ever in Mexican history. Madero was officially elected president, and his followers held most of the positions in the national congress and state governments.[9]

Madero's presidency, however, was short-lived. He attempted to reconstruct democracy in Mexico and this provoked the counterrevolutions that would eventually cause a weakening of his power. He talked about land reform that was sought by Mexican nationalists like Emiliano Zapata, who supported Madero's revolution in 1911. Zapata wanted to break up the large haciendas and distribute its lands among the peasants. It soon appeared to the *Zapatistas*, the followers of Zapata, that Madero was all talk and no action, and that they would have to take matters into their own hands.[10] To the international community, the new Mexican president was too much of a dreamer and an idealist to bring democracy to his country. Even the liberal politicians and professional classes, who were his most ardent supporters, behaved with an unseemly lack of restraint. They began to criticize Madero for not solving all of the problems immediately. He attracted some of the best men into his government, but he tolerated too many supporters of Díaz, and too many of his closest advisers were his relatives.[11] Before Madero could even begin to make any changes, a new revolution began in February 1913 led by Felix Díaz, a nephew of Porfirio Díaz. The revolt failed, and Díaz and many of his supporters took refuge in the military prison. In his haste to suppress the revolt, the new president entrusted the leadership of the armed forces to General Victoriano Huerta. However, Huerta, instead of attacking the rebels, made a secret agreement with them, had Madero arrested, and made himself provisional president.[12]

President Taft followed these events in Mexico closely. His ambassador, Henry Lane Wilson, urged immediate recognition of Huerta, even after the general had Madero and his vice president shot on February 22, 1913. Huerta claimed that they had tried to escape while being transported to prison, but a more likely story was that they were thrown from the car and gunned down.[13] It is interesting to note that four days prior to Madero's and his vice president's murder, Huerta had sent a personal message to Taft that declared "I have the honor to inform you that I have overthrown this Government. The forces are with me, and from now on peace and prosperity will reign."[14]

Taft, on the advice of the State Department, refused to recognize the new Mexican president. The State Department hesitated not because of any revulsion toward the way Huerta had assumed power, but because it wanted to use recognition as a means to obtain prompt settlement of numerous disputes outstanding between Mexico and the United States. Until these issues were resolved, Secretary of State Knox declared that the United States would maintain only *de facto* relations with Huerta's government while withholding formal recognition.[15] However, Great Britain, France, Germany, Japan, and other governments with envoys in Mexico City very quickly recognized the Huerta government on the basis that it was the constitutional government of Mexico.[16]

Henry Lane Wilson played an important role in the events that led to Madero's downfall. It was no secret that Ambassador Wilson despised Madero and did everything he could to destroy his presidency. After Felix Díaz began his rebellion on February 9, 1913, Ambassador Wilson asked immediate protection of foreign lives and property and persuaded the British, German, and Spanish ministers to join him in demanding that Madero resign in order to prevent further bloodshed. The ambassador believed that Madero was totally incompetent and would eventually be overthrown. Wilson, a friend of American oil, was concerned that Madero was unstable enough to do something that would seriously hinder American financial interests in Mexico. According to the American ambassador, it was easier to work with a scoundrel like Huerta, who was practical enough to make deals to benefit American financial interests, than Madero, an unstable idealist, who was capable of anything.[17] When Madero had refused to resign, the American ambassador decided to ally himself with Díaz. Wilson learned of the plot that Díaz and Huerta had made to overthrow Madero and joined the conspiracy. He invited both men to the American embassy on February 18, 1913, and persuaded them to make an agreement where Huerta would be made the provisional president, with Díaz as a possible candidate in the next election. After they agreed, Wilson presented Huerta to the diplomatic corps and promised him U.S. recognition.[18] As we have seen, Wilson failed to keep his promise to General Huerta, but he continued in office for the remainder of Taft's term.

On February 21, 1913, one day prior to Madero's murder, and several weeks before taking office as Woodrow Wilson's secretary of state, Bryan discussed the Mexican crisis. He opposed American military intervention in Mexico, urging the Taft administration to mediate the dispute. He lay the foundation, however, for future intervention by stating that the United States was responsible to foreign nations for Mexico's conduct and declared that if Mexico was incapable of protecting American and foreign property, then the United States would be forced to intervene.[19]

When the Wilson administration took office in March 1913, Ambassador Wilson continued to plead for recognition of Huerta. He denied any complicity in the overthrow of Madero and insisted that he did not know of Huerta's intention to assassinate Madero.[20] The ambassador assured Bryan that Huerta's accession to the presidency was perfectly legal, explaining that Madero and Pino Suárez, the vice president, had resigned and their resignation was accepted by the Mexican Congress. The minister of foreign relations had become provisional-president, and he had appointed Huerta Secretary of Gobernación, and when the minister of foreign relations had resigned, Huerta had succeeded him.[21]

The so-called experts on Latin American affairs in the State Department supported Ambassador Wilson, arguing that Huerta's government was the only legitimate government of Mexico, and if the United States continued to withhold recognition, it would only encourage revolutionary elements and make it difficult for Huerta's government to protect American property and lives.[22] Counselor John Bassett Moore sent Bryan a note attempting to explain when diplomatic recognition was granted to a government. He stated:

The government of the United States having originally set itself up by revolution has always acted upon the *de facto* principle. We regard governments as existing or not existing. We do not require them to be chosen by popular vote. Our deprecation of the political methods which may prevail in certain countries can not relieve us of the necessity of dealing with the governments of those countries. We look simply to the fact of existence of the government and to its ability and inclination to discharge the national obligations.[23]

Henry Wilson continued to praise Huerta as "a man of iron mold, of absolute courage," who if given the chance, could bring peace and progress to Mexico.[24] The ambassador also pointed out that most of the Americans living in Mexico had feared and hated Madero and expected Huerta to restore the old order.[25]

President Wilson and Bryan refused to recognize Huerta and continued to suspect Ambassador Wilson of involvement in the *coup* of February 1913. They not only opposed the usurpation of the lawfully elected Madero government by an army general, but also abhorred the manner in which Madero was assassinated.[26] Bryan supported Wilson's non-recognition policy. Like Wilson, he was a moralist, but he was also an ardent pacifist, opposed to violence and bloodshed. He believed that "just government rests always upon the consent of the governed, and that there can be no freedom without order."[27]

While Bryan and Wilson were deciding on what to do with Huerta, a full-scale revolution was well underway. Venustiano Carranza, the governor of Coahuila, and Doroteo Arango, better known as Francisco "Pancho" Villa of Chihuahua, had gathered forces to overthrow Huerta. Emiliano Zapata, of Morelos, also took the field against Huerta. These revolutionary forces met at Guadalupe on March 26, 1913 and called themselves the Constitutionalists. They drew up a platform that demanded the restoration of constitutional government and appointed Carranza as "First Chief." Four days later, on March 30, 1913, Carranza declared himself provisional president of Mexico.[28]

In July 1913, President Wilson decided upon a plan of action. He first recalled Ambassador Wilson, who had continued to remain friendly to Huerta and insist upon his recognition. Then the president sent ex-Governor John Lind of Minnesota to Mexico as his envoy. Lind, appointed at the suggestion of Bryan, carried a plan formulated by Wilson to end the Mexican crisis. It called for the immediate cessation of all fighting, free elections, and a promise by Huerta not to be a candidate and to abide by the results.[29]

Though Bryan had supported Wilson's plan, he still believed that the best way to settle the Mexican crisis was through mediation. He wrote Wilson in August 1913, offering the president another plan, that embodied four possible courses of action: (1) recognition of Huerta; (2) support of the Constitutionalists; (3) direct intervention; (4) mediation.[30] Bryan opposed the first three as unsound. Huerta was a usurper and murderer; there was no guarantee the Constitutionalists would hold free elections if they succeeded in overthrowing Huerta; and direct intervention would unite the Mexican factions against the United States.[31] Through mediation, however, it might be possible to bring all of the warring actions together, since Huerta and the Constitutionalists would be influenced by the views of diplomats of other nations who also wanted peace in Mexico.[32]

In August 1913, Bryan became obsessed with the safety of American citizens residing in Mexico. The fighting between the Constitutionalists and Huerta's forces had escalated, and neither side would guarantee the protection of American lives and property. Bryan asked all U.S. citizens to leave Mexico, since nothing, short of military intervention, could be done to protect them in Mexico. Bryan wrote the president and asked him to provide transportation at government expense for those wishing to leave. Wilson, wanting to avoid possible international incidents that could involve the United States in the revolution, quickly agreed.[33]

In August 1913, the secretary of state asked the House of Representatives to appropriate $100,000 to pay the fare for distressed Americans wishing to leave Mexico.[34] At the same time, Bryan issued a warning to both Huerta and the Constitutionalists that the United States would hold them responsible for the safety of Americans residing there.[35] This warning was only for American public consumption and perhaps to instill some fear into the Mexican factions, but could not be enforced unless the United States was willing to intervene militarily, which he and Wilson had no intention of doing as yet. Bryan would not even consider a build-up of American forces on the border between the two countries.[36] Throughout his tenure as secretary of state, he vigorously opposed American military intervention in Mexico, fearing that it would ignite all the warring factions against the United States, and the end result would be full scale-war.[37]

On August 27, 1913, Wilson addressed a joint session of Congress to explain his Mexican policy to the American people. He declared that the United States only wanted to help the Mexican people establish peace and elect a constitutional government that represented the will of the people. He condemned the Huerta government as incapable of running Mexico and demanded that Huerta relinquish power. Wilson stated to Congress that "it was our duty at least to volunteer our good offices—to offer to assist, if we might, in effecting some arrangement which would bring relief and peace and set up a universally acknowledged political authority there."[38]

The month after Wilson's statement to Congress, the president was praised by newspapers, congressional leaders, and public figures for showing patience and restraint toward Mexico. Bryan wrote Wilson praising his noninterventionist policy toward Mexico: "I cannot allow this hour to pass without telling you how gratified I am with your message on Mexico and its reception by Congress. If I am competent to judge of merit in the domain of morals and statesmanship you have set the record for both. I have heard nothing but praise from those with whom I have spoken."[39]

Huerta was pleased with Wilson's neutrality; he had expected that the American president would openly support the Constitutionalists or attempt to overthrow his government by military force. However, neutrality was more than Huerta could hope for, since his forces controlled all the seaports of Mexico and could import arms from Europe and Japan, while the Constitutionalists were totally landlocked.[40]

With military intervention ruled out, Bryan waited anxiously for Congress to pass the appropriations resolution. On September 12, 1913, both the House and Senate not only voted for the original $100,000, but for an additional $100,000 that Bryan had asked for in case of unexpected expenses.[41]

In September 1913, the Mexican situation appeared to be improving. Bryan wrote Wilson that Huerta had agreed to hold free elections and not be a candidate.[42] Huerta in a speech to the Mexican Congress on September 16, 1913, stated: "I will spare no effort and no sacrifice to obtain the coveted peace and to guarantee fully in the coming election the free casting of the ballot. You may be sure it will constitute the greatest possible triumph for the interim Government to surrender office to its successor if the latter, as is expected, enters upon its functions with public peace and order an accomplished fact."[43] Both Bryan and Wilson were overjoyed that Huerta had accepted their suggestions on free elections. Bryan saw this as a triumph of moral force—passive persuasion over intervention.[44]

Bryan and Wilson were premature in their conviction that Huerta had been persuaded by moral force. On October 10, 1913, Huerta dismissed the Chamber of Deputies, arrested 110 members, mainly Maderistas, and imposed a military dictatorship.[45] Paolo Coletta, a Bryan historian, claimed that Huerta felt more secure, since he now had the full support of the British government. The new British minister, Sir Lionel Carden, the spokesman for Lord Cowdray, the British oil magnate in Mexico, had recognized and fully supported the Huerta government.[46] Carden had arrived on October 9, 1913, a day before the *coup* and waited until October 11 to present his credentials to Huerta.[47]

Bryan was outraged by the Huerta *coup* and especially by Carden's recognition. First, he and Wilson composed a letter that was sent to Nelson O'Shaughnessy, the U.S. chargé d'affaires in Mexico. O'Shaughnessy was ordered to submit the letter to the Mexican foreign office as an official protest of the Huerta *coup*. The letter stated:

The President is shocked at the lawless methods employed by General Huerta and as a sincere friend of Mexico is deeply distressed at the situation which has arisen. He finds it impossible to regard otherwise than as an act of bad faith toward the United States General Huerta's course in dissolving the Congress and arresting the deputies. It is not only a violation of constitutional guarantees but it destroys all possibility of a free and fair election. The President believes that an election held at this time and under conditions as they now exist would have none of the sanctions with which the law surrounds the ballot and that its results therefore could not be regarded as representing the will of the people. The President would not feel justified in accepting the result of such an election or in recognizing a President so chosen.[48]

Bryan then sent an immediate note of protest to the British Foreign Office, since he firmly believed that British oil interests were responsible for Huerta's recognition.[49] The note made it clear that the United States would not recognize any election under Huerta. It was now evident to both Bryan and the president that Huerta could no longer be trusted and must be removed from office as quickly as possible.[50]

Bryan and Wilson decided that the best way to rid themselves of Huerta was to isolate him. The president wanted to send immediate requests to the major European powers to withdraw recognition of his government, but Bryan desired to wait until after the Mexican elections. He believed that Huerta was bound to be elected, and it would be more practical for them to withdraw recognition then. The secretary of state also told Wilson that Great Britain's recognition of Huerta covered only to the date of the election, and it might be easier to convince them not to renew their recognition if the official American requests were withheld for only a few more days. The president deferred to his secretary of state and decided to wait until after the Mexican elections before taking the offensive against Huerta.[51] The elections took place on October 26, and as expected, Huerta was chosen president *ad interim* by the congress and continued to rule Mexico with absolute power.[52]

Bryan and Wilson now attempted to convince the British of their cause—the isolation and overthrow of General Huerta. In November 1913, Wilson met in Washington with British Foreign Secretary Sir Edward Grey and his private secretary, Sir William Tyrrell. Shortly afterwards, British recognition of Huerta abruptly ended, and one month later, Sir Lionel Carden was transferred to Brazil.[53] Why did the British transfer Carden and support American policy in Mexico? Arthur S. Link mentioned two possible reasons: (1) the United States agreed to repeal the exemption of American coastwise ships from payment of tolls through the Panama Canal in return for British support; and (2) the British government needed and sought American friendship, especially when the European situation seemed so uncertain.[54] The first he repudiated as did another historian, William S. Coker.[55] We will deal with the tolls controversy in chapter 8. The second reason, that the British sought American friendship, appeared more plausible. Walter Hines Page, the American ambassador to England, wrote Bryan that the whole British government's attitude toward Huerta had changed, especially after Page had assured the British foreign secretary that after Huerta's elimination, the United States would take the responsibility of protecting all foreign property against the ensuing chaos that might follow. Page told Grey that the only question here was whether Huerta would be eliminated with or without the moral support of Great Britain.[56]

As the year 1913 came to a close, Bryan clarified his own position on Mexico. He called for Huerta to surrender his authority, claiming that the United States could never accept his dictatorial rule. He forecasted that Huerta was doomed, but at the same time, he made it clear that the United States would take no active armed intervention against him. Both Bryan and Wilson preferred to eliminate Huerta through diplomatic and moral pressure rather than military force.[57]

The president, on November 1, 1913, sent a memorandum to Huerta's minister of foreign affairs declaring that unless Huerta retired from office immediately, the United States would actively support his enemies, the Constitutionalists. Wilson wanted Huerta to form a provisional government, stocked with elderly men who were in retirement and who were unaffiliated with the Huerta government, and to arrange for early general elections at which both a new congress and new president would be chosen. Above all, Wilson demanded that the new government "be put upon a constitutional footing."[58]

Immediately after Huerta had received the Wilsonian memorandum, he appeared ready to retire. However, after reading in the American press that the memorandum was an ultimatum, he decided to remain in office. Huerta was angered by Wilson's incessant demands, and on November 8, 1913, he sent a note to the European powers reaffirming the constitutionality of his government and declared that he would remain in power until he was able to pacify the country.[59] Two days later, on November 10, Wilson instructed William Bayard Hale, a member of his inner circle, to proceed to Nogales, Mexico, and meet with the leader of the Constitutionalists, Carranza. Since Wilson could no longer deal with Huerta, he would begin talking with his enemies.[60]

While negotiating with Huerta in September 1913, Bryan's Mexican policy was criticized by a prominent American citizen living in Mexico and in January 1914 by a member of Congress. In September, James Brown Potter, the head of a large agricultural concern in Mexico, ridiculed Bryan for urging all Americans living in Mexico to return to the United States. He also attacked Wilson's special envoy to Mexico, John Lind, for lack of experience in Latin American affairs. Lind had no knowledge of the Mexican people, their language, or their customs.[61] Potter, an ardent supporter of Huerta, characterized American policy as "grape-juice" diplomacy. The term was meant as a direct insult to Bryan's policy of serving grape-juice instead of wine at formal State Department functions.[62] In January 1914, Frederick H. Gillett, a Republican member of the House from Massachusetts, declared that the Wilson administration was floundering along in its Mexican policy and blamed it entirely on Bryan. He noted that the State Department, by its nonrecognition of Huerta, made the United States the "laughing stock of the world." He also criticized Bryan's choice of Lind and the American diplomat's total unfamiliarity with Mexico.[63]

On January 2, 1914, Wilson met with Lind aboard the U.S.S. *Chester* off Gulfport, Mississippi. The central issue of their conversation was finding ways to help the Constitutionalists without becoming directly involved in the fighting. Without arms to continue the fighting, the Constitutionalist war against Huerta had come to a virtual standstill. Wilson had to decide whether to allow them to obtain the needed arms in the United States (the United States had refused to sell arms to any of the belligerents) or to directly intervene in the Mexican revolution in order to depose Huerta.[64]

By the end of January 1914, the president had decided to recognize the belligerency of the Constitutionalists. Bryan began talks with Luis Cabrera, Carranza's agent in Washington on January 27, 1914. Once Cabrera agreed not to confiscate foreign property and to acknowledge foreign claims for damages growing out of the civil war, there were no longer any stumbling blocks toward belligerent recognition.[65] Cabrera declared that "the Constitutionalists meant to accomplish radical social and economic reforms; but they would use constitutional and legal methods, respect the rights of property, uphold just and equitable concessions, and eschew confiscation and anarchy."[66]

Wilson now made a radical change in his Mexican policy—he abandoned his plan to create a provisional government in Mexico, and supported the Constitutionalists.[67] He sent a message to the British Foreign Office explaining his new policy. It read:

The President fears that the revolution in Mexico has reached such a stage that the sort of settlement proposed, namely the elimination of General Huerta and the substitution of others in authority at Mexico City, would be without the desired effect of bringing peace and order. The men in the North, who are conducting a revolution with a programme which goes to the very root of the causes which have made constitutional government in Mexico impossible, and who are not mere rebels, would still have to be reckoned with. No plan which could be carried out at Mexico City at the present juncture could be made the basis of a satisfactory settlement with them. No plan which could not include them can now result in anything more than a change in personnel of an irrepressible contest. If the European powers would jointly or severally inform General Huerta in plain terms that he could no longer expect countenance or moral support from them, the situation would be immensely simplified and the only possible settlement (the triumph of the Constitutionalists) brought within sight.[68]

Public opinion in the United States generally favored Wilson's new Mexican policy. The Senate Foreign Relations Committee had favored the end of the arms embargo.[69] But in Great Britain, the press had a low regard for the Constitutionalists, who were viewed as murderers and rapists. The United States now began to sell arms to the Constitutionalists and waited for the downfall of Huerta.[70]

While Wilson waited for the Constitutionalists to quickly defeat Huerta with the arms acquired from the United States, events were occurring in Mexico that worked in Huerta's favor. The unity within the Constitutionalists' ranks had weakened as Pancho Villa began scheming to seize power from Carranza. Villa became less interested in defeating Huerta than in preparing himself for eventual warfare with Carranza to see who would become the next president of Mexico.[71] In January 1914, both the Catholic Church and the propertied classes, who feared that a Constitutionalists' victory would bring suppression of the Church and the break up of the large estates, gave large sums of money to Huerta's cause. His treasury now replenished, he began to order arms from Germany and other European powers.[72]

Until April 1914, Bryan and Wilson were in general agreement on United States policy toward Mexico. They both wanted to oust Huerta, institute free elections, and pacify the country; they both opposed American military intervention. The only difference between the two men was the means to obtain these results. Bryan favored outside mediation, while Wilson preferred to follow a course of watchful waiting. Bryan, more than Wilson, was concerned about Americans residing in Mexico, and it was he who initiated action for their safe return.[73]

In April 1914, during the Tampico affair and the ensuing United States landing at the port of Veracruz, the differences between the secretary of state and the president became more discernible. Briefly, seven American sailors were arrested by Huerta's forces at Tampico while loading supplies they had purchased. They were released almost immediately and given an explanation that the Mexican soldier, who had made the arrests, had been ignorant of the rules of war.[74] Admiral Henry T. Mayo, in charge of American naval forces in the area, demand-

ed an apology. General Morelos Zaragoza, without hesitation, apologized pro-
fusely to Mayo for the action of his subordinates. Mayo, however, wanted more,
as he was in no mood to tolerate this incident, which he referred to as an
"insult."[75] Without consulting with his superiors, Mayo sent the following dispatch to Zaragosa:

> I must require that you send me, by suitable members of your staff, formal disavowal of and
> apology for the act, together with your assurance that the officer responsible for it will
> receive severe punishment. Also that you publicly hoist the American flag in a prominent
> position on shore and salute it with twenty-one guns, which salute will be duly returned by
> this ship. Your answer to this communication should reach me and the called-for salute be
> fired within twenty-four hours from 6 p.m. of this date.[76]

Huerta refused to consider Mayo's demand, claiming that his government was not
obligated to salute any country that did not recognize him.[77]
    When the news of this incident reached Washington, the president was not
there to receive it. He had gone to White Sulphur Springs, West Virginia, to be
with his family. Bryan, who was in the capital at the time, read the message that
had been sent to Zaragoza. He immediately sent Wilson a telegram in which he
defended Mayo's actions. He said, "I do not see that Mayo could have done
otherwise."[78]
    Though Bryan continued to support Mayo's demand for an apology, he did
not believe that it had to be a twenty-one gun salute. When Huerta issued a virtual
apology shortly after General Zaragoza's apology, Bryan considered that sufficient
to end the affair. Huerta promised to investigate the matter personally, and if the
inquiry showed that the arresting officer had acted improperly, he would be
punished. It was the Navy Department and Wilson who pressed for the twenty-one
gun salute. On April 15, 1914, the president ordered all navy vessels in the
Pacific Fleet to sail to the western coast of Mexico and await further orders.[79]
    Negotiations between the Huerta government and the United States continued
over the necessity of the twenty-one gun salute. Finally, on April 19, 1914, Huerta
told the Wilson administration that he could never agree to consenting to this
demand. On the following day, Wilson went before a joint session of Congress
and asked for a resolution permitting him to use the armed forces to compel
Huerta to respect American rights. Wilson emphasized that the United States had
no desire to interfere in Mexican affairs, did not want war with Mexico, and
"sought only to maintain its own dignity and influence unimpaired for the uses of
liberty, both in the United States and wherever else it may be employed for the
benefit of all mankind."[80] The resolution was overwhelming passed by both
houses of Congress—the House passed it that same evening and the Senate on
April 22.[81]
    What Wilson did not tell the Congress on April 20 was that a German
warship, the *Ypiranga* was steaming toward Veracruz with arms for the Huerta
government. According to historians Howard Cline and Robert Quirk, the main
reason for intervention at Veracruz was to prevent the arms from falling into

Huerta's hands, but the president was uncertain as to how Congress would react to sending Americans into action over an arms shipment. It was far better to make this a great moral crusade against Huerta and his thugs who had insulted the honor of the United States.[82]

Bryan was against the use of the American military in Mexico. During the Tampico crisis, he opposed the idea of military intervention, and in this case, it was not for any moral reason, but for one that was quite practical—he feared that intervention would array all of Mexico against the United States by uniting the warring factions.[83] While Wilson was reading his address to the joint session of Congress, Bryan, in attendance, looked very uneasy, "white and worn and suffering under great strain."[84] Nonetheless, he supported Wilson, since he did not wish to divide the administration over the issue.

Shortly after eleven o'clock in the morning of April 21, 1914, about 1,000 marines and sailors landed at Veracruz unopposed and quickly seized the customhouse and other public buildings. About one hour later, the Mexican garrison of about 800 men left their barracks and spread throughout the central part of Veracruz, where they were met by Mexican naval cadets from the naval academy. Together these Mexican forces opened fire on the Americans from windows and housetops. By noon the following day, the U.S. forces were clearly in control of the city, after having taken light casualties. The United States suffered only 19 dead and 71 wounded compared to the Mexicans, who had 126 killed and 195 wounded.[85]

When Bryan heard of the number of dead and wounded suffered by both sides, he wanted to terminate the American occupation as soon as possible.[86] However, he was opposed by Secretary of War Lindley Garrison, who wanted to extend the military operations in Veracruz by increasing the number of troops.[87] At a cabinet meeting, Bryan and Garrison argued about the consequences of the occupation, with the secretary of state warning Garrison that extension of the military occupation would eventually lead to war with Mexico. Huerta had already broken off diplomatic relations with United States on April 22, 1914, and had sent all the troops he could gather to the Veracruz area. The final decision on expanding the military occupation of Veracruz rested with Wilson, and the president supported Garrison and reinforcements were sent to Veracruz.[88]

Before the end of April 1914, Brazil, Chile, and Argentina offered to mediate the U.S.-Mexican crisis. Wilson really did not want to accept the offer of mediation, but hostile public opinion in Latin America and Europe forced him to agree. For example, there were anti-American riots and demonstrations in Costa Rica, Guatemala, Chile, and Ecuador. The liberal press in Europe condemned the Wilson administration for making war on its smaller neighbor. It was a low point for Wilson and the American people, who claimed the moral leadership of the world.[89]

The delegates met in Niagara Falls, Canada, from May 20 until July 2, 1914. They first discussed plans for ending the civil war. Their end objective, however, was the formation of a strong conservative provisional government that would be capable of uniting the country.[90]

Though Wilson followed the mediation closely, he refused to commit himself to its results. In fact, the president had formed his own plan, which he revealed to Bryan in a confidential memorandum. It called for the elimination of Huerta and the establishment in Mexico of a provisional government acceptable to all parties. This government would pave the way for free elections and the formation of a permanent Mexican government. It would all be accomplished in accordance with the constitution of Mexico.[91]

The mediation failed because it did not have the full support of the Wilson administration and the Constitutionalists. Though Carranza had sent a delegation to Niagara Falls, he had refused to commit himself to the results of the mediation. When an agreement was reached in late June 1914, providing for a provisional government, among other things, the Carranza delegation refused to sign it.[92]

After the Niagara Falls conference ended on July 2, events in Mexico moved rapidly. Huerta's isolation and the military victories of the Constitutionalists ended any hope that he could continue as president. On July 15, 1914, Huerta resigned, and five days later, he fled to Europe aboard the steamer *Ypiranga*.[93]

Now that Huerta was eliminated, both Bryan and Wilson believed that the Constitutionalists would cease fighting and choose a president. However, whatever unity existed in the Constitutionalists' ranks ended with Huerta's resignation. Both Carranza and Villa wanted the presidency and began to fight each other for the right to succeed Huerta. The rupture could have occurred as early as April, 1914 but the American diplomat George C. Carothers, attached to Villa's headquarters, prevented a schism.[94]

Wilson, who had great hopes for peace in Mexico after the resignation of Huerta, sent Carranza a stern warning on July 23, 1914. He said that the whole world was watching to see how the Constitutionalists would effect the transfer of power. He warned Carranza about the need to protect foreign lives and property and to meet financial obligations. He talked about the treatment of political and military opponents and wanted Carranza to declare a general amnesty. He even warned Carranza about the need to protect the Catholic Church in Mexico, declaring that the civilized world would not stand for the persecution of priests. Wilson summed up his warning by stating that "nothing ought to be overlooked or dealt with hastily which may result in our being obliged to withhold the recognition of this Government from the new government to be created at Mexico City as we withheld it from General Huerta."[95]

Bryan appeared more favorably disposed toward Villa than Carranza. During the Veracruz incident, Villa did not object to American occupation. He related his views to Carothers, and the latter sent the following to the secretary of state: "That as far as he was concerned, we could keep Veracruz and hold it so tight that not even water could get in to Huerta and that he could not feel any resentment."[96] Bryan replied that "it shows a largeness of view on his part and a comprehension of the whole situation which is greatly to his credit."[97] On the other hand, Carranza had opposed American occupation of Veracruz, warning that the American invasion might cause a war between the two countries. He demanded that American forces withdraw from Veracruz immediately.[98]

From the end of July 1914 until the beginning of 1915, State Department policy favored Villa, since he appeared more friendly toward the United States than Carranza. Lind, an ardent advocate of Carranza, was recalled in June 1914 and officially resigned from Wilson's group of special advisers in August 1914. He was replaced by Paul Fuller. [99]

Aside from Fuller, Bryan began to rely heavily on the advice of Carothers, an ardent Villa supporter. Carothers, in an early report to Bryan, related that Villa feared that Carranza was seeking absolute power, and once he obtained supremacy, he would neglect all social legislation, especially agrarian reform. Carothers praised Villa for his abstention from alcohol and gambling. According to Carothers, Villa was a true leader, idolized by his soldiers and completely without ambition. The secretary of state had full faith in Carothers assessment of Villa. Bryan hoped to persuade Wilson to throw his support to Villa, and he asked the president to speak with Carothers. However, Wilson was not as taken with Villa as Bryan and Carothers, and he refused to commit himself to a Mexican leader.[100]

On August 20, 1914, Carranza, surrounded by his generals, except Villa, entered the city of Mexico to the cheering crowds. He rode on his horse to the National Palace where the crowds broke through the barriers to greet him, while cannons fired the presidential salute. Carranza addressed the crowds from the balcony of the palace and asked for their support. All the while, Villa was outside of Mexico City planning his war with Carranza.[101]

In September 1914, sporadic fighting occurred between the Villa and Carranza forces. Preparation also began for a convention at Aguascalientes—a convention that the United States supported, and Carranza had refused to attend, though he did send delegates.[102] The convention met in October 1914, deposed Carranza as first chief in charge of executive power and Villa as chief of the Division of the North, and called for the election of a provisional president, Eulalio Gutiérrez, a supporter of Villa. However, Carranza refused to accept these conditions. On November 3, 1914, he moved his headquarters from Mexico City to the city of Puebla and declared that since the convention had not complied with his terms concerning his own and Villa's retirement, he would continue to exercise the executive power of the nation. When the convention gave an ultimatum to Carranza to either comply to the terms or be declared an outlaw, he ordered his delegates to withdraw from the negotiations and his generals to return to their commands.[103]

In December, 1914, Bryan continued to praise Villa. He wrote Wilson that Villa and Zapata were working in harmony, and the defeat of Carranza was almost certain.[104] The United States did not officially recognize either Villa or Carranza, but Bryan, believing that Villa would prevail, wanted Wilson to send Villa's provisional president, Gutiérrez, an official message, emphasizing the need to protect religious and property rights and also of allowing political amnesty.[105]

However, Wilson did not share his secretary of state's convictions. He allowed Bryan to send the message, but only on an unofficial basis. It would be embarrassing to give official support to a government that might fall at any moment.[106] When Carranza was forced to make a full retreat from Mexico City in early December 1914, Bryan lauded Villa for his peaceful occupation of the capital.[107] Two weeks later, Bryan wanted to close the port at Naco because Carranza's forces were using it to the disadvantage of Villa. The secretary of state also berated Carranza for showing less regard for American lives than Villa. Wilson, however, told Bryan that he lacked the authority to close the port, and that the United States had to remain neutral in the fighting between Villa and Carranza.[108] Three months later, in March 1915, Bryan again wrote Wilson criticizing Carranza and the virtues of Villa. He told the president that Carranza was taking advantage of the U.S.-Mexican border in his war with Villa. Carranza's men congregated on the border and Villa could not attack without shooting into U.S. territory.[109]

Carranza's hostile attitude toward the Catholic Church also made Bryan more favorable toward Villa. The religious issue was a very sensitive one in Mexico. Since the War of the Reform in the late 1850s, the church had been stripped of its large land holdings and much of its power. During the rule of Díaz, these laws were not seriously enforced. But with the revolution of 1910, Carranza, an anti-Catholic, began invoking the 1859 laws, making it most uncomfortable for the Mexican clergy.[110]

In September 1914, the Catholic Church in the United States protested the treatment of its church in Mexico. Joseph Schrembs, bishop of Toledo, spoke before Cardinal James Gibbons and eight bishops and members of the American Federation of Catholic Societies, berating Bryan for doing nothing to stop the desecration of churches in Mexico.[111] Bryan was sensitive to these pleas, and in February 1915, he sent a strong protest to Carranza on behalf of the 180 Mexican priests who were incarcerated by the Carranza government.[112]

Bryan wrote Wilson, in March 1915, with regard to making recognition of any Mexican government contingent upon religious freedom. He wanted the president to issue a declaration to the Carranza government, stating that recognition had not been decided upon, but when the matter was considered, the United States would have to be assured of religious freedom in Mexico. The president, unlike Bryan, refused to make religious persecution of the church a matter of recognition.[113]

By March 1915, the fighting between the forces of Villa and Carranza became more intense, and property destruction and loss of life grew. Bryan, still favoring Villa, worried about the continued consequences to Americans residing in Mexico. The secretary of state wrote Wilson with his own plan to stop the fighting. He wanted the United States and all of the Latin American nations to issue an appeal to the warring factions to come to terms. He hoped that a joint appeal by all would have more force. Wilson disagreed, claiming that a joint appeal would be in-effective and only cause more resentment.[114]

In early April 1915, Carranza's forces won a major battle against Villa. Álvaro Obregón, Carranza's brilliant general, had his forces entrenched at Celaya about thirty-seven miles from Mexico City. Villa's objective was to wipe out Obregón's army, open the road to Mexico City, and begin a campaign to destroy the rest of Carranza's army. Villa launched his attack on April 6, but after thirty hours of bloody fighting, he withdrew. He returned to Celaya one week later, on April 13, with additional forces and made a deadly frontal assault against the strongly fortified positions of Obregón. After two days of violent fighting, Villa lost over 6,000 men. From then on, he was no longer a serious threat to Carranza.[115] With the Battle of Celaya, State Department policy toward Villa now changed. Until this time, Bryan had favored him over Carranza, but when word reached Bryan about Villa's defeat, he wrote Wilson that "if it should be true that the Carranza forces have defeated Villa, there is much to meditate upon."[116] Bryan told Wilson, who never really cared much for Villa, that the Mexican leader could no longer be depended upon, and from April to June 1915, Bryan attempted to work for an impartial settlement.[117]

In May 1915, Bryan and Wilson made constant appeals to both sides to stop fighting. Mexico City was totally ravaged by war, many people were left homeless and starving, and the rule of law failed to exist. Bryan was particularly sensitive to the plight of the Mexican people and wanted to alleviate their distress. He urged Wilson to make a personal appeal for an organized relief program. As a result, the American Red Cross sent both money and foodstuffs to the distressed Mexican people.[118]

Wilson also decided, in the last days of May 1915, to issue a message to the warring factions to make known the position of the United States. The president sent a rough draft of the message to Bryan and asked him to make revisions if necessary. The message condemned the Mexican leaders of both factions for attempting to gain personal power without regard for the welfare of the Mexican people. It emphasized that the United States could not continue to watch this wholesale bloodshed; the American government would begin searching for a man or group of men who could pull the country together. If the warring factions could not come to an agreement, and the United States could not find a leader, Wilson threatened to take action to save the Mexican people. The last part read as follows: "I feel it to be my duty to tell them that, if they cannot accommodate their differences and unite for this great purpose within a very short time, this Government will be constrained to decide what means should be employed by the United States in order to help Mexico save herself and serve her people."[119] The last four lines of this statement were Bryan's contribution to Wilson's message. When the secretary of state received the copy of the draft, the president had used the words "to look for other means;" Bryan wanted to change that with "to decide what means should be employed," since he believed the latter phrase gave Wilson more flexibility in his dealings with Mexico.[120] One week after this message was sent, Bryan resigned his position, but his interest in Mexico did not diminish, as we shall see in chapter 10.

In conclusion, William Jennings Bryan, though he did not formulate U.S. policy toward Mexico, played an instrumental role in contributing to, and differing with, that policy. Bryan as early as August 1913 suggested mediation to Wilson as a possible solution to the Mexican crisis. Though his plan was rejected, Bryan supported Wilson's plan for free elections and even recommended John Lind to carry that plan to Huerta. It was Bryan who not only urged Americans to leave Mexico, but also provided the means of transportation. Though the secretary of state reluctantly supported the original Veracruz landing in April 1914, he opposed any further increase or extension of American military operations there. After Huerta fled in July 1914, Bryan favored Villa over Carranza because of the former's seemingly more friendly attitude toward the United States and his less hostile reaction toward the Catholic Church. However, Bryan became neutral after April 1915, when Villa began to suffer numerous setbacks—he worked for an impartial solution. In June 1915, he helped Wilson compose a letter of warning to the belligerent factions; he also began a campaign to aid the starving people of Mexico.

NOTES

1. For the best single volume history of Mexico see Henry Bamford Parkes, *A History of Mexico* (Boston: Houghton, 1970).

2. John Edwin Fagg, *Latin America: A General History* (New York: Macmillan, 1977), p. 522.

3. Ibid., pp. 523-524.

4. Ibid., p. 528.

5. Ibid., pp. 529-530.

6. *Commoner*, March 29, 1901.

7. Ibid.

8. Ibid.

9. Ibid., p. 533.

10. Arthur S. Link, *Wilson: The New Freedom* (Princeton, N.J.: Princeton University Press, 1956), p. 347.

11. Ibid.

12. Ibid., pp. 347-348.

13. Ibid.

14. General Huerta to the President, February 18, 1913, *Papers Relating to the Foreign Relations of the United States, 1913* (Washington, D.C.: U.S. Government Printing Office, 1920), p. 721.

15. Link, *Wilson: The New Freedom*, p. 348.

16. Ibid.

17. Fagg, *Latin America*, p. 707.

18. Link, *Wilson: The New Freedom*, p. 353.

19. *Commoner*, February 22, 1913.

20. American Ambassador to the Secretary of State, March 12, 1913, *Foreign Relations, 1913*, pp. 768-776.

21. Ibid.

22. Link, *Wilson: The New Freedom*, pp. 348-349.

23. Ibid., p. 349.

24. American Ambassador to the Secretary of State, March 12, 1913, *Foreign Relations, 1913*, pp. 768-776.

25. Link, *Wilson: The New Freedom*, p. 349.

26. Ibid., p. 350.

27. Paolo E. Coletta, *William Jennings Bryan: Progressive Politician and Moral Statesman, 1909-1915*, vol. 2 (Lincoln, NE: University of Nebraska Press, 1969), p. 148.

28. Link, *Wilson: The New Freedom*, p. 351.

29. *New York Times*, August 5, 1913; George M. Stephenson, *John Lind of Minnesota* (Minneapolis, MN: The University of Minnesota Press, 1935), p. 208; Secretary of State to the American Chargé d'Affaires, August 27, 1913, *Foreign Relations, 1913*, pp. 820-827.

30. Bryan to Wilson, May 27, 1913, Bryan Papers, Library of Congress; Ibid., August 10, 1913.

31. Bryan to Wilson, August 10, 1913, Bryan Papers, Library of Congress.

32. Ibid.

33. *New York Times*, August 2, 1913; Bryan to Wilson, August 11, 1913, Bryan-Wilson Correspondence, National Archives; Wilson to Bryan, August 12, 1913, Bryan-Wilson Correspondence, National Archives.

34. *New York Times*, August 2, 1913.

35. Ibid., August 23, 1913.

36. Bryan to Wilson, August 18, 1913, Bryan Papers, Library of Congress.

37. Ibid., September 1, 1913.

38. Link, *Wilson: The New Freedom*, pp. 360-361.

39. Ibid., p. 361.

40. Ibid.

41. *New York Times*, September 13, 1913.

42. Bryan to Wilson, September 25, 1913, Bryan Papers, Library of Congress.

43. *New York Times*, September 17, 1913.

44. *Commoner*, September, 1913.

45. Coletta, *William Jennings Bryan*, p. 154.

46. Ibid.

47. Ibid.

48. Link: *Wilson: The New Freedom*, p. 366.

49. Manton M. Wyvell to Tumulty, October 10, 1913, Bryan Papers, Library of Congress; Ray Stannard Baker, *Woodrow Wilson: Life and Letters*, vol. 4 (Garden City, N.Y.: Doubleday, Page and Company, 1927), p. 256; Bryan to Wilson, October 24, 1913, Bryan Papers, Library of Congress; Coletta, *William Jennings Bryan*, p. 154.

50. Secretary of State to the American Chargé d'Affaires, October 13, 1913, *Foreign Relations, 1913*, p. 838; *New York Times*, October 15, 1913; Baker, *Woodrow Wilson: Life and Letters*, p. 287.

51. Bryan to Wilson, October 22, 1913, Bryan-Wilson Correspondence, National Archives; Baker, *Woodrow Wilson: Life and Letters*, p. 287.

52. American Chargé d'Affaires to the Secretary of State, October 26, 1913, *Foreign Relations, 1913*, p. 850; Coletta, *William Jennings Bryan*, p. 156.

53. Baker, *Woodrow Wilson: Life and Letters*, p. 287.

54. Arthur S. Link, *Woodrow Wilson and the Progressive Era, 1910-1917* (New York: Harper, 1954), p. 119.

55. Link, *Wilson: The New Freedom*, pp. 304-314; William S. Coker, "The Panama Canal Tolls Controversy: A Different Perspective," *Journal of American History* 55 (December 1968): 555-564.

56. The American Ambassador to Great Britain to the Secretary of State, November 13, 1913, *Foreign Relations, 1913*, pp. 860-861.

57. *Commoner*, December, 1913.

58. Link, *Wilson: The New Freedom*, pp. 380-381.

59. Ibid., p. 381.

60. Ibid., p. 382.

61. *New York Times*, September 9, 1913.

62. Ibid.; Link, *Woodrow Wilson and the Progressive Era*, p. 27.

63. *Congressional Record*, 63 Cong., 2 sess., 1914, LI, pt. 2, 1741.

64. Link, *Wilson: The New Freedom*, p. 388.

65. Ibid., p. 389.

66. Ibid.

67. Ibid.

68. Ibid.

69. Ibid., p. 391.

70. Ibid.

71. Ibid., p. 392.

72. Ibid.

73. Bryan to Wilson, August 10, 1913, Bryan Papers, Library of Congress.

74. Robert E. Quirk, *An Affair of Honor: Woodrow Wilson and the Occupation of Veracruz* (Lexington, KY: University of Kentucky Press, 1962), pp. 22-23.

75. Link, *Wilson: The New Freedom*, p. 395.

76. H. T. Mayo to M. Zaragoza, April 9, 1914, *Papers Relating to the Foreign Relations of the United States, 1914* (Washington, D.C.: U.S. Government Printing Office, 1922), pp. 448-449.

77. Quirk, *An Affair of Honor*, p. 60.

78. Secretary of State to President Wilson, April 10, 1914, *Foreign Relations, 1914*, p. 449.

79. Quirk, *An Affair of Honor*, pp. 42-43; Secretary of State to the Chargé d'Affaires, April 17, 1914, *Foreign Relations, 1914*, p. 446.

80. Howard F. Cline, *The United States and Mexico* (Cambridge: Harvard University Press, 1953), p. 158; Quirk, *An Affair of Honor*, p. 75; Address of the President delivered at the joint session of the two Houses of Congress, April 20, 1914, *Foreign Relations, 1914*, pp. 474-476; Baker, *Woodrow Wilson: Life and Letters*, p. 326.

81. Link, *Wilson: The New Freedom*, pp. 398-399.

82. Cline, *The United States and Mexico*, p. 158; Quirk, *An Affair of Honor*, p. 75.

83. *Commoner*, April, 1914.

84. Baker, *Woodrow Wilson: Life and Letters*, p. 326.

85. Link, *Wilson: The New Freedom*, pp. 399-400.

86. *New York Times*, April 25, 1914.

87. Ibid.

88. Ibid.

89. Link, *Wilson: The New Freedom*, p. 405.

90. Cline, *The United States and Mexico*, p. 161; Coletta, *William Jennings Bryan*, p. 169.

91. Link, *Wilson: The New Freedom*, pp. 407-408.

92. Cline, *The United States and Mexico*, p. 161; Baker, *Woodrow Wilson: Life and Letters*, p. 349.

93. Coletta, *William Jennings Bryan*, p. 171.

94. Secretary of State to Vice Consul Silliman, July 6, 1914, *Foreign Relations, 1914*, p. 564; Link, *Woodrow Wilson and the Progressive Era*, p. 128.

95. Link, *Wilson: The New Freedom*, pp. 414-415.

96. Special Agent Carothers to the Secretary of State, April 23, 1914, *Foreign Relations, 1914*, pp. 485-486; Robert Quirk, *The Mexican Revolution, 1914-1915: The Convention of Aguascalientes* (Bloomington, IN: Indiana University Press, 1960), p. 46.

97. Quirk, *The Mexican Revolution*, p. 46; Secretary of State to Special Agent Carothers, April 24, 1914, *Foreign Relations, 1914*, pp. 486-487.

98. Baker, *Woodrow Wilson: Life and Letters*, p. 348.

99. Stephenson, *John Lind of Minnesota*, p. 275; Link, *Woodrow Wilson and the Progressive Era*, p. 129.

100. Bryan to Wilson, August 2, 1914, Bryan-Wilson Correspondence, National Archives.

101. Link, *Wilson: The New Freedom*, p. 416.

102. Quirk, *The Mexican Revolution*, p. 114; Arthur S. Link, *Wilson: The Struggle for Neutrality, 1914-1915* (Princeton, N.J.: Princeton University Press, 1960), p. 250.

103. Quirk, *The Mexican Revolution*, pp. 118-119.

104. Bryan to Wilson, December 2, 1914, Bryan-Wilson Correspondence, National Archives.

105. Ibid.

106. Wilson to Bryan, December 3, 1914, Bryan-Wilson Correspondence, National Archives.

107. Bryan to Wilson, December 7, 1914, Bryan Papers, Library of Congress.

108. Bryan to Wilson, December 21, 1914, Bryan-Wilson Correspondence, National Archives; Wilson to Bryan, December 23, 1914, Bryan-Wilson Correspondence, National Archives.

109. Bryan to Wilson, March 31, 1915, Bryan Papers, Library of Congress.

110. *New York Times*, February 21, 1915.

111. Ibid., September 28, 1914.

112. Ibid., February 21, 1915.

113. Bryan to Wilson, March 11, 1915, Bryan-Wilson Correspondence, National Archives; Wilson to Bryan, March 17, 1915, Bryan-Wilson Correspondence, National Archives.

114. Bryan to Wilson, March 11, 1915, Bryan Papers, Library of Congress; Wilson to Bryan, March 11, 1915, Bryan Papers, Library of Congress.

115. Link, *Wilson: The Struggle for Neutrality*, pp. 465-466.

116. Ibid., p. 467; Quirk, *The Mexican Revolution*, p. 226; *New York Times*, April 20, 1915.

117. Link, *Wilson: The Struggle for Neutrality*, p. 467; Quirk, *The Mexican Revolution*, p. 226.

118. Bryan to Wilson, May 22 and May 26, 1915, Bryan Papers, Library of Congress; Wilson to Bryan, May 27, 1915, Bryan Papers, Library of Congress.

119. Secretary of State to the Brazilian Minister to Mexico, June 2, 1915, *Papers Relating to the Foreign Relations of the United States, 1915* (Washington, D.C.: U.S. Government Printing Office, 1924), pp. 255-257.

120. Bryan to Wilson, June 2, 1915, Bryan Papers, Library of Congress; Wilson to Bryan, June 2, 1915, Bryan Papers, Library of Congress.

8

The Panama Canal Tolls Controversy

The Panama Canal tolls controversy became a serious obstacle to friendly Anglo-American relations during the Wilson administration. William Jennings Bryan played an instrumental role in ending the controversy and eventually improving relations between the United States and Great Britain. Before discussing Bryan's role in the Panama Canal tolls controversy, we will briefly discuss Anglo-American rivalry in Central America prior to 1913.

ANGLO-AMERICAN RIVALRY IN CENTRAL AMERICA BEFORE BRYAN

The rivalry between the United States and Great Britain in Central American lasted for much of the nineteenth century, since the British were particularly active in this region. As early as 1821, British settlers in Belize (British Honduras) had expanded to the south of the Sibun; in 1841, the British government supported the Mosquito king when he expanded his territory to the mouth of the San Juan River. When Nicaragua protested this intrusion, Great Britain ignored the protest and renamed this territory Greytown.[1]

The United States resented and feared British domination in Central America. The American government hoped to build a canal across the Isthmus in order to shorten the time of a voyage from the Atlantic to the Pacific coast. An Isthmian crossing was not only important for ordinary travel, but it was essential to the security of the West Coast, since the speedy arrival of troops could mean the difference between victory and defeat in time of war (the United States before 1846 was thinking about a war with Mexico).[2]

Britain was interested in an isthmian canal for commercial reasons. Since both the United States and Great Britain coveted a canal and did not trust each other, they drew up the Clayton-Bulwer Treaty in 1850. It stated that Great

Britain and the United States should share equally in the construction and control of any canal across the Isthmus.[3]

From 1865 on, Anglo-American relations improved partly due to Great Britain's withdrawal from parts of Central America. The British government signed treaties in 1859 with both Honduras and Nicaragua: Honduras received the Bay Islands, while Nicaragua's right to that part of the Mosquito territory which lay within its boundary was now recognized.[4]

Though Anglo-American relations improved in the latter half of the nineteenth century, it did not stop the clamor among members of the Democratic and Republican parties for the construction of an American-owned canal. During the administration of William McKinley, Secretary of State John Hay signed with Lord Pauncefote of Great Britain in January 1899, the first Hay-Pauncefote Treaty, giving the United States the right to build an isthmian canal, but prohibiting its fortification or ownership. The British agreed because they wanted and needed American friendship—their naval and colonial rivalry with Germany, and the new alliances that were forming in Europe, forced Great Britain to make new allies in other parts of the world.[5] However, the ardent nationalists, or so-called imperialists, among them Theodore Roosevelt, who was then governor of New York, bitterly attacked the first Hay-Pauncefote Treaty for failing to give the United States the right to fortify. Two years later, Roosevelt became president, and a new Hay-Pauncefote Treaty was signed. This treaty gave the United States the right of ownership, and though it was not stated explicitly, the right to fortify was also implied.[6] However, Article III of this treaty stated the following rights of other nations: "The Canal shall be free and open to the vessels of commerce and war of all nations observing these rules, on terms of entire equality, so that there shall be no discrimination against any such nation or its citizens or subjects, in respect of the conditions or charges of traffic, or otherwise."[7]

BRYAN AND THE PANAMA CANAL

William Jennings Bryan favored equality in the use of the Panama Canal (Panama became the site of the new canal) as early as March 1910, three years before he became secretary of state. In his paper the *Commoner*, he wrote:

The Canal should be open to the commerce of the world, without other charge than that necessary for the expense of operation and maintenance. This policy is demanded in the interest of our own people. Every dollar collected in tolls will increase the rates charged by transcontinental lines; and as the railroad traffic between the oceans increases, this charge will aggregate more and more. The cheaper we can make the water rate, the cheaper will be the railroad rate.[8]

However, this was not the only reason why Bryan favored a free canal. He believed that it was to our advantage, since it would deter other governments from undertaking similar projects in the western hemisphere. He said:

A free canal can be justified on the grounds that, as our country objects to other nations gaining a foothold on this hemisphere, it owes it to the world to do the work itself at the least possible expense to other countries. A free canal would set at rest all discussion of other canal routes and effectually prevent the building of another canal by any other country, while a toll would lead to a perpetual dispute as to the fairness of the interest rate as well as to the reasonableness of the construction cost taken as the basis.[9]

In August 1912, the American congress passed the Panama Canal Act, which provided that "no tolls shall be levied upon vessels engaged in the coastwise trade of the United States."[10]   Shortly after President Taft signed it, the British government declared that the new bill was a clear violation of Article III of the Hay-Pauncefote Treaty.[11] Taft quickly replied to the British protest by boasting "that the United States owned the canal and could charge what rates it pleased for American vessels."[12]   However, British Foreign Secretary Sir Edward Grey continued to argue treaty violation and asked that the Taft administration submit the issue to arbitration, if the two governments could not reach an agreement.[13]

A plank in the Democratic platform of 1912 supported the Panama Canal Act. It stated that "we favor the exemption from tolls of American ships engaged in coastwise trade passing through the Panama Canal."[14] Bryan stood solidly behind the platform, although three years earlier he favored equal treatment and hoped that tolls would be unnecessary.[15] There was no reason for Bryan's support of the exemption clause except that he was a good Democrat and stood firmly behind the party platform. It should also be remembered that the issue of exemption was not a major one in 1912 when compared with the Democratic party's demands for revision in the tariff, antitrust legislation, and new banking legislation. Bryan understood that the priority of his party was to elect Woodrow Wilson as president. If that succeeded, he would then deal with the Panama Canal tolls issue.[16]

The Taft administration, even after it was defeated in the November 1912 election, continued to defend the exemption, arguing that since the canal had been constructed by the American people, with American capital, there was no reason American ships in coastwise trade should not be exempted. In January 1913, Philander Knox, Taft's secretary of state, responded to Grey's protest of the exemption by claiming that it was merely a subsidy granted by the United States to its trade. He declared that there was nothing to arbitrate since the president had established equal tolls for United States and foreign vessels engaged in foreign trade. Knox then reminded Grey that the British Foreign Secretary had earlier conceded that the tolls exemption for American coastwise shipping did not necessarily violate the Hay-Pauncefote Treaty.[17]

It should be noted that Knox exaggerated Grey's alleged concession on the issue of exempting American coastwise shipping from the payment of tolls. The British Foreign Secretary had agreed that the exemption of coastwise ships in such a way as not to increase the tolls on foreign shipping might not violate the Hay-Pauncefote Treaty. However, he had then proceeded to argue that it was impossible to exempt coastwise shipping from tolls without also giving a major advantage to American foreign shipping. Grey told Knox that the power of the

American congress to fix lower rates for American shipping amounted to flagrant discrimination against British commerce.[18]

In the last days of the Taft administration, Anglo-American relations needed rejuvenation. Although the tolls issue did not affect the vital interests of either country, to many Americans and most English it involved the good faith and honor of the United States. Some publications in the United States such as the *New York World* sided with the Great Britain on this issue. An editorial in December 1912, stated that "Sir Edward Grey's argument has both dignity and solemnity, but more important than either, it has truth. Never before was a nation more easily or more conclusively proved to be in the wrong. It is a humiliation to reflect that nation is our own."[19]   Since both Taft and Knox had refused to consider arbitration of the Panama Canal Act of 1912, the British government now awaited the inauguration of President Wilson and hoped that he would see things differently.

BRYAN AND THE TOLLS CONTROVERSY

When Bryan became secretary of state, the British Ambassador, James Bryce, soon to be replaced by Cecil Spring Rice, continued to urge arbitration of the tolls dispute. On April 15, 1913, Wilson's cabinet discussed not only the tolls question, but also the Arbitration Treaty under which the British wished to resolve the dispute.[20] This treaty had been formulated in 1908 and was coming up for renewal in June 1913. Bryan and Wilson both wanted the treaty renewed and realized that the British would not consider the matter until the tolls dispute was settled.[21] Wilson, at this time, believed that repeal of the exemption was the only fair course of action. Like Bryan, Wilson had hastily approved the tolls exemption during the campaign of 1912. However, the president, after attending a meeting in late January 1913 of the Round Table Dining Club in New York, had changed his mind. Wilson was impressed by two speakers, Joseph H. Choate, who had helped to negotiate the Hay-Pauncefote Treaty while ambassador to England, and Senator Elihu Root of New York. Both of these men gave logical reasons why the British government was right and the United States was wrong. From that time on, Wilson took the position that exemption was morally wrong and would have to be repealed.[22]

Although Wilson favored repeal of exemption as early as April 15, 1913, Bryan warned the president that the United States should not rush into this matter, which could have political ramifications for the president's domestic program.[23] In late April 1913, Bryan met with Bryce to discuss numerous matters, but mostly the Panama Canal tolls controversy. Bryce told him that since Congress had no intention of repealing the exemption, he wanted it submitted to arbitration. Bryan, always the politician, replied to the British ambassador that the Democrats had just assumed power after sixteen years and that there were vital domestic matters that took precedence over the tolls question. He stressed that Wilson could not risk splitting the Democratic party over the tolls controversy when he needed votes to pass new tariff, antitrust, and banking legislation. He urged the British to wait until 1914 when these domestic matters hopefully would be settled.[24]

It was Bryan who had convinced Wilson to wait at least a year before repealing the exemption. In all of the cabinet meetings in April 1913, the secretary of state when the decision was made to delay repeal of exemption, had grave doubts about the practicality of precipitate action. At the cabinet meeting on April 15, Bryan urged Wilson to wait until he could talk with Bryce.[25] By April 18, at the next cabinet meeting, he had spoken with Bryce and told the president of that conversation. It was also at that meeting that Bryan urged a delay, at least until the new tariff law was passed.[26] Wilson, on the other hand, had favored immediate action as early as April 15, but after speaking with his secretary of state on April 18, he agreed to a delay.[27]

Another reason for Bryan's insistence on deferring action on the tolls question was his fear that the Arbitration Treaty of 1908 would not be renewed.[28] Great Britain had threatened not to renew it if the tolls dispute was not settled, either through repeal in Congress or by use of this treaty. However, Bryan in April 1913, had assurance from Bryce that his government would renew the Arbitration Treaty, if the Wilson administration kept its promise to begin repeal of the exemption within a year.[29] Thus, the threat not to renew the Arbitration Treaty did not emanate as much from Great Britain as from another source. Certain recalcitrant senators, led by James O'Gorman of New York, chairman of the Committee on Interoceanic Canals; an Irish-American; and an ardent opponent of repeal, feared that the Arbitration Treaty, if renewed, would be used to repeal exemption. These senators opposed both repeal and renewal of the Arbitration Treaty.[30] Bryan, a great proponent of arbitration, worried that any action to repeal exemption now would mean almost certain death for the Arbitration Treaty. He told Wilson that the opposition senators feared that renewal of the treaty would be an endorsement of Great Britain's position.[31] Bryan, to alleviate the fears of these senators, proposed a resolution declaring that renewal of the treaty would not mean that the United States accepted Great Britain's position on this matter.[32] The president, who favored the Arbitration Treaty, lauded Bryan for his foresight and approved the resolution.[33]

Wilson and Bryan did not take action toward repeal until early 1914. However, before discussing repeal, something should be said about the motives behind it. Both Bryan and Wilson (as mentioned in chapter 7 on Mexico) did not make repeal of exemption contingent on British support of their Mexican policy. They did not demand that if the British did not recall Lord Carden (the British ambassador, a spokesman for British oil interests, and a supporter of Victoriano Huerta) they would refuse to consider repeal.[34] Bryan and Wilson both knew that the British oil interests were behind Huerta, and the Wilson administration was eventually successful in obtaining British support, but this support came seven months after Wilson had committed himself to repeal. Both the president and Bryan had favored repeal on moral grounds as early as April 1913, and they had promised action within the year.[35] The British sent Grey's private secretary, Sir William Tyrrell, to the United States in November 1913, and it was only after his mission that the British supported United States policy in Mexico.[36]

In January 1914, Wilson decided that it was time to take up the tolls question. The Underwood-Simmons tariff bill had been signed in October 1913, as well as the Federal Reserve Act in late December 1913, so two major domestic obstacles were now cleared away.[37] The Arbitration Convention of 1908 was signed for renewal on May 31, 1913, one day before it would have expired. However, it remained in the Senate until February 1914, when it was finally passed (the British ratified it in March 1914, after Wilson initiated action on the tolls question).[38]

On January 6, 1914, Wilson wrote to his ambassador to Great Britain, Walter Hines Page, and told him that he would begin working on the tolls controversy. He said: "You may be sure I will strive to the utmost to obtain both a repeal of the discrimination in the matter of the tolls and a renewal of the arbitration treaties, and I am not without hope that I can accomplish both at this session. Indeed this is the session in which these things must be done if they are to be done at all."[39] About three weeks later, on January 26, 1914, Wilson decided to test the opinion of the members of the Senate Foreign Relations Committee on the tolls question. He summoned them to the White House for a three-hour conference, where he reviewed the unsatisfactory condition of American foreign policy throughout the world. He pointed to the growth of anti-American sentiment in Japan and to the precarious state of Mexican-American relations. It was difficult, he said, to conduct normal diplomacy in this atmosphere of tension and distrust. He told the committee members that repeal of the exemption might improve relations between Europe and the United States, but that his main goal was to retain the friendship of Great Britain. He said, in no uncertain terms, that American exemption violated the text of the Hay-Pauncefote Treaty and that he wanted the exemption repealed.[40]

On February 5, 1914, Wilson, for the first time, came out publicly for repeal of the exemption. He said: "The exemption seems to me in clear violation of the terms of the Hay-Pauncefote Treaty."[41] He began to confer frequently with Representative William C. Adamson of Georgia, chairman of the House Commerce Committee—the committee that had charge of the bill in the House, and with other Democratic leaders, to build support for the bill in the Congress. It appeared that most House Democrats were falling into line behind the president until March 3, 1914, when Oscar W. Underwood, the House Majority Leader announced that he opposed repeal and would lead the opposition in the House against its passage. Underwood criticized both Wilson and Bryan for violating their pledge to support the Democratic platform in 1912, which supported toll exemption for American coastwise shipping.[42]

Underwood's opposition forced the president to address a joint session on March 5, 1914, where he forcefully urged repeal. He said, "We ought to reverse our action without raising the question whether we were right or wrong, and so once more deserve our reputation for generosity and for the redemption of every obligation without quibble or hesitation."[43]

Wilson needed all the leadership qualities he could muster in his fight for repeal of the exemption. Numerous lobbyists for the coastwise shipping interests swarmed into the capital prepared to do battle with the president. Hundreds of petitions, from Irish-American societies, denouncing Wilson's surrender to British interests found their way to Congress. The anti-British Hearst press criticized the president, demanding that he stand up for national sovereignty. Then on March 26, 1914, in the midst of all of this anti-repeal sentiment, an almost fatal blow to Wilson's plan for repeal occurred when Champ Clark, the Speaker of the House of Representatives, joined Underwood and took personal command of the anti-repeal forces. Now the two most powerful Democrats in the House of Representatives stood against the president on this issue.[44]

Wilson now turned to Bryan to help him get the repeal of exemption bill through the Congress. The secretary of state still had influence among the Democrats in the House, Senate, and party, and he became an invaluable asset to Wilson. Bryan, as stated before, supported repeal of the exemption as early as April 1913, and by February 1914, when the president prepared to do battle with Congress, the secretary of state firmly supported him.[45] Wilson attested to Bryan's importance on this matter in a letter sent to William Marbury of Baltimore, a personal friend of the president. He praised Bryan not only for his personal concern, but also for his great ability in dealing with the right people (Wilson was referring to Bryan's influence in the House and Senate). The president wrote:

Not only have Mr. Bryan's character, his justice, his sincerity, his transparent integrity, his Christian principle made a deep impression on all whom he has dealt, but his tact in dealing with men of many sorts, his capacity for business, his mastery of the principles of each matter he has been called upon to deal with, have cleared away many a difficulty and have given to the policy of the State Department a definiteness and dignity that are very admirable.[46]

Bryan supported Wilson's address to Congress, asking for repeal of the exemption. He said, "His message puts the request upon high grounds, and there is no doubt that the public will support him. Our country will not mar the glory of a great enterprise by doing anything that would raise a question as to the nation's honor in its dealings with foreign countries."[47]

The fight for repeal in the House and Senate did not follow party lines. As mentioned before, both Underwood and Clark opposed repeal of the exemption. Throughout most of March 1914, the battle for repeal continued, and as many as thirty-eight speeches were given in a day.[48] Bryan spoke with members of the House urging them to vote for repeal; he also wrote a letter to the House in which he defended repeal on the following grounds:

There is an important distinction between a platform pledge on a domestic question, which is under the control of the country, and a platform pledge of a foreign question where our country must act jointly with others. In this case, no matter what the individual opinion of the Democrats may be; no matter how desirable they may think free tolls to be, they are not at liberty to do just as they please, because they must consider first our treaty obligations, and second the international effect of free tolls.[49]

Bryan's influence helped, and on March 31, 1914, the House approved the Sims bill repealing the exemption clause by a vote of 247-162.[50] The president was overwhelmed by his victory in the House. He wrote: "It will always be deeply gratifying to me to remember how large a number of the members of our party were willing even to change their former votes in this matter in order to support the administration in a matter which had come to wear a new aspect and in which the welfare and honor of the country were involved."[51]

While the House debated repeal, Ambassador Page, not known for his political tact, made a speech in London on March 11, 1914, at a dinner given by the Association of the Chambers of Commerce. He told of the commercial advantages the Panama Canal would present to British trade.[52] When word of this speech reached the American press, Irish-American societies, lobbyists for coastwise shipping against repeal, and dissident senators thought they had found an issue—Page's patronage of the British government—that would turn public opinion against repeal and would result in its defeat.[53] Senator George Chamberlain of Oregon, a bitter opponent of Wilson's repeal, led the Senate in adopting a resolution asking the State Department for complete information on the Page speech.[54] Bryan saw this as a trick to stop action on repeal; he not only sent a copy of the speech to the Senate, but stood firmly behind Page, noting that his speech was "harmless and innocent."[55]

Wilson had won the battle in the House, but the fight in the Senate was much more difficult, as the opponents of repeal here were even more determined to defeat the president. Again, the vote did not follow party lines, since Republicans such as Henry Cabot Lodge and Elihu Root supported the president, while Democrats such as James O'Gorman and Thomas Walsh opposed him.[56] Nor was the battle fought along geographical lines—O'Gorman and Root were from New York, Walsh from Montana, and Lodge from Massachusetts. O'Gorman, to make matters worse for the administration, was the chairman of the Committee on Interoceanic Canals, the committee that had to act on all canal bills before they went to the Senate floor for a final vote. He was Wilson's most vociferous opponent on repeal; he was an Irish-American who was responsive to the many Irish voters who opposed any agreement with England until Ireland was given independence.[57] On April 8, 1914, O'Gorman deliberately delayed action on repeal by deciding to hold fifteen days of open hearings.[58]

During these hearings and the ensuing debate in the Senate, Bryan again used his influence to convince Democrats of Wilson's cause. He admitted that the Democratic platform of 1912 pledged exemption for American coastwise shipping, but the conditions had changed since that time. He maintained that we did not anticipate the hostile reaction of Great Britain and would not have approved exemption if its attitude had been known in 1912. The secretary of state not only justified repeal of exemption, but also attempted to convince Democrats that this was not a surrender to England. He defended the British position and especially their right to arbitrate this matter. He emphasized that the British were morally right, having the Hay-Pauncefote Treaty to sustain their argument for repeal; the surrender-to-England slogan used by Anglophobic senators to criticize tariff reduction did not apply to this situation.[59]

Bryan also used another line of reasoning to arouse Democratic antimonopolists. He asserted that the Democratic party had in the past stood for equal rights to all and privileges to none. But if exemption were not repealed, how could this support of special legislation be reconciled with Democratic party tradition? Bryan was concerned that the acceptance of exemption would set a precedent for the future—a precedent that favored subsidies, bounties, and special privileges. He said: "It must be remembered, too, that our coastwise vessels are largely controlled by a monopoly with the exception of the Pacific coast trade, it was shown that the line traffic is handled by a comparatively few companies and that these are largely controlled by railroads and shipping consolidations."[60]

Bryan also fought those who maintained that exemption of tolls would benefit the American public through lower railroad rates. He said: "The advocates of free tolls argue that the subsidies voted to ships in the coastwise trade will come back to the public through decreased freight rates on the transcontinental. This reduction as a matter of fact is improbable because the water rate is so much below the freight rate that a reduction of $1.25 a ton in the water rate will not compel a reduction in the transcontinental rates."[61]

However, as much as Bryan talked about ending bounties and subsidies by repeal of exemption, he always returned to the morality of the issue. He said, "We occupy today a proud position among the nations: we are the foremost advocate of peace and arbitration; we are becoming more and more a moral factor throughout the world."[62]

Bryan worked with Senator Thomas P. Gore of Oklahoma, another supporter of repeal. Gore had taken a poll in April 1914 of fellow Democrats who attended the Democratic convention of 1912 to determine where they now stood on the tolls issue.[63] The secretary of state published the results of the Gore poll in the Commoner. It showed that of 845 answers received, 682 had favored repeal of the exemption, 124 opposed it, and 38 remained noncommittal.[64]

The fight for repeal continued into May 1914, with William E. Borah, a Republican from Idaho, and a bitter opponent of repeal, drawing up a resolution to delay action in the Senate. Borah wanted the question of repeal brought forth in a referendum to the people; after the referendum, Congress would take up the matter when it convened in December 1914.[65] Bryan opposed both the delay and the referendum. He said that "Those who believe with the President in the repeal of the tolls law should not permit the Borah resolution to delay action for a single moment. We have no provision for the submission of the tolls question or any other question to a vote of the people."[66] Bryan informed Borah that a referendum can only apply "when a definite proposition is submitted to the people for approval or disapproval, as in the case of a constitutional amendment, or a statute."[67]

On June 11, 1914, the Senate, by a vote of 50-35, finally passed the Sims bill repealing the exemption clause in the Panama Canal Act of 1912; four days later, Wilson signed it.[68] He gratefully said:

I do not know of anything I ever undertook with more willingness or zest and I think that we have reason to be proud of the way in which public opinion of the United States responded to the challenge. My own feeling is that the whole country is heartened and reassured by the repeal. I am not so much proud of it as deeply grateful that the country I love should be set in the right light, in the light of its real principles and opinion.[69]

There was an amendment to the bill to satisfy those who feared it would invalidate the Hay-Pauncefote Treaty, which simply reaffirmed the rights of the United States under the treaty.[70] Nonetheless, it was quite evident that Wilson had won a victory, and one of the men most responsible for it was Bryan. The *New York Times* recognized Bryan's contribution as early as April 1914, when it praised his article for repeal in the *Commoner*, noting that he spoke "with authority and long experience" and it would be well if the dissident Democrats listened to him.[71]

In conclusion, William Jennings Bryan equivocated on the Panama Canal tolls question until February 1914. As early as 1910, he had favored free use of the Panama Canal for all nations, but at the 1912 Democratic National Convention, he backed the platform plank embodying support for exemption of American coastwise ships. In April 1913, he asked Wilson, who favored immediate repeal, to wait until he obtained passage of his important domestic legislation, primarily the tariff and banking bills, before dividing the House and Senate over repeal. By January 1914, with the domestic legislation secured, Wilson prepared to undertake repeal; and by March 1914, he presented his repeal message to a joint session of Congress. Bryan supported the president by sending messages to the Congress and by giving sensible reasons for Wilson's stand in the *Commoner*. There was no question that Bryan played a major role in the repeal process.

However, the most important outcome of this victory was its impact upon Anglo-American relations. The British government ratified an agreement to extend the Anglo-American Arbitration Treaty of 1908 on March 11, 1914, only days after Wilson's speech to a joint session of Congress. In September 1914, only a few months after the tolls fight, the British ambassador in Washington demonstrated his government's good will toward the United States by joining the secretary of state in signing a conciliation treaty. This occurred only one month after the beginning of World War I, and it showed that the two great democracies were determined to live in peace and friendship.

NOTES

1. J. Fred Rippy, *Latin America in World Politics* (New York: F. S. Crofts and Company, 1931), p. 100.

2. Dumas Malone and Basil Rauch, *Crisis of the Union, 1841-1877*, vol. 3 (New York: Appleton-Century-Crofts, 1960), p. 103.

3. Rippy, *Latin America in World Politics*, p. 101.

4. Ibid., p. 109.

5. Samuel Flagg Bemis, *The Latin American Policy of the United States* (New York: Harcourt, Brace and Company, 1943), pp. 144-145.

6. Ibid.

7. Burton J. Hendrick, *The Life and Letters of Walter H. Page*, vol. 1 (Garden City, New York: Doubleday, Page and Company, 1922), p. 241.

8. *Commoner*, March 11, 1910.

9. Ibid.

10. Hendrick, *The Life and Letters of Walter H. Page*, p. 242; Ray Stannard Baker, *Woodrow Wilson: Life and Letters*, vol. 4 (Garden City, New York: Doubleday, Page and Company, 1927), pp. 395-396.

11. Baker, *Woodrow Wilson: Life and Letters*, pp. 395-396.

12. Arthur S. Link, *Wilson: The New Freedom* (Princeton, New Jersey: Princeton University Press, 1956), p. 304.

13. Ibid., p. 305.

14. *New York Times*, July 3, 1912.

15. Ibid.; Baker, *Woodrow Wilson: Life and Letters*, p. 396; Paxton Hibben, *The Peerless Leader William Jennings Bryan* (New York: Russell and Russell, 1967), p. 333.

16. E. David Cronon, ed., *The Cabinet Diaries of Josephus Daniels, 1913-1921* (Lincoln, NE: University of Nebraska Press, 1963), p. 44.

17. Baker, *Woodrow Wilson: Life and Letters*, pp. 395-396; Secretary of State to the American Chargé d'Affaires, January 17, 1913, *Papers Relating to the Foreign Relations of the United States, 1913* (Washington, D.C.: U.S. Government Printing Office, 1920), pp. 540-547.

18. British Ambassador to the Secretary of State, February 27, 1913, *Foreign Relations, 1913*, pp. 547-549; Link, *Wilson: The New Freedom*, p. 305.

19. *New York World*, December 11, 1912.

20. William S. Coker, "The Panama Canal Tolls Controversy: A Different Perspective," *Journal of American History* 55 (December 1968), 558; Cronon, *Cabinet Diaries of Josephus Daniels*, p. 36; Edward S. Kaplan, "William Jennings Bryan and the Panama Canal Tolls Controversy," *Mid-America: An Historical Review* 56 (April 1974): 103.

21. *New York Times*, May 11, 1913.

22. Coker, "The Panama Canal Tolls Controversy," pp. 556-557; Link, *Wilson: The New Freedom*, p. 306.

23. Link, *Wilson: The New Freedom*, p. 306; David F. Houston, *Eight Years with Wilson Cabinet, 1913-1920*, vol. 1 (Garden City, N.Y.: Doubleday, Page and Company, 1926), p. 59; Cronon, *Cabinet Diaries of Josephus Daniels*, p. 36.

24. Cronon, *Cabinet Diaries of Josephus Daniels*, pp. 44-45.

25. Ibid., p. 36; Houston, *Eight Years with Wilson's Cabinet*, p. 59.

26. Cronon, *Cabinet Diaries of Josephus Daniels*, p. 45.

27. Houston, *Eight Years with Wilson's Cabinet*, p. 59.

28. Bryan to Wilson, June 12, 1913, Bryan-Wilson Correspondence, National Archives.

29. Cronon, *Cabinet Diaries of Josephus Daniels*, p. 45; Coker, "The Panama Canal Tolls Controversy," p. 559.

30. Coker, "The Panama Canal Tolls Controversy," p. 559.

31. Bryan to Wilson, June 12, 1913, Bryan-Wilson Correspondence, National Archives.

32. Ibid.

33. Wilson to Bryan, June 13, 1913, Bryan-Wilson Correspondence, National Archives.

34. Coker, "The Panama Canal Tolls Controversy," pp. 555-564; Link, *Wilson: The New Freedom*, pp. 304-314.

35. Houston, *Eight Years with Wilson's Cabinet*, p. 59; Cronon, *Cabinet Diaries of Josephus Daniels*, pp. 44-45.

36. Link, *Wilson: The New Freedom*, p. 307.

37. Houston, *Eight Years with Wilson's Cabinet*, p. 74.

38. Coker, "The Panama Canal Tolls Controversy," p. 561; Link, *Wilson: The New Freedom*, p. 314.

39. Link, *Wilson: The New Freedom*, p. 307.

40. Ibid., pp. 307-308.

41. Ibid., p. 308.

42. Ibid., p. 310.

43. *New York Times*, February 6, 1914; Address of the President delivered at a joint session of the two Houses of Congress, March 5, 1914, *Papers Relating to the Foreign Relations of the United States, 1914* (Washington, D.C.: U.S. Government Printing Office, 1922), p. 317.

44. Link, *Wilson: The New Freedom*, pp. 310-311.

45. *Commoner*, February 1914.

46. Woodrow Wilson to William L. Marbury, as quoted, Ibid.

47. *Commoner*, March 1914.

48. Baker, *Woodrow Wilson: Life and Letters*, p. 414.

49. *New York Times*, March 28, 1914.

50. *Congressional Record*, 63 Cong., 2 sess., 1914, LI, pt. 6, pp. 6087-6089.

51. Link, *Wilson: The New Freedom*, p. 312.

52. *New York Times*, March 13 and March 26, 1914.

53. Link, *Wilson: The New Freedom*, p. 311; *New York Times*, March 13, 1914.

54. Ibid.

55. Ibid., March 25, 1914.

56. Baker, *Woodrow Wilson: Life and Letters*, p. 417.

57. *New York Times*, April 8, 1914; Link, *Wilson: The New Freedom*, pp. 312-313.

58. *New York Times*, April 8, 1914.

59. *Commoner* April, 1914.

60. Ibid.

61. Ibid.

62. Ibid.

63. *New York Times*, April 13, 1914.

64. *Commoner*, May 1914.

65. Ibid.

66. Ibid.

67. Ibid.

68. *Congressional Record*, 63 Cong., 2 sess., 1914, LI, pt. 10, pp. 10247-10248; Baker, *Woodrow Wilson: Life and Letters*, p. 418.

69. Woodrow Wilson to James Bryce, July 6, 1914, Wilson Papers, Library of Congress.

70. *Congressional Record*, 63 Cong., 2 sess., 1914, LI, pt. 10, pp. 10247-10248; *New York Times*, June 12, 1914; Link, *Wilson: The New Freedom*, p. 314.

71. *New York Times*, April 14, 1914.

9

The Colombian Treaty

In his negotiations to secure redress for the Colombian government for the treatment it received from the Roosevelt administration during the Panama revolution, William Jennings Bryan attempted to end the strained relations between the two countries, promote an atmosphere of goodwill, and set a pattern for future U.S.-Latin American relations. He had long been convinced that the Roosevelt administration had acted rashly and wrongly in this matter.[1]

ROOSEVELT AND THE PANAMA CANAL

On February 22, 1902, the United States and Great Britain signed the Hay-Pauncefote Treaty permitting the American government to build and fortify an isthmian canal without British interference. Now there were other problems to overcome before the canal could be built. One was the acquisition of a suitable site, and another was the cost of the project. The Walker Isthmian Canal Commission, formed in 1899, reported that both Nicaragua and Panama were suitable sites for the new venture.[2] At first, Nicaragua was favored because it was nearer the United States, health and sanitary conditions were somewhat better, and the dam construction would be easier.[3] However, Panama also had advantages; for instance, the canal would be 134 miles shorter, and it would have fewer locks and curves. Labor was also more accessible in Panama and work could begin a year sooner.[4] The estimated cost of construction was less in Panama, $144,233,358, as compared to $189,864,062 in Nicaragua.[5]

On June 25, 1902, Congress passed the Spooner Act, which called for the construction of a canal through Nicaragua unless the French New Panama Canal Company would sell its concession to the United States.[6] The concession had been transferred to the French company after Ferdinand de Lesseps and his group had gone bankrupt in 1889. (He was the French engineer who had built the Suez

Canal from 1859 to 1869). However, the French company had been unable to complete work on the canal project due to its own financial difficulties and great loss of manpower suffered from yellow fever.[7] As early as 1896, it had hired William Nelson Cromwell, an American counsel, to convince the U.S. government of the benefits of the Panama route. The French company wanted to sell out at a good price.[8]

A campaign of intense lobbying began, with both Cromwell and Philippe Bunau-Varilla, a stockholder in the French company, putting increasing pressure on the American congress and the State Department on behalf of the Panama site.[9] They frightened members of Congress by distributing Nicaraguan postage stamps depicting smoking volcanoes; two weeks before the vote on the Spooner Act, Mont Pélee in Martinique and La Soufrière on St. Vincent erupted (the Pélee blast was so powerful that it exploded the entire island). This awakened the American public and Congress to the dangers of volcanoes and might have been the deciding factor in favor of the Panama site.[10]

Although negotiations with the French company had proven successful (the American government had paid the French company $40 million for the canal concession), a new treaty would have to be drawn up with Colombia, who owned the Panamanian isthmus. The last treaty of 1846 gave the United States the right of free transit, and in return, Colombia retained its sovereignty over any future canal site. This treaty did not give the United States authority to build a canal.[11]

Although Colombia's consent was needed for the transfer of the French company's concession to the United States, the Colombian government refused to consider the transaction. A civil war had broken out in 1899 between the liberals and conservatives for control of the government, and the conflict was still going on in 1902.[12] Nonetheless, negotiations began in Washington toward the end of 1902 between Tomás Herrán, the Colombian chargé d'affaires, and Secretary of State John Hay, and on January 22, 1903, they signed the Hay-Herrán Treaty. It provided that Colombia would receive $10 million and an annual payment of $250,000. In return the United States gained control over the six-mile wide canal zone for a 100 years, a privilege renewable at the "sole and absolute option" of the North American republic. It also gave the United States the right to construct and fortify the canal.[13] This treaty was approved by the U.S. Senate in March 1903, but the Colombian government, although genuinely desiring American construction of a canal, moved very slowly. Faced with a treasury drained by a long and costly civil war, opposition mounted in the new Colombian congress, as opponents of the Hay-Herrán Treaty wanted more money. The United States had paid $40 million to the French company for the concession, and Colombia now wanted the French company to pay it for the right of transferring that concession to the United States. In June 1903, the Colombian government asked for $10 million from the French company and $15 million from the United States. When the United States refused to consider this request, the Colombian senate rejected the Hay-Herrán Treaty in August 1903.[14]

When negotiations failed, President Theodore Roosevelt became indignant at the Colombian senate. In a conversation with Hay, he blamed them for holding up the entire canal project. He said that "those contemptible little creatures in Bogotá ought to understand how much they are jeopardizing things and imperiling their own future."[15] Roosevelt came to believe that "you could no more make an agreement with the Colombian rulers than you could nail currant jelly to the wall."[16] The president now began looking for the fastest solution to the canal problem. On June 13, 1903, Cromwell met with the president, and shortly afterwards, the lawyer planted a story in the *New York World* stating that, if Colombia rejected the treaty, Panama would secede and grant the United States "the equivalent of absolute sovereignty over the Canal Zone."[17]

By October 1903, Roosevelt decided upon seizure of the Isthmus; he related that the Treaty of 1846 was drawn up for the specific purpose of obtaining a canal and if Colombia would not consent, then the United States had the right to take action.[18] At the same time, Cromwell and Bunau-Varilla were in touch with dissident Panamanians who were anxious to break away from Colombia. Bunau-Varilla was particularly active in fomenting trouble in this area. How much association Roosevelt had with the rebels remains uncertain; however, it was known that the president wanted to build a canal there and was tired of the futile attempts to convince Colombia of the merits of the Hay-Herrán Treaty.[19]

When the Panama revolution began in late October 1903, there were about 300,000 people living in the region. Though there had been revolts before 1903, the people were not nationalists striving for their freedom but regionalists who rebelled for a number of different reasons. National feeling did not exist among the numerous immigrants who lived there, many of them blacks from the West Indies.[20]

When word of the revolt reached Colombia, troops were ordered to suppress it. If its troops had succeeded in landing and crossing the Isthmus, the revolution would have probably failed. It so happened that American warships were present in the area with orders to "maintain free and uninterrupted transit." Interruption meant the landing of Colombia's troops and their crossing the isthmus by railroad. The *Nashville*, an American cruiser, prohibited Colombia's troops from sailing to the isthmus on November 3, 1903, and the revolution succeeded. The United States recognized the New Republic of Panama only three days later on November 6, 1903, and signed a treaty with its representative, Bunau-Varilla.[21]

Roosevelt, in his annual message to Congress after the Panamanian revolution, urged swift ratification of the Hay-Bunau-Varilla Treaty. He told Congress that the canal project would benefit the United States as well as the rest of mankind. When Senate Democrats had the audacity to ask the president what role he played in the revolution, he answered that "no one connected with this Government had any part in preparing, inciting, or encouraging the late revolution."[22] The Senate, obviously satisfied with Roosevelt's reply, ratified the treaty on February 23, 1904, by a vote of sixty-six to fourteen.[23] Seven years later in 1911, Roosevelt reportedly boasted that "I took the Canal Zone and let Congress debate; and while the debate goes on the Canal does also."[24]

Construction of the canal began in 1904, and it was finally opened for traffic on August 15, 1914. There was little question that there was a need for a canal and that its creation was a great feat of the United States. However, the methods used by Roosevelt to accomplish his task will always remain controversial. William Harbaugh, a Roosevelt historian, declared that his handling of the Panama Canal issue constituted "one of the ineradicable blots on his record."[25]

From 1903 until 1913, when the Wilson administration came to power, Colombian-American relations were at their lowest point. There were some attempts by the Taft administration to reconcile these differences through a series of treaties. In January 1909, the Root-Cortés-Arosemena treaties were drawn up. They were all separate and independent of one another. One was between the United States and Colombia, another between Panama and the United States, and a third between Colombia and Panama.[26] The Colombian senate refused to ratify the treaties with Panama and the United States because public opinion in Colombia was hostile toward the United States. Any attempt at reconciliation could foment a new revolution in Colombia.[27] Instead, Colombia's foreign minister, Francisco José Urrutia, asked either for arbitration of the whole Panama question or a direct proposition from the United States to compensate Colombia for all its losses suffered from the separation of Panama in 1903. The Taft administration refused to consider these suggestions; it would amount to an approval of Colombia's position in 1903 and reflect badly on the Roosevelt administration.[28]

In February 1913, one month before the Wilson administration assumed power, Taft and Knox made one last attempt to reach an agreement with Colombia. They instructed the American minister to Colombia, James T. Du Bois, to hold preliminary conferences with the Colombian government to discuss (1) the completion of the Root-Cortés and Cortés Arosemena treaties; (2) the construction of a canal over the Atrato route and the privilege of coaling stations on the islands of San Andreas and Providencia for payment to Colombia of $10 million; (3) the settlement of the boundary dispute between Panama and Colombia; (4) the arbitration for material claims of Colombia regarding the reversionary rights in the Panama Railroad; and (5) preferential rights for Colombia on the Panama Canal.[29] Du Bois was also instructed to offer a proposal that went further than any preceding one. The United States would "honestly regret anything should ever have occurred" to interrupt U.S.-Colombian relations.[30] This paper was known as the "Du Bois memorandum," and it became the basis for Bryan's negotiations with Colombia in 1913.

The Du Bois offer of February 1913 was rejected by the Colombian government, and the reason given was that it did not go far enough to meet the demands of Colombian public opinion. However, there was little question that the Colombian government also hoped to secure better terms from the new Democratic Wilson administration.[31]

BRYAN AND THE COLOMBIAN TREATY

In May 1913, only two months after Bryan took office, Colombia's minister to the United States, Julio Betancourt, informed the new secretary of state that all differences between Colombia and the United States emanating from the Panama revolution of 1903 should be submitted to the Hague Tribunal for arbitration. He believed this was the only way Colombia would secure redress.[32]

Bryan thought Colombia had just grievances against the Roosevelt administration. During the 1903 incident, he not only opposed Roosevelt's use of the U.S. Navy to prevent Colombia's soldiers from quelling the uprising, but also criticized Roosevelt's instant recognition of the new Republic of Panama.[33] However, Bryan opposed arbitration; he believed that direct negotiations between the two countries offered the best solution for settlement.[34]

In July 1913, Bryan began his campaign to repair U.S.-Colombian relations. He had Betancourt present Colombia's side of the case and received information from James Du Bois upon his return to the United States.[35] He then told Betancourt that the United States would use its full resources to satisfy Colombia's grievances and to restore friendly relations between the two countries. He said: "Our nation has its own honor at stake in all matters which involve fair dealing toward other nations, and I speak for the President and, I am sure for the whole people, as well as for myself, when I express the earnest desire that we may be able to remove every obstacle that stands in the way of perfect confidence and free intercourse between the two nations."[36]

The Colombian government responded favorably to the idea of direct negotiations between the two countries, and Bryan immediately sent a note of instructions to the new American minister in Bogotá Thaddeus A. Thompson. The note written, by Wilson, said: "The Government and people of the United States sincerely desire that everything that may have marred or seemed to interrupt the close and long established friendship between the United States and the Republic of Colombia should be cleared away and forgotten."[37] Bryan then wrote Wilson that he had authorized Thompson to make an offer of $15 million for payment of all reparations. However, he told Wilson that this should be only the first offer, and that he was willing to go as high as $25 million, but that he was waiting for the Colombian government to make a counter proposal. The secretary of state also sent an expression of regret along with the monetary payment, declaring that the American government felt badly about what had occurred during the Roosevelt administration that strained relations between Colombia and the United States.[38]

Colombia rejected the $15 million offer, and Bryan, on September 29, 1913, made a new offer of $20 million, in settlement of all claims, including those claims the Colombian government held against Panama.[39] On October 23, Colombia made its first counteroffer. It not only wanted a $50 million indemnity and free access to the Panama Canal under all circumstances, but also a sincere apology from the United States for the events of 1903.[40]

When Bryan received this counterproposal, he informed Minister Thompson that it was unacceptable. The cash stipend of $50 million was much too high, and he would not make a formal apology. Bryan told Thompson to make one last offer of $25 million along with an expression of "sincere regret."[41]

Dr. Francisco José Urrutia, Colombia's foreign minister, had no intention at this time of accepting the $25 million. In the last days of October 1913, he sent Bryan a memorandum requesting the $50 million, showing him how he arrived at the figure. Urrutia claimed that Colombia had not only renounced its right to sixty-six annuities of $250,000 in the Panama railway, but also its exclusive ownership. Colombia had ceded the right to ninety-nine payments of $250,000, according to the terms of the canal contract and was forced to yield Panama, its richest province.[42]

Negotiations continued throughout 1913 and into 1914 with neither side yielding. Bryan, in January 1914, informed Urrutia that an apology for the incident of 1903 could not be included in a treaty without endangering its ratification. He reminded Urrutia that a treaty needed the approval of two-thirds of the U.S. Senate.[43] Two months later, Bryan again made his $25 million offer, averring that he would not go any higher. The Colombian government, in the meantime, had reduced its demand of $50 million to $30 million, realizing the impossibility of securing the larger amount. Betancourt, on three different occasions in March, attempted to sway Bryan into accepting the $30 million, but the secretary of state refused to yield.[44] Finally, on March 31, 1914, Colombia agreed to accept the $25 million with the following conditions. The United States, after exchanging ratifications of the treaty with Colombia, must agree to get Panama to negotiate and conclude a treaty with Colombia, settling all disputes between the two countries. Since this presented no problem for Bryan, he quickly agreed, and even offered his services in bringing the two countries together.[45]

On April 6, 1914, the Thompson-Urrutia Treaty, better known as the Colombian treaty, was signed in Bogotá. The first article became the most controversial; it read as follows:

The Government of the United States of America, wishing to put at rest all controversies and differences with the Republic of Colombia arising out of the events from which the present situation on the Isthmus of Panama resulted, expresses, in its own name and in the name of the people of the United States, sincere regret that anything should have occurred to interrupt or to mar the relations of cordial friendship that had so long subsisted between the two nations.[46]

Wilson historian Arthur S. Link pointed to this episode as the one shining example in which Wilson and Bryan acted "honorably in foreign affairs even when it hurt."[47] It was satisfying throughout Latin America to see this great power almost apologizing to the helpless government of Colombia. More than any other act, the signing of this treaty made the United States look good in the eyes of Latin America.[48]

Many supporters of Roosevelt believed that the Wilson administration signed this treaty to embarrass Roosevelt. There was no evidence in any of the Bryan-

Wilson correspondence that this was true. On the other hand, we have evidence in Wilson's own writing that he was sincerely trying to correct an injustice. The president wrote: "My personal interest in that treaty has been of the deepest and most sincere sort. I believe that it constitutes a just and honorable understanding between two friendly peoples. The more the matter is studied the more evident it becomes that such a treaty is based upon equity and is the natural outcome of genuine friendship between the two countries."[49]

Though the first clause of the treaty just quoted was not an apology, it, nonetheless, turned numerous Roosevelt supporters in the Senate, including the former president himself, against the treaty and caused great delay, as we shall see later. The remainder of the treaty stated the rights of Colombia in the Panama Canal, called for the payment of $25 million to Colombia within six months after the exchange of ratifications (the Roosevelt supporters also opposed this in no uncertain terms), and called for recognition of Panama by Colombia, and the settlement of all outstanding disputes between those two countries.[50]

Though the treaty was signed April 6, 1914, Bryan refused to make it public until the Colombian congress acted upon it. He did state, however, that the treaty could not, in good faith, be rejected by either the Colombian congress or the U.S. Senate.[51] His optimism in the first instance proved correct, for on June 6, 1914, the Colombian house accepted it by five to one and the Colombian senate by three to one.[52]

When Bryan heard of the ratification by the Colombian congress, he was overjoyed. He now prepared to send the treaty to the U. S. Senate. He wrote the president on June 12, justifying the $25 million given to Colombia in the treaty and at the same time assuring him that the treaty should be ratified without much opposition. He said: "We could not have reasonably offered less, in view of the expectations that were aroused. While this sum was not offered by the Taft administration, it was so nearly offered that it amounts to the same thing, and the regular Republicans ought to assist us in ratifying the treaty."[53] Bryan believed that the Progressive Republicans would present the largest obstacle to the ratification, since they were ardent supporters of Roosevelt. However, not all the Progressive Republicans had supported Roosevelt's Panamanian policy, and Bryan hoped that he would be able to divide the Progressive vote.[54] In fact, Bryan was so optimistic about instant ratification that he urged Wilson to send the treaty to the Senate immediately. On June 16, 1914, Wilson sent the treaty to the Senate Foreign Relations Committee where proceedings began.[55]

Bryan's optimism was, to say the least, premature and unwarranted. Wilson's friend George L. Record perhaps best understood the difficulty the treaty would encounter in securing ratification. He wrote the following to Wilson several weeks before the treaty was submitted to the Senate Foreign Relations Committee.

The campaign this fall will turn upon a general attack on your policies. I have not found anybody who approves of the proposition to either apologize or pay money to Colombia on account of the Canal matter. I wish to drive home merely the political point that five out of six men disapprove of this treaty. The Canal has been such a tremendous achievement that the public are in no mood to criticize Roosevelt for any short-cut methods that he chose to adopt in getting the Canal started. The difficulty you will have will be that a lot of people will, rightly or wrongly, assume that the Colombian treaty arises out of a mean and small desire on the part of Bryan to slap at Roosevelt.[56]

Newspapers also took sides in this controversy. The *New York World* was the leading proponent of the treaty, while the *Washington Post* became its chief opponent. The *World* ran a series of articles from July 5 through July 12, 1914, attempting to prove that the United States was in the wrong in its relationship with Colombia.[57] Opposition also came from the British government, which disliked the idea that the Colombian merchant marine would receive privileges on the canal.[58]

On June 17, 1914, Bryan appeared before the Senate Foreign Relations Committee to defend the treaty. He told the committee members that the expression of "sincere regret" came from the Du Bois memorandum of the Taft administration; he also declared that the treaty was necessary to restore good feelings between Colombia and the United States and to alleviate the anxieties of all Latin America that such an incident as occurred in Panama in 1903 would not happen elsewhere.[59]

Notwithstanding Bryan's eloquent speech, the committee decided not to take precipitate action but instead to hold a lengthy investigation into the facts relating to the establishment of the Republic of Panama and the acquisition of the Canal Zone. They also wanted information on how Colombia proposed to use the $25 million. Opponents of the treaty, such as Henry Cabot Lodge of Massachusetts, William Borah of Idaho, and Albert Fall of New Mexico, all members of the Senate Foreign Relations Committee, believed that it would be spent on arms for war with neighboring countries, though the Colombian government denied this.[60]

Bryan defended the treaty by stressing that Article One containing the expression of "sincere regret" was formulated by the Republican Taft administration in February 1913; the $25 million was not an excessive amount to pay for the restoration of friendly relations with Colombia; all of Latin America would judge the United States by its action in this matter.[61] Lodge and other dissidents of the treaty admitted that Du Bois had written the expression of "sincere regret" but denied that it had been sent to the Colombian government. Bryan, on the other hand, claimed that Colombia had received this.[62]

On June 25, 1914, Roosevelt attacked the Wilson administration in a 2,000 word statement. He called the proposed payment of $25 million, with the expression of "sincere regret," as "the belated payment of blackmail with an apology to the blackmailers." He criticized sharply Bryan's handling of the Colombian situation and added that the secretary of state was making the United States the "laughing stock" of world politics.[63] Bryan did not comment on Roosevelt's statement; he would not, at this time, enter a public controversy but would relate anything that had to be said to the Senate Foreign Relations Committee.[64]

On June 27, 1914, James Du Bois testified before the committee. He admitted that he had given the note of regret to Colombia but that it had been sent on his own initiative. He pointed out that it became part of the informal negotiations to get Colombia to reach an agreement.[65]

On June 28, Francis B. Loomis, former assistant secretary of state under Roosevelt from 1902 to 1905, excoriated Bryan's treaty at a committee hearing. He said:

Bryan's Colombian treaty is a covert attempt to loot the United States Treasury by lobbyists and political brigands into whose hands the Secretary of State is playing. Bryan and the President are trying to besmirch and discredit one achievement of the previous administration, which made the canal a reality. The treaty is one of the most stupendous blunders made by Bryan who is running wild with his world peace theories. The United States owes Colombia nothing either by treaty or otherwise.[66]

Beginning in July 1914, proponents of the treaty, including Bryan, came to its defense. On July 13, Francisco Escobar, the consul general of Colombia to the United States, wrote an article in the *Independent*, an American weekly periodical, insisting that only by ratification of this treaty could American friendship be restored throughout Latin America. He emphasized that all of Latin America waited upon the United States to show its goodwill in this matter.[67]

On July 9, 1914, the *Nation*, a supporter of the treaty, berated Roosevelt for his statement of June 25, calling the $25 million payment to Colombia "blackmail." It contended that Roosevelt's former secretary of state, Elihu Root, though he thought that $25 million was too high, believed that some payment should be made. Root felt that Roosevelt's offer of $2.5 million, made shortly after the incident of 1903, was sufficient compensation.[68]

Bryan tried to save the treaty by making an eloquent appeal on July 12, 1914. In a formal statement to the press, he argued that the United States was "big enough and generous enough to accord Colombia the expression of regret."[69] He spoke about the previous split between Colombia and the United States, stemming from the 1903 incident, and hoped that ratification of the treaty would restore friendly relations between the two countries. He said: "As normal relations between nations is one of friendship, it is desirable that differences shall be adjusted and cordial relations resumed. It is not necessary to discuss the events which gave rise to this estrangement, because it does not matter which party was at fault. The estrangement exists, and this is the fact that must be dealt with."[70] Bryan declared that the United States had refused Colombia arbitration and therefore owed Colombia some satisfaction. He said:

Our Nation, being much the larger nation, and having refused to arbitrate, takes upon itself the responsibility of doing justice to Colombia. Not only is it our duty to do justice to Colombia, but in case of doubt as to what is just, we must reserve that doubt against ourselves and in favor of Colombia. Colombia feels that she has been aggrieved, and whatever may be said as to whether or not this feeling is justified, no one will deny that she has sustained great financial loss in the separation of Panama from her.[71]

Two weeks later, Bryan publicly criticized Loomis, Lodge, Borah, and others who maintained that the United States was not responsible for the events that led to the independence of Panama in 1903. He insisted that a detailed account of these events should not be taken into consideration for the justification of the treaty. The treaty should be ratified to show our goodwill toward Colombia and to restore friendly relations for the future. The United States would benefit from the Panama Canal and should pay the $25 million to Colombia "no matter what the facts."[72]

Though the proponents of the treaty worked hard for its ratification, the Senate Foreign Relations Committee delayed action until it heard from numerous witnesses. In August 1914, Minister Thompson wrote Bryan that Colombia desperately needed the $25 million due to financial difficulties. The government deficit was $3 million and the treasury was almost empty. Thompson wanted Bryan to push harder for ratification, or if the delay continued, he hoped the secretary of state would attempt to amend the treaty, so as to make payments by installment.[73] Bryan informed Thompson that he had nothing new to report; the treaty had been referred to a Senate subcommittee, and hearing would continue to delay action. He promised to study the idea of payments by installment (the treaty, as it stood, called for the entire payment of the $25 million six months after exchange of ratifications) and might favor such a plan if he could find enough support for it.[74]

However, Bryan was unable to get the treaty by the Senate Foreign Relations Committee in any form—the $25 million, whether it was paid in installments or at one time, was considered excessive, and the expression of "sincere regret" was demanding. By December 1914, Bryan became very pessimistic. He wrote Wilson in December asking him to put pressure on the Senate; the president agreed to do what he could but made no promises or concrete proposals.[75]

In January 1915, Bryan, once more, appeared before the Senate Foreign Relations Committee and urged ratification of the Colombian treaty. He warned that if the United States failed to act, trade relations with South America would be affected, and there was also a good chance that Colombia would refuse to participate in the upcoming Panama Exposition.[76] But Bryan's request, once again, proved unsuccessful. The treaty was sent to a Senate subcommittee made up of five members that would study it and make recommendations for revision.[77]

In January 1915, Bryan also became very sensitive to Colombian public opinion; he read the Colombian press and kept important clippings. For example, El Nuevo Tiempo, on January 21, 1915, criticized the long delay of the Colombian treaty in the Senate. It claimed that the $25 million was the least that could be accepted; it argued that if the treaty, in its original form, was amended, it should be rejected by the Colombian government.[78] La Tribuna, another Colombian paper, was of the same opinion; it opposed any amendment to the Colombian treaty. It said: "Let us wait, and let our waiting attitude be serene; and let our own effort constitute the basis of our redemption, that by the paths of order and honest labor, we may reach the position where we may stand face to face, without having to bow, as we have to at present, before the compelling imposition of this Uncle Sam, of Punic faith, with muscles of gold and of steel."[79]

In February 1915, Bryan pleaded with Senator William J. Stone, chairman of the Senate Foreign Relations Committee and a fellow Democrat, to use his influence in obtaining approval of the Colombian treaty. Stone, a supporter of the treaty, told Bryan that it was impossible to expect ratification during the remainder of the session—he hoped to get it approved next session.[80] With this information at hand, Bryan informed the Colombian government on March 4, 1915, that action on the treaty would have to wait, but that chances of its passage were good.[81] Bryan now waited anxiously for Colombian public reaction. On March 19, 1915, the chargé d'affaires to Colombia, Leland Harrison, wrote the secretary of state that his March 4 explanation on the treaty had been printed in *El Nuevo Tiempo* and it caused a favorable impression on the people.[82]

Bryan resigned from the State Department in June 1915 with the Colombian treaty still pending. Nonetheless, he continued to work as a private citizen for its ratification. We shall discuss the ratification of the Colombian treaty and Bryan's role in chapter 10.

In conclusion, Bryan was convinced that the United States should give redress to Colombia for its loss of Panama in 1903. As secretary of state, he began negotiations with Colombia in July 1913, which culminated in the signing of the Colombian treaty in April 1914. From June 1914 to his resignation, one year later, he worked arduously to get the Senate to ratify the treaty. Though his efforts, as secretary of state, proved unsuccessful, he continued his work for ratification as a private citizen.

NOTES

1. *Commoner*, November 20, 1903.

2. Dana G. Munro, *Intervention and Dollar Diplomacy in the Caribbean, 1900-1917* (Princeton, N.J.: Princeton University Press, 1964), p. 39.

3. Ibid.

4. Ibid.

5. Ibid.

6. Samuel Flagg Bemis, *The Latin American Policy of the United States* (New York: Harcourt, Brace and Company, 1943), p. 148.

7. Munro, *Intervention and Dollar Diplomacy in the Caribbean*, p. 39.

8. Ibid.

9. Ibid., p. 42.

10. Ibid.

11. Ibid.

12. Ibid.

13. Ibid., p. 45; Bemis, *The Latin American Policy of the United States*, p. 149.

14. Munro, *Intervention and Dollar Diplomacy in the Caribbean*, pp. 48-49; Bemis, *The Latin American Policy of the United States*, p. 150.

15. Henry F. Pringle, *Theodore Roosevelt* (New York: Harcourt, Brace and Company, 1931), p. 311.

16. Howard K. Beale, *Theodore Roosevelt and the Rise of America to World Power* (Baltimore, MD: John Hopkins University Press, 1956), p. 33.

17. *New York World*, June 14, 1903.

18. Munro, *Intervention and Dollar Diplomacy in the Caribbean*, p. 50.

19. Ibid., pp. 52-53.

20. John Edwin Fagg, *Latin America: A General History* (New York: Macmillan, 1977), p. 619.

21. Munro, *Intervention and Dollar Diplomacy in the Caribbean*, pp. 53-54.

22. James D. Richardson, ed., *A Compilation of the Messages and Papers of the Presidents, 1789-1915*, vol. 9 (Washington, D.C.: U.S. Government Printing Office, 1916), pp. 6919-6923.

23. Walter LaFeber, *The Panama Canal* (New York: Oxford University Press, 1978), p. 38.

24. *New York Times*, March 25, 1911.

25. William H. Harbaugh, *The Life and Times of Theodore Roosevelt* (New York: Oxford University Press, 1975), p. 197.

26. Paolo Coletta, "William Jennings Bryan and the United States-Colombia Impasse, 1903-1921," *Hispanic American Historical Review* 47 (November 1967): 487-488.

27. Ibid., p. 489.

28. Ibid.

29. American Minister to the Secretary of State, February 5, 1913, *Papers Relating to the Foreign Relations of the United States, 1913* (Washington, D.C.: U.S. Government Printing Office, 1920), pp. 287-294.

30. Chester Lloyd Jones, *The Caribbean since 1900* (New York: Russell and Russell, 1970), p. 326; American Minister to the Secretary of State, February 5, 1913, *Foreign Relations, 1913*, pp. 287-294.

31. Jones, *The Caribbean since 1900*, pp. 326-327.

32. Minister of Colombia to the Secretary of State, May 3, 1913, *Foreign Relations, 1913*, pp. 309-316.

33. *Commoner*, November 20, 1903.

34. Secretary of State to the Minister of Colombia, July 18, 1913, *Foreign Relations, 1913*, p. 316.

35. Coletta, "William Jennings Bryan and the United States-Colombia Impasse," p. 490.

36. Ibid.; Secretary of State to the Minister of Colombia, July 18, 1913, *Foreign Relations, 1913*, p. 316.

37. Arthur S. Link, *Wilson: The New Freedom* (Princeton, N.J.: Princeton University Press, 1956), p. 321.

38. Bryan to Wilson, September 15, 1913, Bryan-Wilson Correspondence, National Archives; Coletta, "William Jennings Bryan and the United States-Colombia Impasse," p. 490.

39. Secretary of State to the American Minister, September 29, 1913, *Foreign Relations, 1913*, p. 321; American Minister to the Secretary of State, October 8, 1913, *Foreign Relations, 1913*, pp. 321-322.

40. American Minister to the Secretary of State, October 23, 1913, *Foreign Relations, 1913*, pp. 323-325.

41. Coletta, "William Jennings Bryan and the United States-Colombia Impasse," p. 492.

42. American Minister to the Secretary of State, October 25, 1913, *Foreign Relations, 1913*, pp. 325-327.

43. Coletta, "William Jennings Bryan and the United States-Colombia Impasse," p. 492.

44. American Minister to the Secretary of State, March 24, 1914, *Papers Relating to the Foreign Relations of the United States, 1914* (Washington, D.C.: U.S. Government Printing Office, 1922), pp. 152-153; Secretary of State to the American Minister, March 27, 1914, *Foreign Relations, 1914*, p. 153; Coletta, "William Jennings Bryan and the United States-Colombia Impasse," p. 493.

45. American Minister to the Secretary of State, March 31, 1914, *Foreign Relations, 1914*, pp. 153-154; Secretary of State to the American Minister, April 2, 1914, *Foreign Relations, 1914*, p. 154.

46. American Minister to the Secretary of State, April 6, 1914, *Foreign Relations, 1914*, pp. 154-155; Copy of the treaty between the United States and Colombia, June 16, 1914, *Foreign Relations, 1914*, pp. 163-164.

47. Link, *Wilson: The New Freedom*, p. 322.

48. Ibid.

49. Ibid.

50. Copy of the treaty between the United States and Colombia, June 16, 1914, *Foreign Relations, 1914*, pp. 163-164.

51. *Commoner*, May 1914.

52. Coletta, "William Jennings Bryan and the United States-Colombia Impasse," p. 493.

53. Bryan to Wilson, June 12, 1914, Bryan-Wilson Correspondence, National Archives.

54. Ibid; Coletta, "William Jennings Bryan the United States-Colombia Impasse," pp. 493-494.

55. Bryan to Wilson, June 12, 1914, Bryan-Wilson Correspondence, National Archives.

56. Coletta, "William Jennings Bryan and the United States-Colombia Impasse," p. 494.

57. Ibid.

58. Ibid.

59. *New York Times*, June 18, 1914.

60. Ibid.; Coletta, "William Jennings Bryan and the United States-Colombia Impasse," p. 499.

61. Bryan to Wilson, June 12, 1914, Bryan-Wilson Correspondence, National Archives; *New York Times*, June 18, 1914.

62. *New York Times*, June 25, 1914.

63. *New York World*, June 26, 1914.

64. Ibid.

65. *New York Times*, June 28, 1914.

66. Ibid., June 29, 1914.

67. Francisco Escobar, "Why the Colombian Treaty Should Be Ratified," *Independent*, July 13, 1914, pp. 60-61.

68. "Roosevelt and Wilson," *Nation*, July 9, 1914, p. 35.

69. *New York Times*, July 13, 1914.

70. Ibid.

71. Ibid.

72. Ibid., July 31, 1914; *Commoner*, July 1914.

73. American Minister to the Secretary of State, August 29, 1914, *Foreign Relations, 1914*, p. 168.

74. Secretary of State to the American Minister, September 5, 1914, *Foreign Relations, 1914*, p. 168.

75. Bryan to Wilson, December 3, 1914, Bryan Papers, Library of Congress.

76. *New York Times*, January 14, 1915.

77. Ibid.

78. *El Nuevo Tiempo*, January 21, 1915, as quoted, Bryan Papers, Library of Congress.

79. *La Tribuna*, January 23, 1915, as quoted, Ibid.

80. Bryan to Wilson, February 23, 1915, Bryan-Wilson Correspondence, National Archives.

81. Secretary of State to the Minister to Colombia, March 4, 1915, *Papers Relating to the Foreign Relations of the United States, 1915* (Washington, D.C.: U.S. Government Printing Office, 1924), pp. 259-260.

82. Chargé d'Affaires to the Secretary of State, March 19, 1915, *Foreign Relations, 1915*, p. 261.

10

Latin America after June 1915

William Jennings Bryan resigned as secretary of state on June 9, 1915 because he did not agree with President Wilson on the proper response to the sinking of the *Lusitania*. The president had asked Bryan to send a note of stern warning to the German government that any further violations of neutrality at sea would have dire consequences. Rather than send it, which he believed would involve the United States in World War I, Bryan left the Cabinet.[1] Thus, it was the European war that caused him to differ with Wilson; he and the president were in general agreement on Latin American affairs.

BRYAN'S ATTITUDE TOWARD LATIN AMERICA AFTER JUNE 1915

Though Bryan had left the State Department, his interest in Latin America did not cease. In January 1916, the former secretary of state delivered a speech before the Pan American Scientific Congress in Washington, D.C. He spoke about the need to increase cultural exchange and stressed the importance of more trade between the two continents. He even talked about using similar monetary units with Latin America.[2]

In April 1916, Bryan praised the substitution of cooperation for dollar diplomacy under the Wilson administration. He discussed other accomplishments of the Wilson government, such as the raising of the Argentine and Chilean posts from legations to embassies and the formulation of his Nicaraguan and Colombian treaties, both of which were not yet ratified.[3]

In July 1917, Bryan favored a loan sought by the Carranza government in Mexico. Once again, he revived his loan scheme of 1913, which Wilson had rejected. He wanted Mexico to issue a 5 percent bond to be exchanged for 3.5 percent bonds of the United States. The 1.5 percent difference would be put into a sinking fund to retire the principal of the Mexican bonds.[4] By March 1920, Bryan not only supported this plan for all of Latin America, but openly criticized the Wilson administration for completely neglecting Latin America in favor of Europe. He complained that the United States loaned too much money to Europe and not enough to Latin America.[5]

Thus, Bryan did not completely forget Latin America, and his general attitude toward it remained friendly. However, as much as the former secretary of state spoke of cultural exchange and loans for Latin America, he still supported Wilsonian interventionist policies there.

Mexico

In Mexico, at the time of Bryan's resignation, both he and Wilson agreed that the United States must "lend its active support to some man or group of men" who would stop the fighting and unify the country. Wilson said, "I, therefore, publicly and very solemnly, call upon the leaders of factions in Mexico to act, to act together, and to act promptly for the relief and redemption of their prostrate country."[6]

In September 1915, when interventionist sentiment rose in the United States, Bryan emphatically opposed any such course. He blamed the cry for intervention on special interest groups (the American oil men) and the warlike *Chicago Tribune,* which clamored for protection of American lives. He said that "it is one thing to protect our citizens from lawless bands that cross the border, but it is quite a different thing to invade Mexico and visit punishment upon a whole nation because a few irresponsible bandits have committed depredations on this side of the line."[7] What Bryan was referring to were the numerous raids that occurred across the border by Mexican bandits such as Luis de la Rosa and Pancho Villa. These bandits attacked towns such as Brownsville, Texas, where they destroyed American property and murdered American citizens. De la Rosa constantly menaced life and property on the American side of the border. He and his men caused a wreck of a southbound train of the Gulf Coast Railroad near Tandy's Station, five miles from Brownsville in October 1915, killing one American soldier and two civilians.[8]

In October 1915, when the Wilson administration gave recognition to Carranza and supported him over Villa, Bryan, who had always liked Villa, supported the president. He contended that it was worth trying to recognize Carranza and hoped that the Mexican leader would be able to end the incessant fighting.[9] However, the recognition of Carranza did not pave the way for peace and stability in Mexico. When Villa first learned about this from a newspaperman on October 31, 1915, he became very anti-American, especially after the American government had permitted Carranza to transport his troops across United States territory for the defense of Agua Prieta, which was under siege by Villa's forces.[10] Villa now vowed to make the Americans pay for their new Mexican policy. In an interview, an American correspondent reported that Villa "became very angry and declared he was through with them all and that was how he was to be repaid for the protection he has given to Americans and other foreigners; that he would take Agua-Prieta if he had to fight the whole Carranza army and the United States combined."[11]

Villa, after a series of defeats, retired to the mountains of Chihuahua and began his attacks against American citizens in December 1915. He seized thirty Americans in Chihuahua and threatened to kill them if the United States did not stop supporting Carranza.[12] On January 10, 1916, Villa's soldiers stopped a Mexican-Northwestern train at the cattle station of Santa Ysabel fifty miles west of Chihuahua City. They removed eighteen Americans from the train and shot seventeen of them.[13] Wilson, outraged by these attacks against Americans, wrote Carranza and asked him to protect American citizens and property in Mexico and to reinforce his border patrols to prevent the Villistas from crossing. He then warned the Mexican president that if Villa was permitted to run rampant, the United States would have to take measures to stop him.[14]

On March 9, 1916, the Villistas raided the town of Columbus, New Mexico, with a force estimated at between 1,000 and 3,000 men. As they rode into the town, they shouted "Viva Villa" and "Viva Mexico," firing indiscriminately, robbing stores, and setting houses ablaze. American troops came to the rescue within the hour and the Mexicans were driven across the border. The U. S. troops did not stop at the border but followed the Villistas about fifteen miles into Mexico where they spent three hours looking for them unsuccessfully. Total Mexican casualties, including those killed by the pursuing American forces, were sixty-seven dead and seven wounded. About nineteen Americans, civilian and military, lost their lives as consequence of this action.[15]

There was no attempt by Villa to hide the fact that he was responsible for these raids. George C. Carothers, a special agent of the State Department who was at the scene, said:

I was in Columbus the afternoon of the day the attack took place, and examined the papers that were in the two wallets Villa lost on the battlefield during his retreat. The papers fully connect him with the Santa Isabel massacre, and also establish the fact that he decided to declare war on us last December. He is crazy, from what I could find out among the prisoners, goes about with his mouth open, and looks dazed. His obsession is to kill Americans, and he has undoubtedly what the Mexicans call "Delirio de Grandesa" or Delirium of Greatness.[16]

These attacks were well planned and had a purpose. Villa hoped that his assaults on American citizens in Mexico and the United States would provoke American military intervention, and he could then proclaim himself the true defender of Mexican independence, since he was already fighting the United States. The result would be a full-scale war between the two countries, giving Villa an opportunity to seize power.[17]

Wilson called a cabinet meeting on March 10, 1916, to discuss the Mexican situation. He realized that an organized expedition into Mexico might result in war between the two nations. Carranza had warned him that if American troops crossed the border they would meet resistance.[18] Neither Carranza nor Wilson wanted a confrontation that might lead to war. Wilson realized what Villa was trying to accomplish, and he refused to take the bait. However, the problem for Wilson was that Congress, much more belligerent than the president, was prepared to adopt a resolution calling for armed intervention unless Wilson could head them off.[19] At this time, both countries decided to broaden the 1882 agreement that allowed either country to pursue Indians across the other's border. Wilson believed that this enabled him to send forces into Mexico, though Carranza did not interpret the pact the same way. Whether Carranza really opposed American intervention, under any circumstances, or whether he really wanted to aid Wilson but made statements against American intervention to strengthen his nationalistic standing and keep him one step ahead of Villa, remains uncertain. The latter is the interpretation of the American historian Howard F. Cline.[20]

On March 16, 1916, one week after the Columbus raid, General John J. Pershing crossed the border into Mexico with 6,000 troops. Wilson had made clear to the Carranza government that Pershing was only to pursue Villa with the object of either capturing him or destroying his army and putting an end to his raids. Robert Lansing, who succeeded Bryan as secretary of state, sent the following note to the Carranza government three days prior to the actual intervention:

In order to remove any apprehensions that may exist either in the United States or in Mexico, the President has authorized me to give in his name the public assurance that the military operations now in contemplation by this Government will be scrupulously confined to the object already announced, and that in no circumstances will they be suffered to trench in any degree upon the sovereignty of Mexico or develop into intervention of any kind in the internal affairs of our sister Republic.[21]

Bryan approved emphatically of Wilson's course of action. Immediately after Wilson made known his plan on March 10, Bryan held an interview, lauding the president for his position and maintaining that as long as the troops did not interfere in the affairs of the Carranza government, his action could not be called an invasion.[22] He went on to say that other Latin American countries should understand that the Pershing expedition was one of punishment and not invasion, and it should not affect U.S.-Latin American relations. He said: "This is the first time that we have had sufficient cause to cross the border."[23] This last remark by Bryan was intentional. When he was secretary of state, he had opposed Wilson's military intervention at Veracruz in April 1914 (see chapter 7).

Carranza accepted the entry of the punitive expedition under protest, primarily because his general Álvaro Obregón had counseled cooperation and because of Wilson's statements that the expedition was only temporary. In late March 1916, the American president reiterated in the press that the expedition had one purpose only and that was to capture the bandit Pancho Villa. He stressed that no invasion of Mexico had occurred and urged the press to stress that in their daily reports.[24] However, the longer Pershing's forces stayed in Mexico, the more concerned Carranza became and the more opportunity for an incident to occur that could lead to war. In April 1916, the Mexican president asked Wilson to recall his forces. In fact, there was some discussion in Washington at this time about the need to keep the forces there. Though Wilson's mind was completely occupied with relations with Germany, his chief of staff, General Hugh Scott, firmly believed that Pershing had accomplished about as much as he could and said that "it does not seem dignified for all the United States to be hunting for one man in a foreign country. If the thing were reversed, we would not allow any foreign army to be sloshing around in our country 300 miles from the border, no matter who they were."[25] However, it was Lansing who convinced the president to keep the American forces in Mexico. The secretary of state did not particularly like Carranza, nor did he have any faith in the social changes that Carranza wanted to initiate in Mexico.[26]

The first major incident between American forces and Mexicans occurred on April 12, 1916, at Parral, near the border between Chihuahua and Durango. About one hundred troops of the 13th Cavalry entered the town to find food. Civilians, who had gathered in the town square, began shouting "Viva Villa," "Viva Mexico," and verbal insults. As the Americans began to withdraw, they were pelted with rocks and bullets. About 300 soldiers from a nearby garrison joined the battle, and the American soldiers had to fight their way out of town. American casualties were light considering the circumstances. Only 2 soldiers were killed and 6 were wounded, while 40 to 100 Mexicans were killed.[27]

From April to June 1916, Carranza barely tolerated the American forces and, in fact, had to protect Americans living in Mexico from hostile Mexicans who were becoming more anti-American. Finally, on June 19, 1916, the Mexican president warned Pershing that he would not permit him to continue and that further movement in any direction except north would result in resistance.[28] The Americans evidently did not take this warning seriously, for a few days later, on June 21, a scouting party moved eastward, and near Carrizal encountered a larger Mexican force, which ordered the Americans to halt. They refused, and fighting ensued, resulting in twelve American deaths and a Mexican victory.[29] Pershing received word about the battle at Carrizal on the evening of June 21 and thought that it was the beginning of a major attack against his command. He immediately wired the War Department and asked for permission to seize the Mexican Central Railroad and Chihuahua. However, Secretary of War Newton Baker, after having consulted with Wilson, denied his general's request. The Wilson administration needed more information about Carranza's intentions before it would approve the expansion of military operations in Mexico.[30]

The Carrizal incident caused much consternation among those in both countries who opposed war. On June 23, 1916, Luis Manuel Rojas, a Mexican citizen, and two associates asked the American Union Against Militarism to send three representatives to meet them in El Paso, Texas, to find a solution to the crisis. The

Americans chosen were Frank Walsh of Kansas City, Chancellor David Starr Jordan of Leland Stanford University, and William Jennings Bryan.[31] While Jordan and Walsh accepted, Bryan hesitated—he would make no move, even as a private citizen, in this matter unless President Wilson sanctioned it.[32] He explained that it was ridiculous to send private citizens to any such conference, since it could not succeed without Wilson's cooperation.[33] When Wilson refused to sanction it, Bryan affirmed that the time for a peace conference was inopportune and added that the president was doing all that he could to avoid war with Mexico.[34]

In July 1916, the United States and Mexico began negotiations for the withdrawal of American troops, and by February 1917, the last contingent of American forces left Mexico.[35] The withdrawal of the Punitive Expedition and the resumption of normal diplomatic relations was a major triumph for Carranza. He not only withstood Villa's attempts to overthrow him, but he successfully dealt with a very strong and stubborn American president during a critical time. Though Carranza should be given credit for his diplomatic skill and patience in negotiating with the United States, the impending entrance of America into World War I was a major factor in the decision to withdraw all troops from Mexico. Within two months of the withdrawal, in April 1917, the United States became an active participant in World War I.

The Election of 1916 and the Oil Interests

In June 1916, the Democrats met in St. Louis and renominated President Wilson for the upcoming election. For the first time in many years, Bryan had been refused election as a delegate and attended only as a reporter.[36] Nonetheless, he still had great influence among fellow Democrats, and he remained an ardent supporter of Wilson, urged his renomination, and spoke (the cries for a Bryan speech were so deafening that he had no alternative) in defense of Wilson's Mexican policy.[37] He praised Wilson for not intervening in Mexico (he did not consider the Pershing expedition as intervention), while he berated the special interest groups, ranchers and miners, who "would use the blood of American soldiers to guarantee profits on their investments in a foreign land." He feared that intervention would lead to eventual annexation and to the alienation of all Latin America.[38]

The 1916 Democratic national platform, in regard to Latin America generally and to Mexico specifically, recognized a strong and common relationship between the people of the Western Hemisphere. It condemned the Villistas as outlaws and defended the Pershing expedition. It also reasserted the validity of the Monroe Doctrine.[39]

Bryan campaigned for Wilson's re-election by attacking dollar diplomacy, that very doctrine which he opposed so vociferously when he became secretary of state. He pointed to an editorial in the *Chicago Tribune* that advocated dollar diplomacy and condemned it. He declared that this paper was advocating that exploiters of natural resources should venture into Mexico, purchase property, take risks, and then ask for the aid of the U.S. government when it became necessary to make their investment profitable.[40]

The Republican nominee, Charles Evans Hughes, criticized Wilson's Mexican policy, claiming that the president had blundered in not recognizing Victoriano Huerta in March 1913. He maintained that the present instability in Mexico stemmed from Wilson's moralistic inclination.[41] Bryan defended Wilson by declaring that the Mexican crisis really began with the Taft administration and former ambassador Henry Lane Wilson who supported Huerta. Bryan called Huerta a murderer and traitor, relating in detail how he had Madero assassinated, and then asked if it was proper for the government of the United States to recognize a government of assassins.[42]

Although Wilson won re-election in 1916, American oil men and real estate interests, uncertain about the status of their holdings in Mexico, still demanded that the United States protect their property. During World War I, the oil companies, attacked by local guerrillas, were losing money and presented their case to Wilson, who refused to intervene.[43] As late as 1920, when Carranza was ousted and Obregón took power, special interests still urged intervention. Carranza had promised that American properties, including oil land held before 1917, the date of the promulgation of the Mexican constitution, would not be subject to Article 27, which, among other things, reclaimed all subsoil rights for the Mexican nation.[44] Though Carranza never kept his promise to the oil companies (he taxed the companies heavily and made them apply for drilling permits), Wilson still accorded him recognition and refused to intervene. However, in 1920, by the time of Carranza's downfall and the formal accession of Obregón, Wilson had fallen ill, and the Republicans had won the election of 1920. Thus, the Wilson government left the question of Obregón's recognition for the new Republican administration.[45]

Bryan remained an ardent backer of Wilson's nonintervention policy as late as 1920. In January 1920, when he saw a conspiracy among vested interest groups to annex Mexico through war with the United States, he called upon all those who invested in Mexico or any other country to report their financial holdings to the Department of Commerce in detailed form. He contended that the public should know who these financial interests were and how much they had invested. He declared that "when a pecuniary interest is known, it ceases to be dangerous."[46] He affirmed that the American government was doing all that it could to protect its citizens abroad and that intervention was not the answer. Bryan claimed that if these interests persisted in demanding protection, the United States could pay them for their losses or they could leave Mexico and invest elsewhere; however, above all, a war with Mexico must be avoided.[47] The former secretary of state also opposed any interference in the Obregón *coup* in May 1920. He was against immediate recognition of the new government but maintained that it should be forthcoming when law, order, and stability were restored.[48] It is interesting to note that Bryan had little to say about the murder of Carranza by Obregón's men as he fled Mexico in 1920.

Haiti

Bryan, who had much to say about the Haitian policy of the United States when he had been secretary of state continued to support the Wilson administration in this area. The revolution that occurred in Haiti, and which eventually led to American intervention and occupation in July 1915, actually had its beginnings in the last days of March 1915, when Bryan was still secretary of state.[49]

Vilbrun Guillaume Sam became president of Haiti on March 4, 1915; shortly afterwards, Bryan attempted to force him to accept a financial agreement, including, among other things, control of the Haitian customs. Paul Fuller, Jr. was sent to Haiti in May 1915, offering recognition and protection in exchange for a financial agreement.[50] Though no agreement was made, the rumors of a pending accord swept the country, and on March 28, 1915, Ronsalvo Bobo proclaimed a revolution to prevent a collectorship. For a time, it seemed that the Sam government was strong enough to deal with the revolutionaries. It had a treasury full of paper money that could be used to strengthen his army and enable Sam to take the initiative against the rebels.[51] However, there was not much change in the situation during the next five weeks as neither side was able to claim victory. The French landed marines in Cap Haïtien to protect their citizens, and Admiral William Caperton, the American naval officer, warned both sides in June 1915 that the fighting must not spread to Cap Haïtien where numerous Americans and foreigners resided.[52] On July 3, Admiral Caperton ordered a small guard of marines to land at Cap Haïtien and operate a field radio station, but aside from that, no further action was taken until July 28.[53]

On July 27, 1915, an uprising occurred against the Sam government in Port-au-Prince. An insurrectionary group overpowered the president's guard and besieged the palace. In a panic, Sam escaped the palace and sought asylum in the French legation, while the governor of Port-au-Prince, General Oscar Etienne, ordered the execution of nearly 200 political prisoners. These prisoners were first tortured and then hacked to death by machete. News of the massacre spread rapidly through the city, setting off a wave of hysteria. The angry mob seized General Etienne as he left the palace and shot him in the streets. On the following day, an angry mob invaded the French legation, dragged President Sam from his hiding place off the French minister's bedroom, hacked his body to pieces, and threw the parts to the frenzied crowds outside.[54]

The American chargé d'affaires in the Haitian capital was an eyewitness to the horrid murder of Sam. He said:

Before I reached the French Legation there was one terrific howl of fury from that direction. Turning into the street which runs behind the French Legation, I found my way completely blocked by a mob which filled the street from wall to wall. I could see that something or somebody was on the ground in the center of the crowd, just before the gates, and when a man disentangled himself and rushed howling by me, with a severed hand from which the blood was dripping, the thumb of which he had stuck in his mouth, I knew that the threatened assassination of the President was accomplished. Behind him came other men with the feet, the other hand, the head, and other parts of the body displayed on poles, each one followed by a mob of screaming men and women. The portion of the body that remained was dragged through the streets by the crowd.[55]

As a result of the uprising and chaos that followed, Lansing, after conferring with Wilson, ordered the secretary of the navy to land marines in Haiti.[56] Though an explanation was given to the Haitian leaders that the intervention was launched to restore order, there was much opposition among the Haitian people, who felt that the U.S. troops would remain and control their government.[57] At first, there was little physical opposition, but after elections were held in August 1915, with Sudre Dartiguenave defeating Bobo (rumors were spread that the United States had interfered in the election and worked for Dartiguenave's victory), sporadic fighting erupted throughout the country.[58] There was no doubt that Dartiguenave was the favorite of the United States, since he appeared more cooperative during the early intervention, but there was no proof of American interference in the election.[59]

The opposition to Dartiguenave and American occupation grew, especially after a treaty between the two countries was formulated and finally signed in September 1915. Briefly, the treaty legalized American intervention and occupation, gave the United States the financial control over the customs it had so long sought, and forbade transfer of Haitian territory to any other power.[60] To the Haitian nationalists, it was a surrender of their sovereignty, and during the months of October and November 1915, savage fighting erupted between American marines and Haitian *cacos*, causing numerous casualties.[61]

Bryan supported the position of the United States completely. He had believed that intervention might be necessary as early as April 1915, in order to implement financial control, restore political stability, and ensure against French and German intervention.[62] By October 1915, during the uprising against American occupation, Bryan wrote an article that lauded American intervention as a necessity. He claimed that rival clans were terrorizing the country and that the United States must end the chaos with force if necessary or the situation would invite European interference.[63] He hoped that the Haitian people would learn by this experience that the United States government was more capable of ruling them than their native chiefs and that under American guardianship (which lasted until 1934) everybody would have equal opportunity for economic prosperity.[64]

The Dominican Republic

Although American intervention in the Dominican Republic had occurred almost one full year after Bryan had resigned, the policies that he followed there were responsible for that intervention. Bryan, from the inauguration of Juan Isidro Jiménez in December 1914, attempted to increase American financial control through the appointment of an American financial adviser to the Dominican government and threatened to use force against all who opposed the plan and the new president who seemingly supported it.[65] The major opposition to the plan came from Desiderio Arias, the minister of war, and his followers. Due to increased opposition, the plan was revised in May 1915.[66]

Though Arias remained minister of war against Bryan's wishes, his relationship with President Jiménez deteriorated rapidly. In April 1916, Jiménez decided that Arias was too much of a threat to his position, and with the encouragement of his followers, he finally broke with Arias.[67] In May 1916, when the president had some of Arias's followers imprisoned, the Dominican House of Representatives, the majority of whom were Arias's men, decided to impeach the president. Jiménez, in turn, dismissed Arias from the cabinet, starting a war between the followers of these two men.[68]

Bryan's policy in 1914 and 1915 of supporting Jiménez against Arias was continued in 1916 by Lansing. On May 2, 1916, Minister William W. Russell, with the approval of the State Department, had troops landed at Santo Domingo City and was told to support Jiménez fully.[69]

Though Arias controlled the capital and Jiménez had resigned, the American forces refused to recognize the former minister of war as the new Dominican chief of state. Instead, the State Department ordered Admiral Caperton and Russell not to recognize the impeachment of Jiménez, and to inform Arias that if he did not surrender Santo Domingo City, American forces would seize it. Arias evacuated on May 13, 1916, withdrawing into the interior, and a few days later, American control of Santo Domingo was complete.[70] This occupation lasted until 1924, with the United States attempting to attain the same goals that were successful in Haiti.[71]

Though Bryan had made no comment on the Dominican occupation, it was evident that the policy Lansing followed there in 1916, was very similar to Bryan's. It could be said that Bryan actually laid the foundation for American intervention and occupation in the Dominican Republic.

The Nicaraguan Treaty

Bryan also worked, as a private citizen, to get the Senate to ratify both the Nicaraguan and the Colombian treaties. The Nicaraguan or Bryan-Chamorro Treaty was signed in August 1914, but because of protests from both the anti-imperialists senators on the Senate Foreign Relations Committee and from Costa

Rica and El Salvador, it remained unratified.

Bryan had resigned with the Nicaraguan treaty still pending. In October 1915, he made his first comment on the status of the treaty. He believed that the sum of $3 million, the amount to be paid to Nicaragua for a canal option and naval base on the Gulf of Fonseca, was most reasonable and urged immediate ratification of the treaty.[72]

Costa Rica, which owned much of the south bank of the San Juan River, and which had to be consulted on any canal built on the river, and El Salvador, which objected to the naval base on the Gulf of Fonseca, claiming joint ownership of the waters in the Gulf, continued to lobby against the ratification of the treaty by the U.S. Senate.[73] Nonetheless, due to the persistence of Bryan's writing in *The Commoner*, the incessant entreaties of Nicaragua, and especially the active support of Wilson, the Senate finally ratified the treaty in February 1916.[74]

Because of the protests of Costa Rica and El Salvador, the Senate attached the following reservation to the treaty: "It is declared by the Senate that in advising and consenting to the ratification of the said Convention as amended such advice and consent are given with the understanding, to be expressed as a part of the instrument of ratification, that nothing in said Convention is intended to affect any existing right of any of the said named States."[75] This reservation, intended to placate El Salvador and Costa Rica, proved ineffective, since both of these countries opposed the treaty in any form. In March 1916, Costa Rica brought its case to the Central American Court, asking it to declare the Bryan-Chamorro Treaty null and void; in August 1916, El Salvador also appealed to the court. However, the court in both cases refused to declare the treaty invalid, though it did claim that Nicaragua had violated the sovereignty of Costa Rica and El Salvador. Consequently, Nicaragua denounced the treaty that had established the court, and within a short time that body stopped functioning.[76] Thus, it could be said that the Bryan-Chamorro Treaty helped to destroy the Central American Court.

The Bryan-Chamorro Treaty that was ratified on February 18, 1916, was essentially the same that was signed in August 1914. It called for the payment of the $3 million to Nicaragua for the canal option and naval base.[77]

The Colombian Treaty

The Thompson-Urrutia or Colombian treaty proved much more difficult to ratify. It was signed in April 1914, but remained bogged down in the Senate Foreign Relations Committee. During his tenure of office, Bryan had appeared before this committee urging ratification, but the majority of its members, mostly Theodore Roosevelt supporters, opposed the provisions of paying Colombia $25 million and the expression of "sincere regret."[78]

After he resigned, Bryan continued to work for ratification of the Colombian treaty. In October 1915, he wrote in the *Commoner* that he earnestly believed that the Senate would ratify the treaty when it convened. He called it "the last thing necessary to the perfecting of our relations with Spanish America."[79] However, as hard as Bryan worked for ratification, it would take almost six years before his hope would be realized. Henry Cabot Lodge, William Borah, and Albert Fall, among others, continued to delay passage in the Senate.

Finally, in 1919, various events occurred that eventually ensured ratification. Colombia, pressed for money, agreed on February 27, 1919, to forget the expression of "sincere regret" clause; on January 6, 1919, Roosevelt, the one person who would have been most embarrassed by its ratification, died.[80]

The Senate Foreign Relations Committee recommended passage on July 29, 1919; however, Lodge, Borah, Fall, and Porter McCumber still opposed it. Borah wanted no part of it under any circumstances, while the other three delayed it until an agreement could be made with Colombia over American oil concessions. They had information that the Colombian government intended to nationalize its oil, denying American investors profit. Thus, it took almost another two years before ratification became a reality.[81]

On April 20, 1921, the Colombian treaty, with the full support of President Warren Harding, was ratified by a vote of 69-19. Of the nineteen who opposed it, fifteen were Republicans. The treaty was almost the same as was formulated by Bryan in 1914, except for the deletion of Article One, the expression of "sincere regret." The sum to be paid to Colombia remained at $25 million, but instead of paying the entire $25 million within six months after the exchange of ratifications as Bryan had wished, only $5 million would be paid at that time, with the remaining $20 million paid in four annual installments of $5 million each.[82]

Notwithstanding the deletion of Article One, the ratification of the Colombian treaty was applauded by Bryan. He praised Harding for his support, as the president had opposed the treaty before 1919 when he was a senator from Ohio. After the death of Roosevelt, Harding became a supporter of the treaty.[83] Though Bryan had criticized the deletion of Article One, he maintained that the payment of $25 million, even in installments, was much more important.[84] In June 1921, the *Commoner* had claimed that the ratification of the Colombian treaty was a great victory for Bryan. The former secretary of state had been vindicated and the payment of money "acknowledged Roosevelt's wrongdoing in 1903."[85]

In conclusion, it was clear that Bryan continued to take an active interest in many of the same areas that he had dealt with as secretary of state after his resignation in June 1915. His general attitude toward Latin America was friendly; he not only urged the U.S. government to lend money to Latin America, but also suggested more cultural exchanges between the two regions. Both in Mexico and in Haiti, he continued to support Wilson fully; in the Dominican Republic, he formulated the policy, later used by Lansing and Wilson, that led to American intervention in May 1916. He continued to work for the ratifications of the Nicaraguan and Colombian treaties, and in both cases, his efforts proved success-ful—the Nicaraguan treaty was ratified in February 1916 and the Colombian treaty in April 1921.

NOTES

1. *Commoner*, June 1915.
2. Ibid., January 1916.
3. Ibid., April 1916.
4. Ibid., July 1917.
5. Ibid., March 1920.
6. Ibid., June 1915; Arthur S. Link, *Wilson: The Struggle for Neutrality, 1914-1915* (Princeton, N.J.: Princeton University Press, 1960), p. 477.
7. *Commoner*, September 1915.
8. Arthur S. Link, *Wilson: Confusions and Crises, 1915-1916* (Princeton, N.J.: Princeton University Press, 1964), pp. 195-196.
9. *Commoner*, October 1915.
10. Link, *Wilson: Confusions and Crises*, p. 196.
11. G. C. Carothers to the Secretary of State, *Papers Relating to the Foreign Relations of the United States, 1915* (Washington, D.C.: U.S. Government Printing Office, 1924), p. 775.
12. Link, *Wilson: Confusions and Crises*, p. 200.
13. Ibid., p. 201.
14. Ibid., p. 202.
15. Ibid., p. 205; Clarence C. Clendenen, *The United States and Pancho Villa: A Study in Unconventional Diplomacy* (Ithaca, N.Y.: Cornell University Press, 1961), pp. 239-242.
16. Link, *Wilson: Confusions and Crises*, p. 206.
17. Clendenen, *The United States and Pancho Villa*, p. 245.
18. Howard F. Cline, *The United States and Mexico* (Cambridge: Harvard University Press, 1953), p. 176.
19. Ibid.
20. Ibid., p. 177.
21. Link, *Wilson: Confusions and Crises*, p. 212.
22. *Commoner*, March 1916; *New York Times*, March 11, 1916.
23. *New York Times*, March 11, 1916.
24. Ibid., March 26, 1916.
25. Link, *Wilson: Confusions and Crises*, p. 282.
26. Ibid.
27. Ibid., pp. 282-283.
28. Cline, *The United States and Mexico*, p. 181.
29. Ibid.
30. Link, *Wilson: Confusions and Crises*, p. 306.
31. *New York Times*, June 24, 1916.
32. Ibid., June 26, 1916.
33. Ibid.
34. Ibid., June 27, 1916.
35. Cline, *The United States and Mexico*, pp. 182-183.
36. Arthur S. Link, *Wilson: Campaigns for Progressivism and Peace, 1916-1917* (Princeton, N.J.: Princeton University Press, 1965), p. 44.
37. Ibid., p. 47.
38. *Commoner*, June 1916.

39. Ibid.

40. Ibid., July 1916.

41. *New York Times*, August 3, 1916.

42. *Commoner*, October 1916.

43. Cline, *The United States and Mexico*, pp. 186-187.

44. Ibid., p. 205.

45. Ibid., p. 192.

46. *Commoner*, January 1920.

47. Ibid.

48. Ibid., July 1920.

49. Dana G. Munro, *Intervention and Dollar Diplomacy in the Caribbean, 1900-1921* (Princeton, N.J.: Princeton University Press, 1964), p. 351.

50. Ibid., p. 350.

51. Ibid., p. 351.

52. Arthur C. Millspaugh, *Haiti under American Control, 1915-1930* (Boston: World Peace Foundation, 1931), p. 34.

53. Ibid.

54. Ibid., p. 35; Munro, *Intervention and Dollar Diplomacy in the Caribbean*, p. 352.

55. Link, *Wilson: The Struggle for Neutrality*, p. 533.

56. Munro, *Intervention and Dollar Diplomacy in the Caribbean*, p. 352.

57. Millspaugh, *Haiti under American Control*, pp. 36-37.

58. Munro, *Intervention and Dollar Diplomacy in the Caribbean*, p. 355-357.

59. Ibid.

60. Ibid., pp. 356-358; Millspaugh, *Haiti under American Control*, pp. 42-43.

61. Munro, *Intervention and Dollar Diplomacy in the Caribbean*, p. 359.

62. Selig Adler, "Bryan and Wilsonian Caribbean Penetration," *Hispanic American Historical Review* 20 (May 1940): 224-225.

63. *Commoner*, October 1915.

64. Ibid.

65. Sumner Welles, *Naboth's Vineyard: The Dominican Republic, 1844-1924*, vol. 2 (New York: P. P. Appel, 1966), pp. 744-751.

66. Adler, "Bryan and Wilsonian Caribbean Penetration," p. 220.

67. Munro, *Intervention and Dollar Diplomacy in the Caribbean*, p. 305.

68. Ibid.

69. Ibid., p. 306.

70. Ibid.

71. Ibid., p. 307.

72. *Commoner*, October 1915.

73. Munro, *Intervention and Dollar Diplomacy in the Caribbean*, p. 402.

74. *Congressional Record*, 64 Cong., 1st sess., 1916, LIII, 3, 2770-2771; Munro, *Intervention and Dollar Diplomacy in the Caribbean*, pp. 401-402.

75. Samuel Flagg Bemis, *The Latin American Policy of the United States* (New York: Harcourt, Brace, and Company, 1943), pp. 188-189; *Congressional Record*, 64 Cong., 1st sess., 1916, LIII, 3, 2770-2771.

76. Munro, *Intervention and Dollar Diplomacy in the Caribbean*, pp. 402-403.

77. Ibid., p. 402.

78. Paolo Coletta, "William Jennings Bryan and the United States-Colombia Impasse, 1903-1921," *Hispanic American Historical Review* 47 (November 1967): 495-496.

79. *Commoner*, October 1915.

80. Chester Lloyd Jones, *The Caribbean since 1900* (New York: Russell and Russell, 1970), p. 330.

81. Ibid.; J. Fred Rippy, *The Capitalists and Colombia* (New York: The Vanguard Press, 1931), pp. 117-120.

82. *Congressional Record*, 67 Cong., 1st sess., 1921, LXI, 1,. 486-487; *New York Times*, April 21, 1921; Coletta, "William Jennings Bryan and the United States-Colombia Impasse," p. 501.

83. *Commoner*, May 1921.

84. Ibid.

85. Ibid., June 1921; Coletta, "William Jennings Bryan and the United States-Colombia Impasse," p. 501.

11

Conclusion

William Jennings Bryan's Latin American policy was predicated on his firm commitment to the security of the United States (the prevention of European nations from acquiring naval bases in the western hemisphere) and his sense of moral obligation to enhance friendship and understanding between the peoples of the United States and Latin America. In pursuing these aims, Bryan unwittingly followed an inconsistent policy. He acted imperialistically toward Nicaragua, Haiti, and the Dominican Republic, while repudiating imperialism and declaring a moral obligation with regard to Mexico, the Panama Canal tolls controversy, and the Colombian treaty.

The inconsistency of Bryan's policy was due to his failure to explain moral obligation. This term had two different meanings depending upon the situation. For instance, as a private citizen, Bryan defined *moralism* as meaning, among other things, antimilitarism; he opposed American military intervention throughout the world and criticized the militaristic Latin American policies of Theodore Roosevelt and William Howard Taft. Bryan asserted that these policies were imperialistic and declared that the United States had a moral obligation to eradicate imperialism. He reasoned that since the United States possessed overwhelming military power, it should not use this power unless it was attacked. He believed that all political issues could be resolved by peaceful diplomacy.

In speeches and in public statements to President Wilson, Bryan declared a new policy for Latin America. He stated that the Latin American republics must be able to solve their own problems without United States interference. However, he also wanted the United States to "protect the people of these republics in their right to attend to their own business free from external coercion, no matter what the form that external coercion may take."[1]

However, at the same time Bryan and Wilson talked about allowing the Latin American governments to determine their own destiny, they both realized that this new humane Latin American policy must fit in with the security needs of the

United States. When Bryan took over as secretary of state in March 1913, he assumed new responsibilities and the most important of these was the security of the United States. Believing that Great Britain, Germany, France, and Italy coveted coaling stations and naval bases in Latin America, and that debt collection and political instability were used as pretexts to intervention, Bryan attempted to prevent European intervention—he insisted upon political stability and economic responsibility in the Western Hemisphere.[2]

Bryan's preoccupation with security forced him to alter his definition of moral obligation with regard to Nicaragua, Haiti, and the Dominican Republic. In these instances, it meant that the United States should help these politically unstable countries govern themselves. Bryan decided that since the United States was a politically mature and stable democracy, it was duty bound to interfere in Nicaragua, Haiti, and the Dominican Republic. Obligation not only applied to politics, but it was also used to defend American interference in the economic institutions of these countries. Bryan came to believe that the United States must insist that these Latin American countries meet their financial obligations to their European creditors—he thought it was the responsibility of the United States, which had the best political and financial institutions in the world, to give aid to these distressed countries.[3]

Bryan was never able to distinguish between his double definition of moral obligation. The reason for this was that both definitions were always part of his early mental development. At the same time Bryan opposed the use of American military power against weaker nations, he also praised American political and economic institutions, claiming that the United States should set an example for other nations to follow. Before he became secretary of state, he was never explicit on how to set the example, but once he assumed responsibility in 1913, the problem of security forced him to become explicit.

In Nicaragua, Bryan feared that European intervention to collect debts would threaten American security. He worked to obtain a loan, through a treaty, to enable the Nicaraguan government to repay foreign creditors, especially those of Great Britain, France, Italy, and Germany. As secretary of state, he was also concerned about the political instability, and he kept American marines there to ensure free elections.

American security was also Bryan's chief concern in Haiti. He believed that French and German business interests incited the numerous revolutions and that these countries coveted the harbor Mole St. Nicholas to use as a naval base. To end the political instability, Bryan, again, insisted upon free elections, and sent James Fort and Charles Cogswell Smith to Haiti with orders to supervise the elections. The secretary of state also wanted to set up a receivership in Haiti, similar to the one in the Dominican Republic, in order to promote fiscal responsibility.

Bryan's fear that German creditors were seeking to interfere in the Dominican government forced him into imperialistic action. He not only insisted upon free and orderly elections, but sent State Department personnel to supervise the constitutional election in December 1913; in October 1914, Fort and Smith were sent to the Dominical Republic to direct the presidential election. Bryan also attempted to increase American economic control in the Dominican Republic (the United States already supervised the receivership) by appointing an American financial adviser to the Dominican government with absolute power of the budget.

Bryan acted differently with regard to Mexico, the Panama Canal tolls controversy, and the Colombian treaty—he saw no danger of foreign political domination. Since American security was not an issue, he followed an anti-imperialistic policy. He continued to speak of moral obligation, but it no longer meant sending troops or electoral commissions to supervise elections. Instead, Bryan asserted that the United States must right the wrongs of the past, be above reproach, and gain the friendship and trust of Mexico, Great Britain, and Colombia. This definition of moral obligation was anti-imperialistic—it was a reiteration of his anti-imperialistic sentiments of earlier years.

Mexico was not an indebted island republic, and there was little danger of foreign political domination; if there was to be interference here, it would come from the United States. Bryan disapproved of military intervention in Mexico; he regretted the Veracruz incident in April 1914, fearing that it would unite the warring factions against the United States. Bryan, unlike Wilson, favored arbitration, hoping that this would end the fighting in Mexico and demonstrate to all of Latin America that the United States would not use military force to settle disputes.

The Panama Canal tolls controversy was another matter of moral obligation. Again, it was not a question of foreign domination in the Canal Zone, but whether the United States would honorably abide by the Hay-Pauncefote Treaty of 1902, promising equal treatment to all nations in the Canal Zone. When Bryan worked for repeal of exemption, he continually stressed the morality of the issue.

The best example of Bryan's moral obligation to improve United States-Latin American relations was his Colombian treaty. The treaty would compensate Colombia for its loss of Panama and would demonstrate to Latin American states that the United States was anxious to right the wrongs of past administrations.

Bryan's inability to understand the inconsistency of his Latin American policy was due to his failure to define clearly what he meant by moral obligation. While he claimed that his Latin American policy differed from that of his predecessors (it opposed military and political interference in Latin America), he never really understood that the awesome responsibility of maintaining American security in Nicaragua, Haiti, and the Dominican Republic altered his definition of moral obligation. Bryan not only followed the same imperialistic policies of the Roosevelt and Taft administrations in these three countries, but he did so for the very same reason—the concern of American security in the Western Hemisphere.

NOTES

1. Louis W. Koenig, *Bryan: A Political Biography of William Jennings Bryan* (New York: G. P. Putnam's Sons, 1971), p. 513.

2. Ibid.

3. Ibid., p. 515.

Bibliography

UNPUBLISHED PAPERS

Papers of the Department of State, 1913-1915, National Archives. Washington, D.C.
Papers of William Jennings Bryan, 1913-1915, Library of Congress. Washington, D.C.
Papers of Woodrow Wilson, 1913, Library of Congress. Washington, D.C.
William Jennings Bryan-Woodrow Wilson Correspondence, 1913-1915, National Archives. Washington, D.C.

PUBLIC DOCUMENTS

Papers Relating to the Foreign Relations of the United States, 1913-1915. 3 vols. Washington, D.C.: U.S. Government Printing Office, 1920-1924.
U.S. Congressional Record. Vols. LI, LIII, LXI. Washington, D.C.

NEWSPAPERS

Commoner. 1901-1921.
New York Herald Tribune. 1913.
New York Times. 1898-1920.
New York World. 1910-1915.

ARTICLES AND PERIODICALS

Adler, Selig. "Bryan and Wilsonian Caribbean Penetration." *Hispanic American Historical Review* 20 (May 1940): 198-226.
Coker, William S. "The Panama Canal Tolls Controversy: A Different Perspective." *Journal of American History* 55 (December 1968): 555-564.
Coletta, Paolo E. "William Jennings Bryan and the United States-Colombia Impasse, 1903-

1921." *Hispanic American Historical Review* 47 (November 1967): 486-501.

Curti, Merle F. "Bryan and World Peace." *Smith College Studies in History* 16 (April-July 1931): 113-254.

Escobar, Francisco. "Why the Colombian Treaty Should Be Ratified." *Independent*, July 13, 1914, pp. 60-61.

Holbo, Paul S. "Presidential Leadership in Foreign Affairs: William McKinley and the Turpie-Foraker Amendment." *American Historical Review* 72 (July 1967): 1321-1335.

Kaplan, Edward S. "William Jennings Bryan and the Panama Canal Tolls Controversy." *Mid-America: An Historical Review* 56 (April 1974): 100-108.

"Roosevelt and Wilson." *Nation*, July 9, 1914, p. 35.

BOOKS

Ashby, Leroy. *William Jennings Bryan: Champion of Democracy*. Boston: Twayne Publishers, 1987.

Baker, Ray Stannard. *Woodrow Wilson: Life and Letters*. 8 vols. Garden City, N.Y.: Doubleday Page, and Company, 1927-1939.

Beale, Howard K. *Theodore Roosevelt and the Rise of America to World Power*. Baltimore, MD: John Hopkins University Press, 1956.

Beisner, Robert L. *Twelve Against Empire: The Anti-Imperialists, 1898-1900*. New York: McGraw-Hill, 1968.

Bemis, Samuel Flagg. *American Secretaries of State and Their Diplomacy*. 10 vols. New York: Pageant Book Company, 1929.

Bemis, Samuel Flagg. *The Latin American Policy of the United States*. New York: Harcourt, Brace, and Company, 1943.

Bryan, William Jennings. *Speeches of William Jennings Bryan*. 2 vols. New York: Funk and Wagnalls Company, 1909.

Clendenen, Clarence C. *The United States and Pancho Villa: A Study in Unconventional Diplomacy*. Ithaca, N.Y.: Cornell University Press, 1961.

Cline, Howard F. *The United States and Mexico*. Cambridge: Harvard University Press, 1953.

Coletta, Paolo E. *William Jennings Bryan: Progressive Politician and Moral Statesman, 1909-1915*. Lincoln, NE: University of Nebraska Press, 1969.

Cox, Issac J. *Nicaragua and the United States*. Boston: World Peace Foundation, 1927.

Cronon, E. David, ed. *The Cabinet Diaries of Josephus Daniels, 1913-1921*. Lincoln, NE: University of Nebraska Press, 1963.

Fagg, John Edwin. *Latin America: A General History*. New York: Macmillan, 1977.

Glad, Paul W, ed. *William Jennings Bryan: A Profile*. New York: Hill and Wang, 1968.

Harbaugh, William. *The Life and Times of Theodore Roosevelt*. New York: Oxford University Press, 1975.

Hendrick, Burton J. *The Life and Letters of Walter H. Page*. 3 vols. Garden City, N.Y.: Doubleday, Page, and Company, 1922-1925.

Hibben, Paxton. *The Peerless Leader William Jennings Bryan*. New York: Russell and Russell, 1967.

Houston, David F. *Eight Years with Wilson's Cabinet, 1913-1920*. 2 vols. Garden City, N.Y.: Doubleday, Page, and Company, 1926.

Jones, Chester Lloyd. *The Caribbean since 1900*. New York: Russell and Russell, 1970.

Koenig, Louis W. *Bryan: A Political Biography of William Jennings Bryan*. New York: G. P. Putnam's Sons, 1971.

LaFeber, Walter. *The Panama Canal*. New York: Oxford University Press, 1978.

Link, Arthur S. *Wilson: Campaigns for Progressivism and Peace, 1916-1917*. Princeton, N.J.: Princeton University Press, 1965.

Link, Arthur S. *Wilson: Confusions and Crises, 1915-1916*. Princeton, N.J.: Princeton University Press, 1964.

Link, Arthur S. *Wilson: The New Freedom*. Princeton, N.J.: Princeton University Press, 1956.

Link, Arthur S. *Wilson: The Road to the White House*. Princeton, N.J.: Princeton University Press, 1947.

Link, Arthur S. *Wilson: The Struggle for Neutrality, 1914-1915*. Princeton, N.J.: Princeton University Press, 1960.

Link, Arthur S. *Woodrow Wilson and the Progressive Era, 1910-1917*. New York: Harper, 1954.

Malone, Dumas, and Basil Rauch. *Crisis of the Union, 1841-1877*. 3 vols. New York: Appleton-Century-Crofts, 1960.

Millspaugh, Arthur C. *Haiti under American Control, 1915-1930*. Boston: World Peace Foundation, 1931.

Morgan, H. Wayne. *America's Road to Empire: The War with Spain and Overseas Expansion*. New York: Wiley, 1965.

Mowry, George E. *The Era of Theodore Roosevelt and the Birth of Modern America, 1900-1912*. New York: Harper and Row, 1958.

Munro, Dana G. *Intervention and Dollar Diplomacy in the Caribbean, 1900-1921*. Princeton, N.J.: Princeton University Press, 1964.

Parkes, Henry Bamford. *A History of Mexico*. Boston: Houghton, 1970.

Pringle, Henry. *Theodore Roosevelt*. New York: Harcourt, Brace, Jovanovich, 1956.

Quirk, Robert E. *An Affair of Honor: Woodrow Wilson and the Occupation of Veracruz*. Lexington, KY: University of Kentucky Press, 1962.

Quirk, Robert E. *The Mexican Revolution, 1914-1915: The Convention of Aguascalientes*. Bloomington, IN: Indiana University Press, 1960.

Richardson, James, ed. *A Compilation of the Messages and Papers of the Presidents, 1789-1915*. 20 vols. Washington, D.C.: U.S. Government Printing Office, 1916.

Rippy, J. Fred. *The Capitalists and Colombia*. New York: The Vanguard Press, 1931.

Rippy, J. Fred. *The Caribbean Danger Zone*. New York: G. P. Putnam's Sons, 1940.

Rippy, J. Fred. *Latin America in World Politics*. New York: F. S. Crofts and Company, 1931.

Stephenson, George M. *John Lind of Minnesota*. Minneapolis, MN: The University of Minnesota Press, 1935.

Unger, Irwin. *These United States: The Questions of Our Past*. 4th ed. Englewood Cliffs, N.J.: Prentice-Hall, 1989.

Welles, Sumner. *Naboth's Vineyard: The Dominican Republic, 1844-1924*. 2 vols. New York: P. P. Appel, 1966.

Index

About the Author

EDWARD S. KAPLAN is Professor in the Social Science Department at New York City Technical College of the City University of New York. He is a specialist in the economic history of the United States, and is coauthor of *Prelude to Trade Wars*: *American Tariff Policy, 1890–1922* (Greenwood, 1994) and author of *American Trade Policy, 1923–1995* (Greenwood, 1996).

ISBN 0-313-30489-0

90000>

9 780313 304897

EAN

HARDCOVER BAR CODE